IN SEARCH OF A
BETTER
LIFE

IN SEARCH OF A
BETTER
LIFE

BRITISH
AND
IRISH
MIGRATION

EDITED BY GRAHAM DAVIS

First published 2011

The History Press
The Mill, Brimscombe Port
Stroud, Gloucestershire, GL5 2QG
www.thehistorypress.co.uk

British Library Cataloguing in Publication Data.
A catalogue record for this book is available from the British Library.

ISBN 978 0 7524 5954 7

Typesetting and origination by The History Press
Printed in Malta

Contents

Notes on Contributors

John Fripp

John retired in 1998 after an academic career in three industries. Brief spells in the energy, aero engine and gas industries were followed by a move to Ashridge Business School, Hertfordshire, as lecturer, researcher and management consultant. John holds a BSc in Physics and Mathematics, a PhD in Management Studies and, since retiring, an MA in History and Culture from Bath Spa University. He has published widely in business and management literature, including several books and many journal articles. Since retiring to Dorset and completing his MA in 2007 he has written a number of articles on Dorset history: 'The Sherborne Riot of 1831: Causes, Characters and Consequences', *Proceedings of the Dorset Natural History and Archaeological Society*, 127, 2005; 'Mobility in Victorian Dorset', *Proceedings of the Dorset Natural History and Archaeological Society*, 129, 2008; 'Weymouth over the long eighteenth century: urban renaissance or new leisure town?' *Proceedings of Dorset Natural History and Archaeological Society*, 129, 2008.

Lynda Brown

Lynda went to Bath Spa University as a mature student to study English and History in 1996. Having studied a variety of modules involving the Irish during the nineteenth century, she developed a love of the Irish in Britain and graduated in 1999 with a 2:1. On completion of her degree Lynda then continued to study at Bath Spa University and gained a Masters in Local and Regional History, graduating in 2002, the subject of her dissertation being the Irish in Wiltshire during the nineteenth century.

Since completing her Masters, Lynda spent some time teaching genealogy on the internet with the University of Bath whilst continuing her research on the Irish in Wiltshire. Lynda now hopes to further this research, especially with regard to the railway workers and the development of the railway towns along the Paddington to Bristol line.

Celia Martin

Celia was educated at Millfield School and later went to Bristol Old Vic Theatre School to study Stage Management. She married David Ralph Martin, the writer, and is the daughter of the writer Denis Constanduros. It was not until the age of 50 that she entered the education system of her own volition and was fortunate to be under the tutelage of Graham Davis at Bath Spa University. She was awarded her MA in Local and Regional History in 2005. Having been widowed, she later moved to France to live with the television chef, Keith Floyd, where she was able to further her interest in researching and writing about emigration from England in the early nineteenth century.

Sara Moppett

After completing an MA in Irish Studies at Bath Spa University in 1999, Sara trained as a history teacher at the University of the West of England. Sara is currently working as a classroom teacher in a small special school in outer Christchurch, New Zealand, and is working towards a Graduate Diploma in the Education of Students with Special Teaching Needs. She lives in Christchurch with her husband and two children, James and Sophie.

Emily Slinger

Originally from London, Emily Slinger now lives in Bath with her husband and two grown-up children. In the 1970s, having left school with A-levels in Art and History of Art, Emily lived and worked in Italy for two years. During this time she studied Italian and Art History. Although primarily based in the city of Florence and the Etruscan town of Cortona, Emily also travelled extensively throughout the rest of Italy experiencing her own modern-day 'Grand Tour'. After two years she returned to the UK where she continued her studies with the Open University. After bringing up a family, Emily attended Bath Spa University where she gained her degree in History which she followed with a Masters in Irish Studies.

Tessa English

Tessa English was awarded her MA in Irish Studies from Bath Spa University in February 2009. A university researcher and administrator, she undertook it while working as a manager of the university's Wessex Partnership with local and regional further education colleges. Her first degree was in English Literature; however, her keen interest in Irish history was fuelled by stories of her Irish ancestry. In the far distant past, an ancestor on her mother's side settled in Galway where the family flourished until the early twentieth century. She undertook the MA both as a challenge and to further her knowledge of Ireland's history. She is now exploring further avenues of historical research.

Matthew Goulding

Matthew went to Bath Spa University in 2006 to study History with an elective in Philosophy. During his time at university he took part in the Sealed Knot and worked in many offices. He graduated in 2009 with a History degree and subsequently moved to Brighton with university friends. He currently works at an insurance company and is considering taking a Masters course in the future.

Graham Davis

Graham is Emeritus Professor of History at Bath Spa University and was course director for the MA in Local and Regional History and the MA in Irish Studies. He has written extensively on Irish migration: *The Irish in Britain, 1815–1914* (1991); and the award-winning *Land! Irish Pioneers in Mexican and Revolutionary Texas* (2002). He has also written a number of books and articles on the history of Bath, including: co-author with Penny Bonsall, *A History of Bath: Image and Reality* (2006); editor of *Bath Exposed!* (2007); and author of *Bath as Spa and Bath as Slum* (2010). He is currently editor of the journal *Bath History*.

Introduction

The partition of Ireland in 1922 and the creation of the Irish Free State not only saw the break-up of the Union between Great Britain and Ireland, but rendered its 120-year legitimacy null and void. Inevitably it also brought a retrospective separation of the histories of Britain and Ireland, which for good or ill had been closely entwined since 1800. The story of nineteenth-century Ireland became dominated by the divergent histories of nationalism and unionism. However, in comparing patterns of emigration from Ireland and Britain, it is clear that contemporary authorities were sensitive to the impact of Irish migration to Britain and viewed state emigration policy formation in terms of relieving 'redundant' population in both countries. In turn, it was thought that state-assisted migration would further colonial settlement in Canada and Australia, and would provide a demand for British goods. So in modern parlance, the advocates of emigration saw positive advantages at home and abroad.

In the 1820s, parliament recognised a common problem of what was termed a 'redundant' population of agricultural labourers in extensive districts of Ireland and in certain districts of Scotland and England. It was maintained in a select committee report that the effect of this redundancy was to reduce the wages of labour below the proper level, by which much destitution and misery were produced in particular places and, as a consequence of the labourers' consumption exceeding production, this tended to diminish the national wealth.[1] The remedy recommended by the select committee was an extensive programme of emigration: 'it is not for the separate interests of Ireland, where redundancy is proved to exist in a greater degree, but for the interests of Great Britain, and for the general advantage of the whole Empire, that such an experiment be made.'[2]

For the government, the emigration of redundant pauper labour would have the merit of reducing the increasing problems within Ireland, but also prevent the alarming prospect of pauper migrants pouring into Scotland and England and thereby effecting a deterioration of the condition of native labourers.

A further House of Commons inquiry into the state of the Irish poor in 1830 identified the cause of Irish migration as the higher rate of wages available in Britain. Colonisation from Ireland would tend to raise wages in Ireland and therefore diminish the flow into Britain. However, as George Nichols made clear in his report in 1837, it was essential that emigration should be limited to British colonies. Instead of being a burden at home, they could become 'productive powers of the Empire, as well as enlarge the demand for British produce'.[3]

Up to this point, in the aftermath of pilot schemes of state-assisted emigration in the 1820s, such as the Peter Robinson scheme with Irish emigrants from Cork and Kerry going to Canada, officials believed they could control and direct the emigrant flow. However, by 1847 it was clear that the scale of voluntary emigration completely dwarfed the scale of state schemes, and far from heeding official advice, most emigrants went to the United States rather than to British colonial settlements in Canada or Australasia.

It was finally conceded that 'The question of Emigration from Ireland is decided by the Population itself'.[4] The concern that remained in the absence of state-assisted emigration was that it was still open to the legislature to:

decide whether it shall be turned to the Improvement of the British North American colonies, or whether it shall be suffered and encouraged to take that which will be its inevitable Course, to deluge Great Britain with Poverty, and gradually but certainly, equalize the state of the English and Irish Peasantry.[5]

Here we can identify a clear divergence between the imagined perspective on colonisation abroad and pauperism at home, and the real pattern of emigration that was taking place. Events were also prompting a further divergence in the shape of the accelerating Irish emigration to the United States during the successive years of famine in Ireland between 1845 and 1852. During the period 1815–35, while governments and commentators were worried about

the rise of the pauper population (increasingly seen as a burden on taxpayers), a sizeable proportion of actual emigrants from both Ireland and Britain were not poor, redundant labourers, but farmers looking to prosper from opportunities to acquire land in the New World.

In 1835, an extensive survey was carried out in Ireland that enquired into the reasons for emigration over the previous three years.[6] The responses from magistrates and clergy throughout the country revealed that demand for emigration was high and that a large proportion were taking their capital with them in search of better opportunities overseas.

> Emigration has been very considerable among all classes of late years: many persons possessed of capital have gone after the expiration of old leases of farms held by them at a low rent, and of which they could not expect a renewal on the same profitable terms. (Barony of Mohill, Co. Leitrim.) I am convinced that one-third of the entire population of my parish would start immediately if they had a free passage offered to them. (Rev. Geraghty, P.P.)
>
> Most of those who departed were persons possessing small capital, hardly any destitute persons, inasmuch as they had no profitable mode of investing their capital, which they found continually diminishing of late years, since the decline of the linen trade. (Mr McDonnell, Barony of Murrisk, Co. Mayo.)
>
> For some years the emigration of labourers and small farmers has been considerable, but, unfortunately for Ireland, they have generally been the most industrious, well-behaved, and in most cases the most monied of their class, thus leaving the worst, and all the riff-raff, as an increased burden on the country. They have emigrated, some from want of employment, or other means of subsistence, at home; others from the hope of considerably improving their condition, excited by the success of their relatives and friends who had emigrated a few years before and who had, in many cases, assisted them to join by paying their passage out. (Barony of Balrothery, Co. Dublin.)

While this is a well-known phenomenon in pre-famine Ireland, there are also some similarities in the pattern of emigration from Britain. Charlotte Erikson has concluded that those fearful of encroaching poverty and loss of status in England were the most likely to be motivated to emigrate.[7]

From 1835 in Ireland, when mass emigration began, tenant farmers from the north-east and south-east of the country were joined by artisans, labourers and would-be female servants from all over Ireland to swell the emigrant tide. It was the availability of remittances from the 1830s, increasing dramatically during the famine years, that allowed more labourers to leave Ireland, destined primarily for America. These movements of people, which rose from

100,000 a year to a peak figure of 250,000 in 1852, were overwhelmingly voluntary and self-financed. The association between famine and the Irish exodus to America, instead of Canada (which virtually closed its doors in 1847 after the tragic loss of 5,000 lives at Grosse Isle), explains the commonly held American belief that all their Irish ancestors arrived during the famine.

Official language describing the 'redundant' and 'feckless' poor can also be distinguished from those among the labouring poor who were most likely to emigrate – the respectable and independent labourers. Those who managed to obtain state-assisted passage still had to find their way to a port and provide themselves with some of their needs for a sixteen-week voyage to Australia. 'Free passage' to Australia was by no means free. The middle-class lobby, campaigning successfully for assisted emigration, wanted the emigrants themselves to contribute towards their costs. In this way, private aid combined with assisted passage to finance emigration and encourage the resourceful among the labouring poor. In practice, assisted passage was selective in encouraging only certain occupations – married agricultural labourers, shepherds, herdsmen, mechanics, single female domestics and farm servants. The Australian colonies required particular skills and people who could contribute to the building of the country.

The south-west of England was the most important region of the country affected by the government-assisted stream, representing 41 per cent of the national total between 1846 and 1850.[8] Australia was also the most favoured destination from the rural west. What distinguished the western counties of Somerset, Dorset, Wiltshire and Cornwall was the generally low level of agricultural wages, running at about half the rate of northern counties, such as Durham and Northumberland. It was pointed out forcibly in 1843 that:

> The wages are certainly insufficient. Even where there are only two children it requires good management to keep them decently out of 8s a week … Each person costs 1/6d weekly on average, a man, wife, and two children costs 6/- to be properly fed. 1s a week rent at least, and fuel will nearly swallow up the remainder. But there are still soap, candles, clothes and shoes. A man's boots cost 12/- a pair, a serious expense, and he needs 1 pair a year. When I reckon up these things in detail I am always more and more astonished how the labourers continue to live at all.[9]

The low level of wages in the western counties of England found strong parallels with low wages and the availability of even less work during the year in many parts of Ireland. Given such conditions, the economic incentive to immigrate to the New World for higher wages was clearly powerful. A young lawyer in Washington wrote to his uncle in Ireland in 1853 pointing to the good wages available in America:

> This is a good country for a labouring man … At this time he can earn at least
> one dollar a day, equal to 4 shillings British. He is in good demand for this sum.
> He can board himself well – having meat three times a day, for ten dollars a
> month – two dollars and a half a week, or ten shillings British.[10]

Official understanding of the emigration of the labouring classes from England retained a belief in the twin blessings of removing a 'redundant' part of the workforce and settling communities with a vital human resource to build the colonies in a mould that reflected the mother country. The loss of the emigrant population was not felt adversely as Britain's population expanded (quadrupling between 1801 and 1901), along with the process of urbanisation and industrialisation. In Ireland, the peak year of population was 1841, with 8.2 million – a figure that halved by 1901. So emigration was deplored as part of a serious population loss that clearly diminished the human capital of the country. The explanation differed according to the view from the rural south or the industrial north, the position of Catholic nationalism or Protestant unionism, each side looking to make political capital out of a fundamentally economic phenomenon. The *Cork Examiner* proclaimed with engaging certainty:

> As to the causes of the decrease in the population … it is perfectly clear that
> in a large measure, if not wholly, it may be attributed with certainty to a want
> of manufactures, the absence of that business enterprise which a paternal
> Government would do much to foster … and to the oppressive laws which
> reduced tenant farmers to a condition of continuous and hopeless struggle, and
> to the labourers to a permanent and degrading destitution … People do not fly
> at the rate of seventy thousand a year from a self-governed country of the size
> of Ireland and possessing the same natural advantages … And we are convinced
> that the beneficial influence of Irish self-government will in no direction be
> more conspicuous than in the cessation of the fearful drain on the population
> of the country, which has been doing its deadly work for the past half-century.[11]

This contrasted with a cold blast of realism from the *Belfast News-Letter* that challenged the reasons for the lack of enterprise in Ireland and questioned how self-government would solve the problem of a lack of investment perpetuated by religious and political agitation:

> It is no use denouncing the Union with England, and alleging that it is the
> cause of all our misfortunes … The Nationalists might employ their time more
> profitably if, instead of bewailing the connection with Great Britain, which

can never be severed, they endeavoured to find the real causes of the declining population, and endeavour to find a remedy … there can be no doubt that the decrease is due to emigration. Large numbers of our people leave our shores every year, mostly for the United States … Why do they emigrate? Simply to improve their position … Agriculture is depressed. It cannot afford the constant employment and good wages which are obtainable in other industries. This depression is due to several causes, of which the principal is the pressure of foreign competition. But it is attributable in some measure to antiquated methods of cultivation, and to a lack of energy and enterprise. Nationalists say that a parliament in Dublin would remedy all this, but they do not show how it would do so.[12]

In the conflicting perspectives on the problem of Irish emigration within Ireland, it was not appreciated that the process of the concentration of industry that occurred with increased mechanisation produced a decline in domestic handicraft industry that affected parts of England as well as Ireland. The location of the linen cloth industry in Belfast and the north-east of Ireland was matched by the location of the cotton industry in the towns of Lancashire and of the woollen cloth industry in Yorkshire. The corollary of such a concentration of industrial production was a relative decline in the more peripheral areas of domestic textile work in the southern, western and midland counties of Ireland, and in England the losers were the south-western counties and East Anglia, traditional woollen cloth areas since the Middle Ages. The result for those areas in Ireland and England that suffered from a process of deindustrialisation was a population decline in rural areas as the dispossessed labour force migrated to the towns or looked for better prospects overseas.

Throughout the century, while officials and commentators continued to view emigration from Britain and Ireland through the prism of political aspiration, colonial, nationalist or unionist, people voted with their feet, looking to find better opportunities abroad. They should not be viewed primarily as 'redundant' pauper labourers shovelled out to relieve the burden of domestic taxpayers or the oppressed victims of unjust laws forced into 'exile'. Neither were they the mere flotsam and jetsam of global economic forces, compelled by the demand for cheap labour abroad. They made courageous, if dangerous, choices and, on the whole, lived to become established and see the next generation prosper.

This collection of essays on British and Irish migration during the nineteenth century draws on the research of postgraduate students at Bath Spa University. The opening piece by John Fripp on 'Mobility in Victorian Dorset' provides a close analysis of migration within a single county – a process commonly associated with further migration, sometimes overseas. In this study, the national pattern of rural to urban migration is replicated. Rural communities commonly experienced a decline, while Weymouth, a seaside resort, and the Isle of Portland, a naval base and construction site, increased their populations. However, very wide differences can be observed among the sample parishes. Mobility was connected to occupations, with most manual workers tending to move shorter distances. Incomers to Dorset included Irish convicts employed on construction work at Portland, Irish nuns and chaplains at Spetisbury Priory, and military and naval personnel. Interestingly, Dorset women were more mobile than men – a pattern that contrasts with national studies. The importance of local structural changes in the economy and improved trans- port networks in prompting and facilitating mobility are specific conclusions. Individual and family case studies add to the statistical analysis in the study.

The county of Wiltshire, with less than one-quarter of 1 per cent recorded as Irish-born in 1901, might appear an unpromising choice for finding signif- icant patterns of Irish settlement. Yet, Lynda Brown's detailed census study has identified two important groups – railway workers in Swindon and soldiers in the garrison towns of Trowbridge and Devizes – that have been previously marginalised. An analysis of Irish households in Swindon poses a challenge to the old reputation of inveterate slum-dwellers. No evidence of the infamous ghetto Irish was found in a mixed population of English, Scots and Irish in the rapid growth of the railway town of Swindon. Nor, unlike in the cities of Liverpool and Manchester, did the Swindon Irish have much recourse to poor relief. The Swindon experience reflects similar patterns of settlement and poor relief in the south-western cities of Bristol and Bath. Late on in the century, the Irish presence was considerable in the town, with more than a fifth of its population. By 1830, there were more Irishmen than Englishmen in the British army. In Trowbridge in 1851, 58 per cent of soldiers were Irish- born. Numbers declined as the century wore on. Better opportunities and high levels of emigration to the United States reduced the pool of recruits. Among Irish soldiers there was a high level of recruitment from County Cork. This geographical link between south-western Ireland and English south-western counties is again repeated in the patterns of Irish settlement in the cities of Bristol and Bath.

The importance of the link between the south-west of England and migration to Australia is featured in Celia Martin's chapter, 'Politicians, Philanthropists & the People: Early Emigration from Somerset & Dorset to Australia'. As the title suggests, this allows for the agendas of government, landowners and the emigrants themselves to be explored and contrasted. In attempting to reduce pauperism at home and to develop colonial settlements in Australia, government officials saw twin benefits for the nation. Assisted passage for the long journey south was essential and Australian settlements looked to attract specific occupations needed in frontier conditions. The match between the British wish to 'shovel out' paupers and the Australian desire for the recruiting of skilled workers and female domestics was not always one made in heaven. Equally, the emigrants who went on their own resources or were sent as convicts or political rebels could not be selected to meet specific requirements in the emerging colony. What emerges in the individual stories featured illuminates the search for a better life in a more egalitarian Australian society that provided opportunities for farmers, labourers and freed convicts.

A parallel study of '"Great Britain of the South": The Irish in Canterbury, New Zealand' by Sara Moppett employs a different methodology in drawing extensively on surviving passenger lists. It echoes Celia Martin's piece in articulating British colonial policy in the hands of Edward Gibbon Wakefield and the New Zealand Association, founded in 1837. The Canterbury Association, formed in 1848, designated the principal town in the province as Christchurch, named after the Oxford College. In the colonisation of Canterbury, the aspiration was for a Protestant, British settlement. Protestant Ulstermen and women were regarded as ideal Irish migrants. Free and assisted passages were given to agricultural labourers, ploughmen, shepherds, navvies, mechanics and domestic servants. An analysis of ships' passenger lists in the period 1865–69 and 1875–79 reveals that despite government preference for English Protestant settlers, the proportion of Irish migrants was significantly above 35 per cent. A changing balance in Irish recruits between Ulster and the 'South' of Ireland reinforces the conclusions of earlier work on the importance of the links between Munster and New Zealand. Irish migrants, both Catholic and Protestant, took advantage of assisted passage schemes to create a 'Britain of the South' – a classic case of the law of unintended consequences.

The next two studies are examples of assisted emigration from the west of Ireland to Canada. Emily Slinger's account of the Gore-Booth assisted emigration scheme from Sligo to St John's, Quebec, in 1847, tells the compelling and controversial story of a landlord-assisted scheme during the worst of the famine years. It is a well-documented scheme because Gore-Booth gave evidence before a parliamentary committee, detailing the financing and organisation of the emigration of the tenants on his estate. At the time, Gore-Booth was praised for helping poor tenants to escape the plight of rural poverty to seek a new life in Canada. Later, as the political climate turned against landlords as a class, he was vilified for allowing the emigration of his tenants. The surviving letters of some of the migrants and their secondary movement to the United States add fascinating individual responses to an epic adventure.

Tessa English tells the equally fascinating story of James Hack Tuke and the assisted emigration scheme from the west of Ireland to Canada in the 1880s. Tuke, an English, Quaker banker, had a long and distinguished career as a philanthropist and pamphleteer in relieving the poor in the west of Ireland since the 1840s. He believed that emigration offered the chance of a better life in Canada and the USA, and also relieved the plight of those left behind with the consolidation of smallholdings into viable plots. Through influential contacts, Tuke raised the funds to finance his schemes, implemented between 1882 and 1884. However, he was met with resistance by the Catholic Church, nationalist politicians and the receiving countries. If Tuke's scheme was not ultimately supported by powerful interests, it remained popular with his emigrants who left poverty in Ireland for better prospects overseas.

Politicisation of emigration is part of the published work on the migration of hard-rock miners. Drawing on census data in Britain and the United States, Graham Davis and Matthew Goulding trace the differential movement and settlement of copper miners from west Cork to both Cornwall, in south-west England, and Michigan, in the north of the United States, and miners from northern counties of Ireland to Cumbria, in north-west England. In the past, Irish and American scholars have drawn political conclusions from these movements in a narrative that combined poverty and oppression in Ireland followed by exile in America or Orange order hostility in Cumbria. This study recognises that Irish hard-rock miners were part of a global migration of miners that involved Cornish tin miners and a European movement to America that included Scandinavians, Germans and Italians. The emphasis is on global factors – the reduction in the price of copper, new sources discovered in Chile and the American West, cheaper Atlantic crossings and the investment in American mining ventures, and a system of contract recruitment by employers.

The final piece by Graham Davis looks back at Ireland through the prism of emigrant letters. 'Reconstructed Memory: Irish Emigrant Letters from the Americas' draws on a wide range of letters from the 1820s to the 1890s and relates the emigrant experience in Canada, the United States, Mexican Texas and Argentina. It is argued that letters with an eye to the intended audience back home in Ireland require careful interpretation. The memory of Ireland could be set in aspic and fiercely defended in the New World. It could also be rationalised as part of a culture of exile with the dream of one day returning to Ireland. The dream of enjoying better times in America could also be associated with an irritation with the ways of the old country – the drinking culture and an acceptance of enduring hard times. What the letters reveal is a journey of self-discovery: an oppressed and restricted old self in Ireland, a new self in dynamic American societies, and taking advantage of the prospects of a better life.

Notes

1 British Parliamentary Papers: Third Report from the Select Committee on Emigration from the United Kingdom, 1827.
2 Ibid.
3 British Parliamentary Papers: House of Commons Inquiry into the State of the Irish Poor, 1837.
4 British Parliamentary Papers: Third Report of the Select Committee of the House of Lords on Colonization from Ireland, 1847.
5 Ibid.
6 British Parliamentary Papers: Commissioners of Inquiry into the Condition of the Poorer Classes in Ireland, 1836, Reports and Supplement, app. F33.
7 Charlotte Erickson, *Leaving England* (Ithaca: Cornell University Press, 1994), cited in Robin F. Haines, *Emigration and the Labouring Poor: Australian Recruitment in Britain and Ireland, 1821–60* (Basingstoke: Macmillan Press, 1997), p. 21.
8 Haines, *Emigration and the Labouring Poor*, p. 39.
9 British Parliamentary Papers: Report of the Poor law Commission on the Employment of Children, Young Persons and Women in Agriculture, 1843, Vol. 13, Mr Austin's Report.
10 Thomas Bernard Delany to his uncle, 29 August 1853, Washington DC, cited in Arnold Schrier, *Ireland and the American Emigration, 1850–1900*, first pub. University of Minnesota, 1958 (Chester Springs: Dufour Editions, 1997), p. 28.
11 Schrier, *Ireland and the American Emigration, 1850–1900*, p. 54.
12 Ibid., p. 55.

1

People on the Move: Mobility in Victorian Dorset

John Fripp

Times were hard in the nineteenth century for the rural poor, particularly in the southern counties of England. Agriculture went through long periods of depression, wages were low and employment was uncertain. Dorset agricultural wages and living conditions were so poor that they came to national attention.[1] But those contemplating protest were only too aware of the deportations following the Swing Riots and the Tolpuddle Martyrs episodes of the 1830s. However, while employment on the land declined, growing towns offered new opportunities and in the second half of the nineteenth century many country folk were attracted to them.[2] Others left the county and perhaps the country altogether. Surplus labour in the south, particularly in Dorset, provided the incentive to emigrate, and some were assisted to do so by members of the gentry or clergy or by overseers of the poor.[3]

Although emigration and immigration have been studied, little work has been done on internal movements within the country, particularly in Dorset. This essay aims to establish more clearly the extent of movement in Dorset over the Victorian period.[4] A small sample of Dorset rural parishes and two larger settlements are examined to show the extent of mobility, both geographically and socially. Among the topics to be addressed are how movements into and out of small villages compared with those generated by larger centres, for example the Island of Portland and the growing town of Weymouth.

To what extent did Portland or Weymouth offer employment to people from Dorset or more widely? How far did people move and what types of trades or occupations were most likely to move around? Were females or males more mobile? Questions such as these are clearly of interest to those concerned with either the history of families or groups, or of a particular locality. Apart from providing the opportunity to find work, people on the move clearly had a wider impact, contributing to the exchange of ideas and news, and serving as a powerful adhesive force in provincial society, 'integrating towns with the villages of their hinterlands'.[5] In Dorset, the worst areas of depression were to the south and east of Dorchester, and records show many instances of farms being sold, with about one in five farmers leaving the land in the last quarter of the century.[6] Yet, even more than now, relocation from one settlement to another could be a traumatic experience.

Mobility was, of course, not invented in the nineteenth century. Peter Clarke points out the 'profound and pervasive effect' physical mobility had on early modern society, and how in previous centuries poor migrants had roamed across the land, and the difficulties they caused for housing, public order and food supply.[7] Writing about Lincolnshire, Steve Hindle described the widespread hostility to poor migrants in the sixteenth and seventeenth centuries.[8] Parishes were reluctant to accept them because of their effect on the Poor Rates, and vagrancy statutes acted as powerful disincentives among poorer folk. However, the New Poor Law made it easier for the distressed to move around, aided by improving road networks.[9]

Previous mobility studies have focused on a range of different issues, including emigration, internal moves as part of the urbanisation process, marriage or literacy.[10] Many sources can be used to study internal mobility, including apprenticeship records, settlement certificates, removal papers, baptisms, diaries and court records.[11] One approach is to record baptisms and burials in a particular settlement over a period of years and assume that those baptised for whom no burial can be found were 'out-migrants', and those buried for whom there is no baptism were 'in-migrants'.[12] Another method is to count the occurrences of particular names over time in a particular locality. The most sophisticated approach is the longitudinal method using detailed family histories, often documented over several centuries.[13] However, this method is less suitable for mainly within-county movements over a generation or two.

Censuses can only offer snapshots of settlements at ten-year intervals, but they reveal movements of individuals and provide a wealth of detail allowing, for example, movements of occupational groups to be traced. They can be augmented with parish registers and other sources, and several such studies have been published.[14] From 1851 onwards, censuses contain the parish and county of birth, thus allowing movements within a county and from outside it to be deduced. The availability of some censuses, in a digital, searchable form, provides a powerful research tool and the Dorset censuses in this form for 1851, 1881 and 1891, and others in microform, will be used here.[15] The statistical analysis is supplemented by brief histories of some local families, illustrating various types of movements. Also featured are extended accounts of particular developments in the village of Spetisbury and on the Island of Portland, both of which led to unusual patterns of inward migration, particularly from Ireland. Table 1 shows population details of the six Dorset settlements investigated:[16]

Table 1: Population of the six settlements and the county of Dorset, 1831–1901								
Settlement	1831	1841	1851	1861	1871	1881	1891	1901
Hilton	685	730	761	833	800	663	567	502
Milton Abbas	846	833	915	1014	942	956	787	677
Moreton	304	294	227	283	341	309	356	356
Spetisbury	667	654	660	688	673	530	562	457
Isle of Portland	2,670	2,852	5,195	8,468	9,907	10,061	9,443	15,199
Weymouth	7,655	7,708	8,230	10,013	11,361	11,550	11,217	11,970
Dorset (000s)	159	175	184	189	196	191	195	203

The Sample Parishes

Hilton is a large parish about 6 miles west of Blandford, and Milton Abbas lies immediately to the south-east of Hilton. Milton Abbas was wholly owned by Joseph Damer, Lord Milton, and his descendants until 1852, when it was sold to the Hambro banking family. Both parishes are remote from the railway. Moreton is unusual in that its population at first declined and then grew fairly steadily over the second half-century. The parish lies in the valley of the River Frome, about 6 miles east of Dorchester, and was mainly owned by James Frampton. The village has a railway station on the London and South Western Railway. The fourth village, Spetisbury, is a large parish on the banks of the River Stour, 3 miles south-east of Blandford, and is also served by a railway. As Table 1 shows, most Dorset rural parishes grew until around 1860 or 1870 and then declined. The population of the three parishes, excluding Moreton, peaked around 1861. All four are relatively isolated rural parishes and were chosen for their different ownership patterns and for their central location in the county. Inter-parish movements were therefore more likely to be recorded in the Dorset censuses. Seasonal in-migration at harvest time in such parishes should not significantly affect the results since the census dates for 1851, 1881 and 1891 occurred too early in the year.[17] The growing town of Weymouth (including Melcombe Regis) was included as it was one of the largest and fastest growing settlements in the county, and therefore likely to attract a wide range of employment opportunities. The Isle of Portland came to prominence in the nineteenth century as a naval base and for a range of large construction activities employing many people. Fig. 1 shows the positions of the chosen settlements. Table 2 shows the size and ownership of the four small parishes:[18]

Table 2: Size and ownership of the four small parishes					
Parish	Size (acres)	Principal landowner	Acreage owned	Second Landowner	Acreage owned
Hilton	3,044	Hon. Dawson Damer	1,400	Francis Byam Bingham	400
Milton Abbas	2,420	Hon. Dawson Damer	2,420	N/A	N/A
Moreton	2,157	James Frampton	2,000	Rev. William Buller	31
Spetisbury	2,250	Lord Drax	1,000	William Mackrell	540

For the purposes of this research, we define three types of movement into and out of a settlement. 'Stayers' were those who had been born in the census parish; 'joiners' were those who had been born elsewhere and had moved into the parish by the census date; 'leavers' had been born in the parish but had moved out.[19] 'Movers' were defined as the average of leavers and joiners. For comparative purposes, the numbers of people moving shown throughout this chapter are often expressed as a percentage of the relevant settlement population at census date. Table 3 shows movements in and out of the smaller settlements in 1851 and 1891, and 1881 for Moreton.[20]

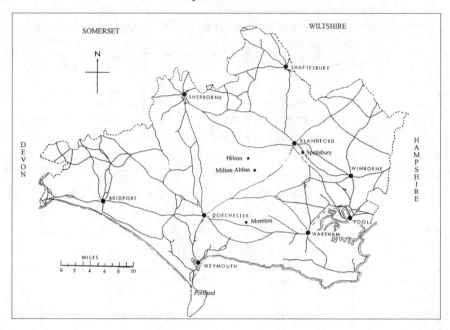

Fig. 1. The settlements discussed

Table 3: Mobility among small settlements (percentage of population)										
Parish	Hilton		Milton Abbas		Moreton			Spetisbury		All four parishes	
Date	1851	1891	1851	1891	1851	1881	1891	1851	1891	1851	1891
Joiners from outside England	0.1	0.4	0.4	1.5	0.4	0.3	3.1	3.0	2.7	1.0	1.8
Joiners from England beyond adjacent counties	0.9	1.1	1.3	4.9	3.5	6.9	11	8.8	5.9	3.3	5.2
Joiners from adjacent counties	0.8	5.0	2.4	6.6	6.2	9.5	7.9	5.6	9.3	3.1	7.1
Joiners from Dorset	59	36	33	41	46	60	58	34	46	42	43

In Search of a Better Life

Parish	Hilton		Milton Abbas		Moreton			Spetisbury		All four parishes	
Total Joiners	61	42	37	54	56	76	81	51	63	49	57
Stayers	39	58	63	46	44	24	19	49	37	51	43
Leavers to Dorset	34	59	17	43	93	76	64	39	45	35	51
Movers	47	51	27	48	74	76	72	45	54	42	54
Leavers to adjacent counties					22						
Leavers to other English counties					28						
Total leavers to beyond Dorset					50						

The first conclusion is that few people had moved into any of the four parishes from outside the county, with the exception of Spetisbury, which will be discussed later. Consider the average movements of all four parishes, shown in the right-hand two columns of the table. Only 7 per cent of parishioners in 1851 and 14 per cent in 1891 had come from outside Dorset. Those travelling from beyond the four adjacent counties (Devon, Somerset, Wiltshire and Hampshire) only amounted to 4 and 7 per cent respectively. This contrasts with the 35 and 51 per cent who left the parishes to go elsewhere in the county. Within-county joiners and leavers indicate a high and increasing degree of mobility. Movers averaged 42 per cent in 1851, and in 1891 over half of the population of the four parishes had not been born where they lived. Barry Stapleton examined the parish registers of Odiham in Hampshire for the period 1541 to 1820, and found broadly similar levels of inward and outward movements.[21] Similar results have been reported before for other parts of the country.[22] In 1891, the increase in Moreton joiners was due to increasing numbers moving from within the county and from beyond it, but those from beyond Dorset were still only a minority, perhaps reflecting the relative inaccessibility of the region or its lack of attraction for employees.

Considering the parishes individually, a number of movements do stand out. In 1851, leavers to Dorset varied greatly, from 17 per cent in the case of Milton Abbas, to 93 per cent for Moreton. Milton Abbas was clearly a comparatively popular place to live. Moreton had an average level of stayers and joiners in 1851 but a very high level of leavers. In 1891, Moreton joiners were the highest observed and stayers were the lowest. Ties to the parish of birth were clearly weakening. Among the Spetisbury movements which seem unusual was the high number of joiners coming from outside England in 1851. These were predominantly Catholic nuns and priests who came over from Ireland to work at St Monica's Priory.[23]

Spetisbury Priory

In 1735 William Hody built what Hutchins described as a 'small but elegant seat' in Spetisbury. The house passed through several hands until in 1800 it was occupied by a group of nuns, the sisters of the Augustinian Order of St Monica. They had abandoned their former convent at Louvain and fled France to avoid the revolutionary French army in 1794. Their French monastery was one of the most ancient of English establishments on the Continent, being founded in 1609, but by the end of the eighteenth century it was in debt and the sisters bought the house in Spetisbury as a school. By 1810, Hutchins reports that the society had thirty-three members and the Superior was Mrs Stonor, of Oxfordshire. The bulk of the house was occupied by the young ladies they educated, about seventy people in all. There was also a separate building in which 'the chaplain and some respectable borders then resided'.[24]

The 1851 census shows where the thirty-three nuns, including the Superior and a governess, originated. Three were from Ireland – one from Newbrook, County Mayo, one from Westport, County Mayo and one from Mount Jerome, Dublin; and one was from Pembroke, Wales. But of the others, only three came from Dorset. The majority came from far and wide in England, five each from Lancashire, London and Warwickshire. The staff outnumbered the sixteen scholars, who were aged between 9 and 17, and who came mainly from the south of England. In an adjoining building lived two Irish Roman Catholic chaplains, a boarder from Berkshire and a female servant from Wiltshire.

The nuns stayed until 1861, when they were succeeded by a group of English Bridgettine nuns, who arrived from Lisbon, their order having been

Nuns and students at Spetisbury Priory, *c.* 1920 (Reproduced courtesy of Dorset County Museum)

founded by St Bridget in Sweden in the late sixteenth century. By 1871, the house had been renamed 'Sion House', and the numbers had shrunk to seventeen in total. Nine of the fifteen nuns had been born in Lancashire, and the chaplain was from Belgium. They employed only one servant, in contrast to the seven employed by the Anglican rector and his ten children at the time. Ten years later, a new priest from Surrey had arrived and of the fifteen nuns (including the abbess and prioress), eleven had been present in 1871. Newcomers were recruited from across England, although none came from Dorset.

The Bridgettines left in 1887 to be succeeded by some Canons Regular of the Lateran, of Bodmin Abbey, who were there until 1907. In 1891, the house was called St Monica's and two Roman Catholic priests lived there, one from Italy and one from Ireland. Of the seven theology students, aged 17 to 21, one was from Ireland and the rest were from England. Also in the household were three elementary teachers, two lay brothers, from Devon and Lancashire, and an Irish kitchen maid. This is a typical example of a religious house where foreign in-migration could be found throughout the century.

Moreton

The 1881 nationwide census makes it possible to trace movers who crossed county borders, and the parish of Moreton was chosen as an example. Moretonians steadily became more mobile over the century, travelling to and from more widespread areas of the country. As Table 3 shows, over 70 per cent had left Moreton in 1881. Then, for every three people who had left Moreton to live elsewhere in Dorset, one had moved to the adjoining counties and one even further. Very few went to the emerging industrial areas of Yorkshire, Lancashire, Derby or Cheshire, preferring either London or elsewhere in south-east England. In all, Moreton-born people were living in twenty-two counties in 1881. Moreton residents had certainly come from all over Dorset. In 1851 they came from fifty-two different parishes, increasing to seventy-one in 1881 and eighty-two in 1891. However, even in 1891, over seven in ten joiners still came from within the county. In that year a mere 19 per cent were stayers in the parish, but 81 per cent had moved to the village from elsewhere, a higher level than anywhere else at the time. Leavers had declined from 93 per cent, the previous highest level, to under two-thirds.

The Parmiters were a farming family living in Moreton who were examples of both joiners and leavers. Edward came from Ludgershall, Wiltshire, and married Lucy from Kimmeridge in Dorset. They had at least three sons and four daughters between 1816 and 1833, one in the nearby parish of West Lulworth. In 1841, the family was in Moreton and Edward had become an overseer of the poor.[25] Ten years later, Edward and Lucy were living in Moreton with two daughters. None of the other children are to be found in Dorset. No more Moreton-born Parmiters appeared in the parish census from 1871 to 1901, but the Moreton registers showed that their four children chose to be married where they had been brought up.[26] In 1842, daughter Mary, born in Moreton, was married to another Parmiter, Samuel, a tradesman and farmer's son from Southampton. Nine years later, daughter Edna married a widower and draper from Wareham. Her father was described as a yeoman and his father as a brewer and they both signed the registers. A year later a third marriage took place. This time, son Thomas Parmiter, a yeoman from Moreton, married another Moreton farmer's daughter, Sophia Henrietta Forss, whose family had been in the village many years. Both fathers were yeomen. Daughter Rebecca made an equally good marriage in 1856, when she married Charles Hudson, a land agent from Devon. Two years later, Eliza Parmiter married a yeoman, also from Southampton. Parents, Edward and Lucy, were both buried in Moreton, and the burial of second son, Thomas, in 1863 brought their association with the village to an end. No more Parmiters were to be found in Moreton up to 1901. The Parmiters are an example of a middle-class family who moved around extensively but many of whom felt ties to their family and the place of their birth and upbringing.

Hilton & Milton Abbas

The differences between the adjacent parishes of Hilton and Milton Abbas are particularly striking. In both years, Hilton leavers to Dorset exceeded those from Milton Abbas, and in 1851 Milton Abbas experienced far fewer joiners from Dorset. These differences are possibly a reflection of their different forms of ownership. The terms 'open' and 'closed' parishes have been defined in a variety of ways, but a key influence is property ownership. In closed parishes like Milton Abbas, the owner was often able to restrict settlement by controlling the supply of housing and discouraging or evicting people thought likely to claim poor relief.[27] The control on joiners, in our terminology, may also have had the effect of ensuring work for those already settled in the parish. Even if additional labour was required, owners of such villages could control rents and limit the number of labourers who gained settlement, thus making it necessary in some cases for workers to walk to work from nearby parishes.[28] Those who may have done so do not count as 'movements' in this chapter, and in any case would be very hard to trace. The idea of the open and closed parish 'system' has been proposed, in which those from a closed parish migrated to a nearby open one, and the closed parish relied for its labour on the open parish. This may have been the case for Hilton and Milton Abbas. Milton Abbas certainly seems to have been a more attractive place to stay than Hilton, and in 1851 movements both into and out of the 'closed' parish were far smaller than for the 'open' neighbour.

By 1891, mobility had increased generally but the margin between joiners and leavers had diminished. The decline in the populations of Milton Abbas, Hilton and Spetisbury by the end of the century was probably due to declining birth rates. In Milton Abbas, it appears that the new ownership of the village had encouraged substantially more movement.

Occupations

People with what kinds of occupations were most likely to move? To address this question, occupations were grouped into four categories: manual workers, including labourers or servants; semi-skilled trades, such as buttoners or

carriers; skilled workers, comprising those undergoing a formal apprenticeship, such as carpenters or blacksmiths; professionals, including bailiffs and
magistrates. Table 4 analyses Moreton leavers and joiners, according to their
occupations in 1851, and lists separately those who moved less or more than
the mean distance of 11km. Straight-line distances were used to approximate
to actual distances moved, an approach also adopted by Pooley and Turnbull.[29]
Distances were measured from modern Ordnance Survey Landranger maps.[30]
Most manual workers moved only shorter distances. Very few, as might be
expected, moved into the county and none came from outside the country.
On the other hand, semi-skilled and skilled workers moved further afield,
perhaps to a larger village or to a town, since in the second half of the century,
cheaper factory-made goods undermined rural industries and many rural
trades began to disappear.[31] There were too few professionals to determine a
clear pattern, but it would be expected that they were even more mobile geographically. This suggests that, scarce though agricultural work was, labourers
were unwilling or unable to move far to find it, or, more likely, that the scar-
city of work was widespread. Skilled workers could find employment by
moving further. Since there were few large towns in the county, skilled workers would have had to move further than agricultural workers. We may test
this hypothesis by comparing the distances moved by groups of agricultural
labourers and skilled workers in 1851.

Table 4: Distance moved by various occupational groups of Moreton people in 1851						
Movement	Distance (Km)	Manual	Semi-skilled	Skilled	Professional	Total
Leavers	<11	33	5	11	3	52
	>11	19	15	25	1	60
Joiners	<11	19	3	8	0	30
	>11	14	3	9	3	29
Movers	<11	52	8	19	3	82
	>11	33	18	34	4	89
TOTAL		85	26	53	7	171

The two sets of data were tested using appropriate statistical methods, and the
results strongly supported the hypothesis that skilled workers moved further
than labourers.[32] The result does not, of course, tell us why they moved further, although we may speculate, as above, that they too moved to find work.
The vast majority of skilled people who left Moreton went to larger villages

or towns. This was partly inevitable since the village was one of the small-
est in the locality. By the same token, Moreton joiners had usually moved
from larger settlements. Out of the thirty-five agricultural labourers who
had left Moreton in 1851, all but three moved to larger villages. Of thirty-
four skilled workers who left, all moved to larger settlements, half going to
the county town of Dorchester or to the growing Weymouth area, both of
which offered a far greater variety of trades and occupations.[33] This supports
the widespread contention that towns offered strong attractions to country-
dwellers, particularly those having skilled occupations. According to Mingay,
'migration from the countryside continued throughout the nineteenth century. The larger towns, with better-paid and more varied occupations, were
a powerful attraction to many country dwellers.' He also claims that most
people who did move into towns did not move far until the second half of
the century.[34]

Weymouth

Weymouth and Portland movements are shown in Table 5, with the average of the four smaller parishes repeated for ease of comparison. Weymouth
stayers were at a level comparable with the four small parishes, but what
stands out is the large number of joiners, particularly from outside Dorset,
and the extremely low levels of leavers. This was an indication of the rapid
population explosion of a town which continued to be attractive throughout
the period (see Table 1). Weymouth was typical of seaside resorts nationally,
whose growth at this time was even more rapid than that of industrial cities.
The town drew people from further afield than the small settlements. While
nearly 39 per cent of joiners were from Dorset in 1851, they had increased to
43 per cent in 1891, and joiners from outside the county had increased from
25 to 31 per cent over the same period, as a result of the town's wider appeal
in England. At both censuses, a far higher proportion of joiners came from
outside England than was the case for the small parishes. In 1851, Weymouth
still enjoyed the boost to its fame given by the visits of George III around
half a century earlier. The 164 who joined the town from outside England
had a very wide range of occupations, including many sailors, ten annuitants,
seven gentlemen/women, many children, a bookmaker, draper, carpenters,
laundresses and many other trades.

Table 5: Mobility of the average of four parishes and the larger settlements (percentage of population)						
Settlement	The four small parishes		Weymouth		Portland	
Date	1851	1891	1851	1891	1851	1891
Joiners from outside England	1.0	1.8	5.2	4.2	6.0	6.7
Joiners from England beyond adjacent counties	3.3	5.2	8.8	14	20	28
Joiners from adjacent counties	3.1	7.1	11	13	5.1	9.5
Joiners from Dorset	42	43	39	43	8.5	10
Total Joiners	49	57	64	74	40	54
Stayers	51	43	36	47	69	46
Leavers to Dorset	35	51	7.7	24	4.7	6.1
Movers	42	54	36	49	22	30

In 1851, the parishes where most joiners had been born were the adjacent ones of Wyke Regis and Portland. Two of our four smaller parishes sent appreciable numbers to the larger settlements: eighteen from Moreton in 1851 and ten from Spetisbury in 1891. Half of those who moved from Moreton

Convicts at Portland, 1904 (Reproduced courtesy of Dorset County Museum)

to Weymouth went there to do skilled or professional jobs, or to become servants. The new Weymouth area residents from Milton Abbas were more diverse, including a cook, two housemaids, a GWR shunter, three bricklayers and an upholsterer. The coming of the railway was as important to some, as well as the growth of leisure.

Portland

The general tendency for rural people to move to the towns has been noted,[35] especially to do building and railway work.[36] Portland was one of those settlements which had very specific needs; for example, naval personnel or builders, which attracted many from Ireland and the colonies to the naval base, to the prison and for construction work. Very few from rural parishes had the required skills.

The Island of Portland lies a few miles south of Weymouth and, over the course of the nineteenth century, was to be the centre of several large construction projects attracting national headlines. In 1843, a Royal Commission considered the construction of a breakwater at an estimated cost of £500,000. This was designed to provide a place of safety for ships at the end of a period of extended shipwreck. But the necessary labour for such a large and long-lived construction was not available locally, and thus the idea of building a prison on the island was born. Prison inmates could provide cheap labour, and Home Secretary Sir George Grey felt that Irish convicts looked upon transportation rather as a 'reward rather than a punishment'. Work on Portland could provide a 'fresh start with a fair rate of pay' and would help to instil an appropriate work ethic. *The Times* agreed that transportation was 'a rightful inducement to the commission of crime'.[37]

As Table 5 shows, compared with the small settlements, Portland attracted more joiners from outside the county and from other countries. However, most of the 5,000 joiners in 1891 were from England. They included many retired people, 127 dressmakers, 100 laundresses, 62 tailors and several lodging-house keepers. By far the most numerous were servants, of whom there were 430. Very few joiners came from Dorset, in both 1851 and 1891, and the proportion of leavers was exceptionally low in both years – perhaps an indication of the historic insularity of the islanders or the variety of occupations and employment available at the time. In 1851, 119 Portland residents were joiners from Ireland. They were employed in a wide range of occupations: fourteen were gunners, nine were warders or assistant warders at the prison, three were coastguards and the others covered twenty different occupations. Forty-seven were convicts.

The Prison

The prison was for category one convicts, who started arriving on the island in 1848. They were to produce the enormous quantities of stone required to build the breakwater to enclose Portland Harbour. The 1851 census shows that the total prison population was 900, including sixty-eight staff and their families. The prison was home to many nationalities. The governor was himself from Bristol and his wife from Nova Scotia. The chaplain was Irish, perhaps to minister to the Irish prisoners, while his assistant was English. The principal warder was born in Jamaica. Of the other warders, four were from England, beyond Dorset, and one was from Ireland. The assistant warders numbered eighteen, including one each from Scotland, Wales and Gibraltar, four from Ireland, one from Dorset and the rest from other parts of England. Table 6 shows the origins of the convicts.[38]

Table 6: Origins of Portland convicts		
Nationality	**1851**	**1891**
Dorset	11	2
England outside Dorset	657	728
Scotland	94	36
Ireland	47	54
Wales	10	14
Canada	3	2
USA	3	7
Germany	2	1
China	1	0
East Indies	1	0
France	1	2
Spain	1	0
West Indies	1	1
Australia	0	1
New Zealand	0	1
Total from outside England	164	121
Total prisoners	832	861

Further analysis of the occupations of convicts is probably not meaningful for our current purpose as they were not, of course, voluntary joiners, but had been moved to Portland, many from other prisons, for reasons mentioned above. It is worth noting that, although the convicts had a wide range of trades and professions, the majority of them were labourers and there was not a single mason among them. In 1851, thirty-five masons, the skilled trade most in demand, lived on the island, with another twenty-six a few miles away in Weymouth. At the time, most stone produced from Portland was carved at its destination, requiring few masons on the island itself. So, most of the masons living nearby were probably engaged on the breakwater, too.

Portland was permanently connected to the mainland in 1885, by a causeway carrying a railway linked to the Great Western and London & South Western Railways. To protect the harbour and its surroundings, extensive fortifications were built in both Portland and Weymouth. The Verne Citadel could accommodate 2,000 men and in Weymouth, the Nothe Fort was completed in 1872, containing heavy batteries. The two fortifications could provide crossfire against any potential enemy fleets. As a result, Portland became one of the most important naval centres on the south coast. Near the breakwater, a hospital was built for navy patients, the 'Royal Sick Quarters'. The military presence in Portland was supplemented by a large group of coastguards and similar occupations by 1891. The resultant joiners are shown in Table 7.

Table 7: Military and similar Portland joiners, 1891									
Occupation/ rank	Outside England						England		Total
	Ireland	Scotland	North America	Europe	Wales	Other countries	Dorset	Beyond Dorset	
Lt Col infantry	1								1
Surgeon RN	1					1		2	4
Major								3	3
Captain						1		5	6
Lieutenant	2	2	1	1	1	1		9	17
Sergeant/ lance sergeant	1	2				1		40	44
Corporal/ lance corporal	1					2		48	51

Occupation/ rank	Outside England						England		Total
	Ireland	Scotland	North America	Europe	Wales	Other countries	Dorset	Beyond Dorset	
Soldier/ private infantry	26	11	1	2		3	2	584	629
Stoker/ leading stoker	1	2			1	1	2	44	51
Gunner	18	2					2	28	50
Petty officer	4	3					1	23	31
Able seaman	3	6		6	1	1	7	26	50
Sailor/ ordinary seaman	3	2	2			3	5	45	60
Bandsman/ master/ drummer	3					2		20	25
Boy sailor	2	5	3	1	2	33	58	441	545
Boy infantry								20	20
Band boy								14	14
Coastguard/ customs boatman	7	1	1		1	4	12	37	63
Other									29
Total	73	36	8	10	6	53	89	1389	1693

One surprising feature of these results is the origins of the 579 'boy' trainees of various kinds. While the boy soldiers and band boys came exclusively from England, forty-six of the young trainee sailors were born outside England, presumably as a result of the high reputation enjoyed by the navy at that time. Both commissioned officers and NCOs were drawn mainly but not exclusively from England.

Males & Females

A number of historians have shown that women had been more mobile than men well before the nineteenth century.[39] Table 8 compares the movements for males and females in the smaller four parishes. The results show that Dorset women were certainly more mobile than men in mid-century. In 1891, however, the situation was more complex. In all four parishes, women were still more mobile than men overall, but there were some differences in leavers. Women were less likely to leave Spetisbury, for reasons of the priory staff and residents, as discussed above. Women were also less likely to move into Moreton than men, for reasons that are unclear. These results contradict other findings, for example those of Pooley and Turnbull, who found that, between 1850 and 1859, men made slightly more moves than women.[40] Also, Friedlander found that, for most of the Victorian period, men left agricultural districts more readily than women, which he attributed to the higher level of under-employment among men than women, and low agricultural wages.[41]

Table 8: Numbers of male and female movers in all four parishes					
Parish	Movement	1851		1891	
		Males	Females	Males	Females
Hilton	Stayers	43	35	60	55
	Joiners	56	65	38	46
	Leavers	28	40	53	66
	Movers	42	53	46	56
Milton Abbas	Stayers	69	56	52	41
	Joiners	32	43	48	59
	Leavers	10	17	34	44
	Movers	21	30	41	52
Moreton	Stayers	48	41	17	22
	Joiners	52	60	83	78
	Leavers	86	92	61	65
	Movers	69	76	72	72
Spetisbury	Stayers	55	44	41	32
	Joiners	43	58	58	69
	Leavers	34	45	45	41
	Movers	39	52	52	55

Parish	Movement	1851		1891	
		Males	Females	Males	Females
Average for all parishes	Stayers	54	44	43	38
	Joiners	46	57	57	63
	Leavers	40	49	48	54
	Movers	43	53	53	59

Age Groups

The age profiles of residents of all four parishes were very similar in 1851 and in 1891, and were close to overall county and national profiles. Table 9 shows the age profiles of Moreton stayers and movers compared with the Dorset people as a whole. [42]

Table 9: Age profiles of Moreton stayers and movers and of the population of Dorset (%)						
Age range (years)	1851			1891		
	Stayers	Movers	Dorset population	Stayers	Movers	Dorset population
0–19	54.0	28.2	46.0	88.4	38.1	44.1
20–29	14.0	20.9	15.9	5.8	14.6	15.5
30–39	6.0	15.7	12.0	1.4	19.6	12.1
40–49	7.0	14.5	9.8	0.0	8.7	9.9
50–59	9.0	9.7	7.3	0.0	9.8	7.9
60–69	4.0	6.4	5.2	1.4	5.4	6.0
70–79	4.0	3.6	3.0	2.9	2.8	3.5
80–89	2.0	0.9	0.7	0.0	0.9	0.9
90–99	0	0	0.1	0.0	0.0	0.1

In 1851, those in the under-19 age group were much less mobile than older people – a finding reported before. [43] This may be partly explained by the presence of a school in the village, funded by Squire Frampton, and a resident schoolmistress. An even stronger effect is to be found forty years later. The youngest group of children, up to the age of 4, was particularly large in 1891, reflecting the increase in births in the parish during the second half of the century. Moreton people became less mobile as they got older. The increased mobility in the 20–49 age groups at mid-century has also been noted elsewhere.[44] However, a fair degree of mobility was evident even among the young and older groups, presumably because some families moved together.

Other Approaches

One of the other approaches to movement studies mentioned above was also used. In 1841, sixty families were living in Moreton whose surnames were legible in the census, forming a total of 282 residents. Ten years later, more than half had disappeared, with only twenty-seven families present, and in 1861 the numbers had dropped to twenty-two. Thereafter, numbers stabilised at around twelve families and forty-five members. These results confirm the high levels of mobility out of the parish found above. Only four names persisted throughout the remainder of the century.

One of these was the Frampton family, who had owned land in Moreton from the fourteenth century.[45] They were prime examples of those whose ties of landownership and local responsibility led them to stay in the parish over many generations, and put down deep roots in the county. James Frampton senior was very active in agricultural improvements and his son, also James, was born in London in 1769, and succeeded as lord of the manor on his father's death.[46] James junior later became a magistrate and colonel commander of the Dorset Yeomanry, owned over 5,000 acres of land in the county and married Lady Harriet Strangways, daughter of the Earl of Ilchester. James, their eldest son, was born in 1802, but died in Weymouth aged 16 and was buried in the family vault in Moreton. Second son William Charlton remained unmarried and was Rector of Moreton from 1842 until his death. James had a third son, Henry, and two daughters. Henry became major in the queen's own regiment of Dorset Yeomanry and lived briefly in the next parish, Affpuddle, as a magistrate, but then moved back into Moreton to become lord of the manor on his father's death in 1855. He and his wife had a daughter, Louisa Mary, in 1834, who married Rupert Pennefather Featherstonhaugh, of Westmead, Ireland, in 1855, and the couple had at least seven more children in Moreton. It was their son, Henry Rupert, who baptised his son Alaric Featherstonhaugh-Frampton, thus continuing the family name and their connection with Moreton to the present day. This family is a good example of the effects of landownership, in which the owners assumed a range of local responsibilities and which led to persistent residence lasting many centuries.

Occupational changes can also be tracked over time. Thirty-nine people, whose ages were stated exactly in the Moreton census of 1841,[47] were traced by name and age in the 1851 Dorset census. One, who had been a female servant, had become a housekeeper, and one previously an agricultural labourer had become a station agent. A servant had gone back to the land as an agricultural labourer. Of those who were shown as students in 1841, eighteen were agricultural labourers in 1851, ten still in Moreton. Five children had become house servants, four having to leave Moreton to do so. Of the six who had achieved semi-skilled jobs or apprenticeships for skilled trades, all had had to find work outside Moreton. One had returned to his birthplace to become an apprentice blacksmith. This appears to support Kerr's assertion that young men were often told stories about the 'good old days' by their grandparents, and some longed to get back to their roots.[48] Two-thirds of adult leavers went to parishes where there were others with their surname. The tendency for migrants to rely on a network of family or acquaintances to help them move has been noted before in the literature, and many will have received help from relatives.[49] Of the thirty-four who moved to new parishes, the majority moved alone and took a wide range of jobs, including many servants and various semi-skilled, skilled or professional jobs. As general levels of prosperity improved over the century, the nationwide demand for servants increased steadily, from 665,000 in 1831 to 908,000 in 1851 and 1.4 million in 1881, 90 per cent of whom were female.[50] Six families moved, all containing agricultural labourers. The average age of adult leavers was only 33 years.

The second half of the century brought renewed problems for agricultural people, one writer claiming that 'the hardy peasantry of bygone times seems to have degenerated into a stagnant mess'.[51] But nationally, rapid urbanisation increased the demand for food and led to buoyant prices, and in the third quarter of the century, agricultural profits improved and the era of 'high farming' dawned. Landowner and tenant alike benefited from a 'generally deferential and passive workforce'.[52] But the period of relative prosperity ended abruptly in the 1870s with the farming depression caused by cheap imports.[53] This lasted well into the twentieth century and was marked by rapidly falling prices and great hardship for landowners and tenants alike. Contemporary writers talked of many minor rural industries having 'completely died out', and the depression having 'left its mark on the county's chief industry'.[54] Traditional forms of secondary employment were disappearing too in the wake of mechanisation.[55]

The Railway

The railways helped farmers to modernise and transformed market towns such as Dorchester and Sherborne. Railways also encouraged farmers to send liquid milk to these market towns, thus killing off small-scale cheese production.[56] Farmers and landowners had to reduce their workforces and many labourers had to find work elsewhere.[57] Railways are reputed to have played a crucial role in allowing many to leave rural villages in the second half of the century,[58] but seem to have had little effect on overall movements among our settlements.

Moreton acquired a railway station in 1851, 1 mile from the village. The line went to Dorchester and Wareham, and reached the outskirts of the growing town of Poole by 1857. However, in 1851, only fifteen leavers from Moreton were living in Dorchester and fifteen in Wareham, out of a total of 210. Even by 1891, only eight were living in Dorchester, three in Wareham and two in Poole, out of 224 leavers. The railway did not reach Spetisbury until 1860,[59] but only eleven Spetisbury people lived in Poole in 1891, out of 125 leavers. Farm labourers were in any case probably unable to enjoy the benefits of rail travel until near the end of the century, when wages had risen and fares decreased.[60] Although seeming remote, this part of Dorset was well served by carriers throughout the century, thus facilitating movements for the less well-off rural population. As the rail network expanded, long-distance carriers disappeared but short-distance ones prospered. In 1859, there were many carriers in the surrounding market towns of Dorchester, Blandford and Poole, and also in

A coach at Beaminster, 1890 (Reproduced courtesy of Dorset County Museum)

Weymouth. By 1889, these had expanded even more in all these towns and there were two carriers in Milton Abbas and one in Spetisbury.[61] Carters and carriers are known to have been important for the transportation of labourers and their families.[62] The illustration opposite shows a horse-drawn carriage laden with passengers and luggage in 1890. These were in use at railway stations and more widely for those unable to afford rail fares.

The railway did, however, bring opportunities for some. In 1841, Uriah Sansom, an agricultural labourer, was living in Moreton with his wife Sophia and their three children. Uriah had been born in Moreton, and Sophia in the adjacent parish of Owermoigne. They were still in the parish ten years later, by which time two of their children had died, but they had had another son and two more daughters. The arrival of the railway in Moreton had allowed Uriah to become a station agent in 1850 and later station master. Ten years later the Sansoms were still in Moreton with four children. Also living with them were two grandchildren, one born in Marnhull, north Dorset, and the other in Surrey. Tragedy overtook the family when Uriah's eldest son was buried in Moreton in 1863. He had been a guard on the London & South Western Railway, and was recorded as having 'died in Guy's Hospital, from injuries received accidentally while looking out of a railway carriage in motion'.[63] In 1867, Sophia died and Uriah married again, to Harriet, born in Stinsford, a nearby parish. Living with them in 1871 was Uriah's daughter by his first marriage. In 1881, Uriah and Harriet were still in the parish with their new daughter, Sophia. From 1891 onwards, there is no trace of the family in Moreton, but two Sansoms were living in the parish, both born elsewhere in Dorset. In 1901, yet another Sansom moved into the parish from Tarrant Crawford.

Conclusions

This research shows that, even by mid-century, Dorset people were surprisingly mobile, including the beleaguered agricultural workers. Contrary to other studies, women were most mobile and mobility increased as the century progressed, for reasons which are not always clear, although the small sample size of the present work allows no firm conclusions. At least until late in the century, men found it harder to move than women. This work has supported the idea, first suggested over 120 years ago, that short-distance moves outnumbered longer ones.[64] The 20- to 50-year-olds were most mobile, and skilled workers most of all. All classes of society were mobile in Victorian Dorset, including labourers, poor or not. Thomas Hardy was probably right in claiming that labourers often had to move because of short-term employment, and annual hiring fairs allowed them to do so.[65] Taking place in market towns, these fairs were the means by which strong labourers who were willing to move could find work. Mingay agrees by saying, 'in areas like Dorset, where the farm hands changed masters every year, the tied cottage does not seem to have deterred them'.[66] Those first to move were often the most enterprising or the fittest, and while two-way movements could obviously be beneficial, the gradual excess of leavers over joiners among small settlements was a cause of village disintegration, which continued for many decades. Dorset rural workers were not slow to move to the towns, and many did so to become servants to the burgeoning middle classes or the urban gentry, or to take apprenticeships or work in the skilled trades needed in a growing town. Yet it is probably true that 'the Dorset labourer remained, with the church mouse, a byword for poverty until after the First World War'.[67]

People did not move around without reason in Victorian Dorset. This chapter has described their widespread and increasing movements in the nineteenth century, and speculated that many of these were the inevitable result of declining rural agriculture and the growing opportunities in new towns. Although movements could be restricted in close villages such as Milton Abbas, Dorset people eventually travelled to all parts of the county and many different counties. Some joined the armed services. To many people the railway does not seem to have influenced movements unduly, and presumably families relied on other forms of transport such as carters and carriers. Although many were prepared to sever links with their home village for the sake of finding work, they often returned to get married, or to take an apprenticeship. At mid-century, within-county mobility levels were comparatively high, but the 1851 national census shows that only 14 per cent of Dorset-born people had left the county and half of them had only moved to an adjacent county.[68] The fact that over 40 per cent of residents in our sample parishes were movers implies a loyalty to the county and a tendency to move around within it rather than leave it, although this loyalty declined as time progressed.

Although many of the movements discussed above will have been voluntary, at least to some extent, this work has illustrated various types of involuntary movement. As we have seen, soldiers and sailors were subject to the enforced movements dictated by military requirements. Prisoners had to go where the prison authorities sent them, and the Church required its people to move wherever they too were required. On the other hand, ties of landownership were strong, as were the ties of birthplace. As for voluntary movements, we can only speculate about the myriad social and cultural forces at work. But whatever the reasons, Dorset people were well and truly 'on the move' in the nineteenth century.

Notes

DHC – Dorset History Centre

PDNHAS – the *Proceedings of the Dorset Natural History and Archaeological Society*

1 J.S. Cox, *The Peasantry of Dorsetshire* (1866, reprint Besminster: Toucan, 1963); B. Kerr, 'Dorset Cottages', *PDNHAS*, Vol. 86 (1964), pp. 186–202.

2 P. Horn, *Labouring Life in the Victorian Countryside* (Dublin: Gill & Macmillan, 1976), p. 6.

3 J.H. Bettey, *Wessex from AD 1000* (Essex: Longmans, 1986), p. 234.

4 This essay is an extended and revised version of: J. Fripp, 'Mobility in Victorian Dorset', *PDNHAS*, Vol. 129 (2008), pp. 39–47, and is published by permission of the editor.

5 P. Clarke, 'Migration in England During the late Sixteenth and early Eighteenth Centuries', *Past and Present*, Vol. 83 (May 1979), p. 58.

6 P.J. Perry & R.J. Johnston, 'The Temporal and Spatial Incidence of Agricultural Depression in Dorset, 1868–1902', *Journal of Interdisciplinary History, Vol. 3, No 2, Economics, Society, and History* (Autumn 1972), p. 310.

7 Clarke, 'Migration in England During the late Sixteenth and early Eighteenth Centuries', *Past and Present*, Vol. 83, p. 57.

8 S. Hindle, 'Power, Poor Relief and Social Relations in Holland Fen, c.1600–1800', *The Historical Journal*, Vol. 41, No 1 (May 1998), p. 67.

9 A. Redford, *Labour Migration in England 1800–1850* (Manchester: Manchester University Press, 1976), pp. 99–105.

10 J. Ferrentzi-Sheppard, 'Migration From West Dorset to Jefferson County, New York 1830–1860: Was Canada the Gateway to Jefferson?', unpublished MA dissertation, Bath Spa University, 2003; P.J. Perry, 'Working-Class Isolation and Mobility in Rural Dorset, 1837–1936: A Study of Marriage Distances', *Transactions of the Institute of British Geographers*, No 46 (Mar. 1969), pp. 121–41; J. Patten, *Rural-Urban Migration in Pre-Industrial England*, Research Paper No 6 (Oxford: University of Oxford, 1973); D. Mitch, 'Literacy and Occupational Mobility in Rural versus Urban Victorian England', *Historical Methods*, Vol. 38, No 1 (Winter 2005), pp. 26–38.

11 This unusual source of such material contains the stories told in courtrooms by the deserted wives of mid-Victorian emigrants. See O. Anderson, 'Emigration and marriage break-up in mid-Victorian England', *Economic History Review*, New Series, No 1 (Feb. 1997), pp. 104–9.

12 B. Stapleton (ed.), *Conflict and Community in Southern England* (Stroud: Sutton, 1992), p. 53.

13 C. Pooley & J. Turnbull, *Migration and Mobility in Britain Since the 18th Century* (London: UCL Press, 1998).

14	D. Mills (ed.), *Victorians on the Move: Research in the Census Enumerators Books 1851–1881* (Milton Keynes: Open University, 1984); D. Mills & J. Mills, 'Rural Mobility in the Victorian Censuses: experience with a micro-computer program', *Local Historian*, Vol. 18, No 2 (May 1988), pp. 69–75.

15	The 1851 and 1891 censuses on CD for Dorset are available from the Somerset and Dorset Family History Society, and the nationwide census for 1881 on CD is available from the Federation of Family History Societies. I wish to thank Dr Diana Trenchard for providing excerpts of the nationwide 1881 census for Moreton.

16	W. Page (ed.), *Victoria History of the County of Dorset*, Vol. 2 (London: Archibald Constable, 1908).

17	The census dates were: 6 June 1841, 30 March 1851, 3 April 1881 and 5 April 1891.

18	Information was gathered from the tithe apportionments for the respective parishes, all of which were dated in the early 1840s (with the exception of Milton Abbas, for which none exists): DHC: T/HIL, T/MTN and T/SPY.

19	It is, of course, quite possible that individuals or families moved more than once between censuses, but it is not possible to track these intermediate movements without more detailed information. The likelihood of movements being missed in this way is least for stayers appearing in the parish in several consecutive censuses, unless we suppose that they moved away from their home parish to another parish, and back again within ten years, and then repeated the process.

20	By definition, stayers plus joiners comprise 100 per cent of the population of each parish.

21	Stapleton (ed.), *Conflict and Community in Southern England*, pp. 54–5.

22	W.A. Armstrong, 'The Flight from the Land', in G.E. Mingay (ed.), *The Victorian Countryside*, Vol. 1 (London: Routledge, 1981), p. 118.

23	A. Taylor, *The Book of Spetisbury, History of a Stour Village* (Tiverton: Halsgrove, 2006), pp. 68–9.

24	W. Shipp & J. Hodson (eds), *Hutchins' History and Antiquities of the County of Dorset*, 3rd edn, Vol. 1, 1861 (E.P. Publishing & Dorset County Library, 1973), p. 519.

25	DHC: D/FRA/R17: correspondence between James Frampton and others and the Poor Law commissioners concerning the sale of Moreton poor house.

26	DHC: MIC/R/1559 Moreton marriages 1837–1994.

27	S. Banks, 'Nineteenth-century scandal or twentieth-century model? A new look and "open" and "close" parishes', *Economic History Review*, Second Series, Vol. 41, No 1 (1988), pp. 51–73.

28	B.A. Holderness, 'Open and Close Parishes in England in the Eighteenth and Nineteenth Centuries', *Agricultural History Review*, Vol. 20 (1972), p. 127.

29	Pooley & Turnbull, *Migration and Mobility in Britain Since the 18th Century*, p. 64.

30	The maps used were: No 183, Yeovil and Frome (Southampton, 1994); No 194,

Dorchester and Weymouth (Southampton, 1994); and No 195, Bournemouth, Purbeck and Surrounding Area (Southampton, 1989).

31 Horn, *Labouring Life in the Victorian Countryside*, p. 7.

32 K.H. Janausch & K.A. Hardy, *Quantitative Methods for Historians* (London: University of North Carolina, 1991), p. 119. The method used was the Chi-squared test, which is a non-parametric test to find the significance of the difference between two or more sets of categorised data. In this case the null hypothesis is that there is no difference in movement distances between the two groups of workers. The result is highly significant with p=0.001, i.e. only in 1 in 1,000 such cases will the observed differences occur by chance. This is very strong support for the alternative hypothesis that skilled workers moved further than agricultural labourers.

33 Post Office Directory of Hants, Wilts and Dorset (London: Kelly & Co., 1859), pp. 610–4 & 672–8.

34 G.E. Mingay, *Rural Life in Victorian England* (London: Heinemann, 1977), pp. 19–20.

35 D. Conway, 'Step-wise Migration: Towards a Clarification of the Mechanism', *International Migration Review*, Vol. 14, No 1 (Spring 1980), p. 4.

36 Armstrong, 'The Flight from the Land', in Mingay (ed.), *The Victorian Countryside*, Vol. 1, p. 118.

37 R. Legg, *The Book of Portland: Gibraltar of Wessex* (Halsgrove Parish History Series, 2006), pp. 63–4.

38 Census summary information on Portland prison was taken from www.opcdorset. org for 1851 and from http://blacksheepancestors.com for 1891, supplemented by details from the census enumerators' schedules, DHC: /R/645 and DHC: /R/F/5/100 respectively.

39 Armstrong, 'The Flight from the Land', in Mingay (ed.), *The Victorian Countryside*, Vol. 1, p. 118; P.J. Waller, *Town, City and Nation, England 1850–1914* (Oxford: Clarendon, 1983), p. 26.

40 Pooley & Turnbull, *Migration and Mobility in Britain Since the 18th Century*, p. 59.

41 D. Friedlander, 'Occupational Structure, Wages, and Migration in Late Nineteenth-Century England and Wales', *Economic Development and Cultural Change* (1992), pp. 303–5.

42 *Census Population Tables – Ages and Conditions of the People*, Vol. 1 (London: HMSO, 1854), pp. 155 & 194–5.

43 Pooley & Turnbull, *Migration and Mobility in Britain Since the 18th Century*, p. 280.

44 D. Mitch, 'Literacy and Occupational Mobility in Rural versus Urban Victorian England', *Historical Methods*, Vol. 38, No 1 (Winter 2005), pp. 26–38.

45 W. Shipp & J. Hodson (eds), *Hutchins' History and Antiquities of the County of Dorset*, Vol. 1, 1861 (E.P. Publishing & Dorset County Library, 1973), p. 395.

46 G.E. Fussell, 'Four Centuries of Farming Systems in Dorset', *PDNHAS*, Vol. 3 (1952), pp. 125–6.

47 DHC: HO 107/278 Moreton census for 1841 on microfilm.

48 B. Kerr, *Bound to the Soil, A Social History of Dorset, 1750–1918* (London: John Baker, 1968), p. 118.

49 J. Patten, *Rural-Urban Migration in Pre-Industrial England*, Research Paper No 6 (Oxford: University of Oxford, 1973), pp. 46–7.

50 T. Wild, *Village England: A Social History of the Countryside* (London: Tauris, 2004), p. 77.

51 Redford, *Labour Migration in England 1800–1850*, p. 97.

52 T. Wild, *Village England: A Social History of the Countryside* (London: Tauris, 2004), p. 70.

53 J.P.D. Dunbabin, 'The "Revolt of the Field": The Agricultural Labourers' Movement in the 1870s', *Past and Present*, No 26 (Nov. 1963), p. 68.

54 Page (ed.), *Victoria History of the County of Dorset*, Vol. 2, p. 275.

55 J.H. Bettey, *Rural Life in Wessex 1500–1900* (Gloucester: Sutton, 1987), pp. 43 & 63.

56 Bettey, *Wessex from AD 1000*, pp. 238–42.

57 J.H. Bettey, *Dorset* (London: David & Charles, 1974), p. 58.

58 Bettey, *Rural Life in Wessex 1500–1900*, p. 88.

59 Taylor, *The Book of Spetisbury, History of a Stour Village*, p. 108.

60 Mingay, *Rural Life in Victorian England*, p. 11.

61 *Post Office Directory of Hants, Wilts and Dorset* (London: Kelly & Co., 1859), pp. 584–678; *Kelly's Directory of Dorsetshire* (London: Kelly & Co., 1889), pp. 1172–332.

62 P.S. Bagwell, 'The Growth of Carriers', in G.E. Mingay (ed.), *The Victorian Countryside*, Vol. 1 (London: Routledge, 1981), pp. 32–7.

63 DHC: MIC/R/1071 Moreton burials 1813–1993.

64 E.G. Ravenstein, 'The Laws of Migration', *Journal of the Statistical Society of London*, Vol. 48, No 2 (Jun. 1885), pp. 167–237.

65 T. Hardy, 'The Dorsetshire Labourer', *Longmans Magazine* (July 1883).

66 Mingay, *Rural Life in Victorian England*, p. 80.

67 Kerr, *Bound to the Soil, A Social History of Dorset, 1750–1918*, pp. 248 & 25.

68 *Census Population Tables – Ages and Conditions of the People*, Vol. 1 (London: HMSO, 1854), p. 176.

2

Irish Railway Workers & Soldiers in Wiltshire

Lynda Brown

The migration of the Irish in Britain during the nineteenth century has been a subject of research since the 1960s. However, most works have concentrated on the major areas of settlement in large cities such as Liverpool, London and Manchester. The county of Wiltshire has always been regarded during this period as an area of stagnation, falling population and outward migration. Yet, a closer inspection of the census returns reveals a different picture, as inward migration into the county did exist and the Irish were among those heading into the area. Moreover, the pattern of Irish migration into Wiltshire has its own particular characteristics.

The Irish in Wiltshire during the nineteenth century were concentrated into two main areas. In the north of the county the building of the Great Western Railway line and workshop in Swindon attracted many Irish into the town. Readily available employment of navvies building the railway line, labouring opportunities within the railway workshop and the building of housing, all provided opportunities for unskilled workers. Although there were no apparent 'little Irelands' within this town, the Irish did form local communities, working and living in overcrowded and unsanitary conditions, alongside labourers from many different locations.

In the south of the county, at a time when the British army was experiencing a period of massive recruitment and growth, the Irish could be found.

Often enlisted in Ireland by scouting parties in public houses, they signed up as a way of escaping the hardships endured in their homeland in the hope of a better life and a regular income. However, the conditions within the barracks in Wiltshire were very sparse and overcrowded. Once their term had been completed, many Irish remained within Wiltshire, preferring to marry and raise a family and work on the land.

As can be seen in Table 10, the percentage of Irish-born living within Wiltshire between 1841 and 1901 was never of any great consequence, and if the Irish had been spread equally throughout the county, they would have been virtually invisible.

Table 10: Source: British census returns for Wiltshire			
Census year	Population of Wiltshire	Irish born	Percentage
1841	248,056	563	0.22%
1851	326,574	781	0.23%
1861	338,939	671	0.19%
1871	360,324	759	0.21%
1881	381,324	808	0.21%
1891	390,747	806	0.20%
1901	415,239	1,078	0.25%

This chapter will concentrate on two main Irish occupations: those employed in the British army in garrison towns and the railway workers in and around Swindon.

In a predominantly agricultural county, Swindon was the main area of Wiltshire to be affected by modern industry during the nineteenth century. Parliament authorised the construction of the London Paddington to Bristol railway line in 1835 and sections of the line were in use by the late 1830s. However, the line was not completed until 1841. This delay was due entirely to the construction of the two tunnels between Chippenham and Bath, Middle Hill Tunnel and Box Tunnel (the latter being some 3,195 yards long) – a massive engineering project.

The arrival of the railway not only brought employment to a once small hill-top village, but also had the effect of changing both its size and economic structure. The associated difficulties of overcrowded housing conditions, illness and squalor, equal to that of any large town at this time, was also prevalent once the labourers arrived. Swindon grew at an astonishing rate throughout the nineteenth century, a trend that continues today with Swindon being one of the fastest growing towns in Europe.

The total population of Wiltshire grew by some 16 per cent during the nineteenth century and, without the attraction of the railways in the north of the county, Wiltshire's population would have declined. Certainly the trend in most towns and villages was for the population to increase during the first half of the century and then fall into decline.[1] Swindon, in the north of the county, proved to be the exception as, having not enforced Acts of Settlement, the population grew from 1,198 in 1801 to 46,006 in 1901, an increase in excess of 3,000 per cent. This population growth was a direct result of the planning and arrival of the railway. This mass increase in populace for just one small area of the county provided Wiltshire with an overall increase in population, whilst the trend in the remainder of the county was one of decline. Swindon, having been chosen to accommodate the engineering workshops, provided employment for a prospective workforce which quickly descended on the area.

The opportunity for gainful employment encouraged people to migrate to Swindon from all parts of the county and beyond, with the hope of a regular weekly wage packet approximately double the rate for agricultural labour. Whilst some moved into the town from the surrounding rural area, others travelled great distances or were relocated from other railway workshops to supply the demand for workers. Those imported into the town by Great Western Railways were required to supply the need of skilled employees to build and design the workshops. Others, experienced within railway engine construction, were required to train the unskilled labourers who flooded into the town.

In 1841 the census only recorded three Irish people as living within Swindon, all described as stone masons. These were employed, presumably, in the construction of the engineering workshops and to provide accommodation for the migrants in Swindon village. Certainly, Irish labour, as E.P. Thompson identified, was often preferred to that of the English as: 'The Irish labourer will work at any time … I consider them very valuable labourers, and we could not do without them. By treating them kindly they will do anything for you.'[2] This certainly appeared to be true in Wiltshire, as although many navvies were engaged, there were small groups of Irish navvies constructing the railway line. There is no evidence that the Irish behaved in any other way than as loyal and hard-working alongside their fellow English navvies. The biggest group of Irish was working just outside Swindon, at Wootton Bassett, where ten Irish excavators were identified within the census data.

Wootton Bassett must have experienced something of a boom, as the census of 1841 reveals that the railway was under construction en route through the small market town. Its total population was only 2,888, but 20 per cent of this figure were navvies drafted in from throughout the country to construct the line. These navvies, totalling nearly 600, appeared to be living throughout the town, renting rooms in nearly every dwelling. Additionally, over 100 unnamed males had occupations listed as 'Not Known' in the census, and appeared to be sleeping in stables at a local inn. The census also contained a note on the side of the page from an account from W. Bailey that '22 Excavators having slept about without any lodgings'.[3] These were accounted for within the census but combined with a large group of men whose names, ages and origins were listed as 'Not Known'.

Despite the harsh working conditions, the draw for men to work on railway construction was the regular pay packet, which was considerably higher than that of the agricultural labourers in the area at this time. However, insufficient workers meant that still more men were needed in 1840 to work on the line. The *Bristol Mercury*, on 1 August 1840, recorded that: 'Many of the men working on the railway at Wootton Bassett are earning 25s. to 35s. per week, and such is the want for more hands that 100 men have been advertised for, to assist at the works at Tockenham, near Christian Malford.'[4]

This large influx of people living in the market town must have changed its make-up by providing prosperity, albeit for a short time. Not only were the inhabitants making money out of providing lodgings for the navvies, but also the shopkeepers and innkeepers must have increased their turnover considerably during this period. Additionally, the census revealed that a small percentage of locals were also listed as excavators in the census, thereby bringing work directly to the local population. Certainly, all ages were employed on the construction and many boys as young as 15 were listed as being excavators.

With this great influx of navvies, the ten listed as being Irish paled into insignificance. These men, having found lodgings at one of the inns in the town, were just incorporated within the group of navvies. Unusually for navvies at this time, two Irish-born wives and one Irish-born child aged 3 years were also staying at the inn with their husbands. However, the true identity of those navvies recorded as being 'Not Known' may well have included further Irish-born who preferred to keep their true identity hidden from the authorities, for fear of being returned to their native country.

Additionally, at Stratton St Margaret, Christian Malford and Lyneham, smaller groups of navvies, including Irish, could be found labouring on the London to Bristol line under construction at this time. The 1841 census also reveals nine more Irish-born labouring on the building of Box Tunnel, but living on the Wiltshire side of the tunnel, along with a civil engineer, Edward Murray.

The building of a railway, without the advantage of modern-day earth-moving machinery, was an amazing feat. The navvies, armed only with a shovel, dug cuttings, tunnels and built viaducts. Working long hours in often dangerous conditions (including the use of explosives), the navvies toiled, travelling around the country wherever the railways took them. The railway building boom of the 1840s proved very useful to the Irish as it coincided with the poor harvests and potato famine in Ireland. The Irish, being a 'mobile people', fitted in with this lifestyle perfectly as they had already severed the ties with home and were prepared to work, and play, hard. The work of a navvy was one of the most strenuous of occupations as:

> each man has to lift nearly twenty tons of earth on a shovel over his head into a wagon. The height of lifting is about six feet. This is taking it at fourteen sets a day; but the navvies sometimes contrive to get through sixteen sets, and ... some men ... will accomplish this astonishing quantity of work by about three or four o'clock in the afternoon.[5]

The Irish were attracted to this employment by the thought of the excellent wage packets paid to the navvies, irrespective of the hazards involved.

By 1851, however, with the completion of the railway in June 1841, the picture of Swindon's inhabitants was very different. An analysis of the inhabitants of the town indicates that work within the railway workshops was the main employer; the vast majority of these men migrating into Wiltshire.

By examining the census data in Chart 1, it is apparent that by 1851, very few of the workers in Swindon's railway industry, only 9 per cent, were natives of Wiltshire, with the remainder migrating into the town in search of employ-

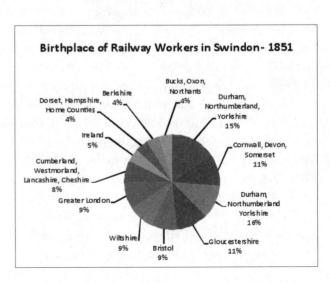

Birthplace of Railway Workers in Swindon - 1851

Bucks, Oxon, Northants 4%

Berkshire 4%

Dorset, Hampshire, Home Counties 4%

Durham, Northumberland, Yorkshire 15%

Ireland 5%

Cornwall, Devon, Somerset 11%

Cumberland, Westmorland, Lancashire, Cheshire 8%

Durham, Northumberland Yorkshire 16%

Greater London 9%

Wiltshire 9%

Bristol 9%

Gloucestershire 11%

Chart 1. Devised by Lynda Brown from census data[6]

ment. The GWR Company brought in experienced workers from other areas to train and manage the workforce. Of the remaining 91 per cent, most were drawn from all over the country with a relatively small percentage, only 5 per cent, being Irish-born.

As can be found in other towns and cities in England at this time, the majority of Irish were engaged in labouring tasks. In working within the railway factory, they encountered the same overcrowded disease-ridden conditions as could be experienced in any industrial town at that time. Like any mixed group of migrants living and working within a new area at that time, they experienced poor living conditions and long working hours.

The railway line through Swindon may have been completed in 1841, but permanent housing for the employees was not begun until 1842. This created an acute shortage of accommodation within the surrounding villages of Swindon, as labourers struggled to find shelter. Alongside the railway workshops, the GWR, realising the plight of the workers, planned housing to accommodate their workforce. The village was designed to be a model village of terraced houses, shops and other amenities. The firm of Rigby's was contracted to build housing using the available quantities of Bath stone, removed from the building of Box Tunnel, along with local Swindon stone. The housing was constructed to a standard which Rigby's thought was affordable for the skilled engineers employed by GWR. The roads were named after the towns the trains were destined to reach. However, this building work proved too little and too late, as the migrants poured into the town looking for work and swamped the available accommodation.

Although the 'railway village was designed with flair and imagination',[7] the terraces of small houses built from 1842 were of poor quality. Friedrich Engels, in *The Condition of the Working Class in England*, identified that in Manchester: 'Workers' cottages are now hardly ever built singly, but always in larger numbers-a dozen or even sixty at a time. A single contractor will build one or two whole streets at a time.'[8] This was certainly the case in Swindon where, like Manchester, the building of terraces proved a cheaper method of providing housing. Additionally, the builder was very rarely the landowner, the land being leased to the builder for a period between twenty and ninety-nine years. Once the lease had expired, the land and buildings would revert back to being the responsibility of the landowner for its upkeep and repair. Therefore, the housing built in Swindon, like many towns during this time, was only designed to last as long as the lease.

The number of houses inhabited in New Swindon was quite small in comparison with the numbers of people working in the railway workshops. To assist in the need for accommodation, 'temporary wooden houses mounted

on wheels scattered about the fields'[9] served as shelter, whilst others inhabited the constructions as they were being built. Edward Snell, a labourer in
Swindon during the early years, described his accommodation as 'rather
queer lodgings mine, at present the house only 1 story high, walls of rough
brick inside, and most of the rooms occupied by a barefooted Scots woman
and her family'.[10]

Daniel Gooch of the GWR reported in 1845 on the urgent need of new
cottages: 'since in some instances 10 or 12 people were living in 2 rooms and
when the night men got up the day men went to bed, and workers were leaving Swindon because they could not get a place of any kind to live.'[11]

The situation did not improve readily as by January 1847, the 182 completed houses accommodated some 1,360 people, averaging 7.5 people per
house. Many of these houses were small, with only two or four rooms, and
designed to accommodate one family each. A further 978 people were living
in lodgings in the surrounding villages and walking several miles to continue their employment within the railway yard.[12] By 1851, as more houses
were built, the occupancy rate reduced slightly to just over six people per
house.[13] By general standards, however, Swindon, being newly built and with
the absence of decaying courts and alleys, was not seriously overcrowded.
In 1841, Midghall-Lane, Liverpool, recorded an average occupancy of 16.4
people per house, whilst Avon Street, Bath, in 1851, fared slightly better at
15.3 people per house.[14]

Reading Street, in the centre of the railway village, was built between 1845
and 1847, and contained some thirty-four units of accommodation, each
having five rooms. It had the highest overall household size within the area
of 7.6 people per house, with one household alone containing some fourteen
people. The high rents required by the railway company determined it was
essential for most houses to contain two families, or else lodgers were taken
in. Within Reading Street, the Irish households contained slightly below the
average at 7.2 people per house, whilst overall, Irish households within the
railway village had an average household size of only 5.7 people.

Despite the reputation of the Irish in Britain as inveterate slum dwellers
living in ghettos, propagated by J.P. Kay and Engels, the limited census evidence in Swindon confirms the findings of Mervyn Busteed and others in
their study of the notorious 'Little Ireland', Manchester in 1851.[15] Within this
one road alone the levels of inward migration into Swindon can be observed
as identified in Chart 2 (see overleaf). This migration into Swindon seems
to be linked directly with the railways as 17 per cent were from Somerset,
mostly from Bristol, and a further 11 per cent from Gloucester. Middlesex was
the next highest recorded birthplace, primarily from Paddington, where four

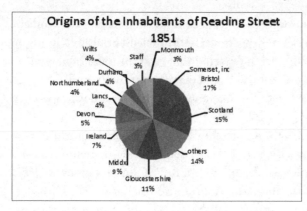

Chart 2. Origins of the inhabitants of Reading Street, 1851. Source: Census of Great Britain (1851)[16]

Irish children were born prior to arrival in Swindon. Scotland also featured highly, with some 15 per cent of the residents of Reading Street recording a Scottish birthplace in the census. The Irish-born, some 7 per cent, were residing amongst people from all areas, including one family sharing a house with a Scottish family. Of the residents who were Wiltshire-born, only seven were adults. The remainder, fifty-four, were all under the age of 8 years, the majority being 3 years old or less, which would correlate with the timing of new housing being completed.

In 1851, the census revealed that 55 per cent of the 2,371 inhabitants of New Swindon came from outside Wiltshire.[17] The census recorded the addresses of the seventy-five Irish-born living in Swindon as being within the railway village and in close proximity to each other. Swindon, having the highest concentration of Irish in Wiltshire at 3.2 per cent, does not show any indications of containing any Irish ghettos, although the opportunity for one to develop was surely possible. However, as Swindon was newly built, the decaying courts and alleys contained within the larger towns in England during this period didn't exist. Certainly, the majority of Swindon's Irish-born inhabitants were living within the small, inferior housing built during the 1840s, adjacent to and employed within the railway workshops.

Westcott, to the west of the railway village, was also an area of great expansion by 1851, mostly due to speculation. The astute owner of Westcott farm bought the land in 1843, and he and his family built many two-storey cottages and twelve shops in Westcott Place. By 1851, the Irish had moved into this area due to the low rents charged for the cheaply constructed premises. Out of these seventy dwellings, the Irish were to be found in five, including a few connected with trades like that of a coal merchant and a master baker. These cottages and shops were in close proximity to the Greyhound Inn which, incidentally, was run by an Irish family at this time.

Extensive building of housing by 1881 accommodated the railway workers in a far less crowded manner. By this time the Irish element, although growing in number to some 130, were dispersed throughout the maze of new roads built in the town, thereby reducing any concentration of Irish in any one area. This dispersal suggests a process of modest, upward social mobility among the Irish within a generation.

Swindon being a 'modern town' had one vital element omitted from its make-up, that of being built alongside a river and thereby supplying a means for gaining access to water, along with the disposal of waste fluids. Swindon's only source of water was the declining Wiltshire and Berkshire canal, used by the railways both for the delivery of coal and used in the engineering works, along with extraction for use in the steam engines. Although the drinking water extracted from the canal was filtered, albeit poorly, this could not remove the pollution produced by the discharge from the works, which was fed directly back into the canal. Even by 1853, when all cottages had their own water supply, this water was still drawn from the polluted canal until 1866, when the Swindon Water Company supplied fresh water.

In common with many towns, a poor water supply and little in the way of sanitation resulted in many outbreaks of typhus, cholera and smallpox. Following the cholera epidemic in the town in 1849, 'caused by the blocked and overflowing cesspools in the rear yards to the cottages',[18] orders were given by the GWR for drains to be cleaned and the cottages whitewashed. Edward Snell recorded his experiences in a diary on arrival to New Swindon in 1843:

> For my part I hate it and haven't been well since I've been here ... Most of the houses very damp and containing only two rooms. Not a drop of water to be had but what comes from the tenders or out of ditches and what little we do get is as thick as mud – not fit for a jackass to drink.[19]

The situation had not improved by 1852 as serious outbreaks of typhoid, typhus and other related diseases affected the town. Over 400 separate cases were reported at this time and resulted in fourteen people losing their lives. Again stagnant pools and overflowing cesspools were seen to be the cause of the problem. Immediate steps were taken to improve the area 'for the purpose of preventing any increase of fever and of averting the dreaded approach of cholera'.[20] Finally, unable to solve the problem of ill health, the GWR decided to pave all the rear yards and passageways within the village reported 'to be indispensable for the preservation of health and lives of the inhabitants'.[21] Although the Highworth and Swindon Union out-relief records indicate that

between the years 1843 and 1870 fever-related illnesses like typhoid and cholera continued to hit the town, only three families in Reading Street made any
claim for assistance.

The course of the railway and the building of Swindon 'New Town', being
at a lower level than the surrounding villages and towns, and with the canal
running through, did, however, create problems in times of heavy rainfall. The
Bristol Mercury and *Daily Post* reported on 28 October 1882 that, following a
period of excessively heavy rain:

> the streets of New Swindon were flooded to an alarming extent, caused by the
> overflow of water from the canal. In the vicinity of the overflow the cottages
> were completely soaked, whilst in other places the flood was caused through
> the inability of the sewer to carry off the storm water … water would rush out
> from under the floors of the houses into the streets.[22]

Within Swindon, with its high employment rate, the Irish made very few
claims for poor relief. This low figure may have been assisted by the existence
of a 'sick club', later known as GWR Locomotive and Carriage Department
Sick Fund Society in 1844, enabling staff to pay money on a weekly basis,
thereby receiving help towards any costs for medication when needed.[23]
In other cities, however, for example Liverpool in 1847, the Poor Law was
unable to cope with the influx of famine migrants from Ireland asking for
assistance. As Frank Neal estimates, some 39 per cent starving Irish applied for
poor relief during that year, overwhelming the systems in existence for such
relief.[24] The port of Bristol also experienced migration; however, the amount
of claims for poor relief were considerably lower at some 2 per cent (102
people) of the Irish population of the city and included both those housed
within one of the workhouses or claiming outdoor relief.[25] The impact of
Irish settlement on the system of poor relief, therefore, varied considerably
from place to place. The negative story of Irish paupers was the one believed
at the time and understood as a universal truth.

Of the Irish living in Swindon, only seven families applied to the parish
for outdoor relief between the years 1843 and 1870, and in the majority of
cases this was for assistance due to work-related injuries. Only the Sheehans,
living in Oxford Street within the railway village, applied for assistance due to
illness. William Sheehan, aged 25 and the head of the house, had contracted
phthisis (consumption) and applied for assistance three times during the latter
part of 1851 and in early 1852.[26] William Sheehan was married to an Irish girl,
Mary, and had a 1-year-old son to support. His 22-year-old younger brother
shared their house in Oxford Street and was also employed as a labourer on

the railways.[27] This high rate of employment, or lack of willingness to ask for assistance, is further shown in the 1851 workhouse census of the Highworth & Swindon Union, where the Irish-born formed only 1 per cent of inmates. By 1881, no Irish-born migrants were to be found within the Highworth & Swindon Union workhouse.[28]

The railway workforce in 1851 was young, with an average age of only 32. Of the Irish, some as young as 12 were employed as messengers or junior clerks, whilst older boys joined as apprentices. A typical example would be that of the Keefe family. Having arrived in Swindon some five years previously from Bristol (evidenced by the birthplace of the children),[29] this family found ready employment on the railways. Edmund Keefe, a widower aged 36, worked as a blacksmith, whilst his two eldest sons, both born in Bristol, Charles, aged 15, and Thomas, 11, found employment as a striker and a clerk respectively. Three younger children also shared the house along with an elderly Irish-born servant. Living in Bath Street, one of the first blocks of houses to be built in 1842, seven family members shared a two-roomed apartment, one up and one down. In 1849, the rent on these cottages was 3s 6d a week, amounting to 29 per cent of a labourer's wages. Edward Snell commented about the high rent: 'The Company make the men pay most extortionate rents for these bits of huts, too – 3s 6d for a single and 7s for a double cottage.'[30] By 1872, the rent for these cottages had risen to between 5s and 8s a week, depending on the size – 'a price too high for the great majority of mechanics to pay'.[31] To cover the costs of accommodation, two or three families often shared a house, living in overcrowded conditions.

Richard Jefferies also observed the cost of accommodation within Swindon. In a letter to a newspaper he compared the wages and housing costs of both rural and urban workers and found them to be comparable. The labourers working on the railways in Swindon, although paid a regular and higher wage throughout the year, also had to pay higher rents for their accommodation. In comparison, those working in agricultural areas experienced fluctuating wages depending upon the time of year. But by taking into consideration 'the extremely low and often nominal rent; and the advantages of a garden … representing a supply of vegetables',[32] there was little difference in the annual wages for either labourer. Jefferies further added that 'the mechanical labourer is usually unable to find lodgings in the town near to his work from their high price, and is therefore, obliged to take a cottage in some village at the distance of two or three miles'.[33] He also noted that some 100 railway employees walked from Wroughton to Swindon, some 4 miles each way, whilst another boy walked from Wootton Bassett, 6 miles outside Swindon. These observations led him to believe that 'The labour and time expended in this walking are equal to half a day's work, so that the mechanical labourer really, for the same money, works a day and a half, as compared with the agricultural labourer'.[34]

Within Swindon's Old Town, the houses were believed to be of superior class, whilst the tenants of these houses connected with the railways were considered to be a 'well behaved and intelligent class of persons'.[35] Of the seven Irish-born living in Old Town in 1851, only one had connections with the railways. His position of working as a railway clerk could well classify him as being on a higher social scale than the labourers within Swindon's New Town. However, the remaining six Irish-born, living in two of the many lodging houses, were not connected with the railways but classified as drapers, a sailor and two errand boys.

The recording of female occupations in the Victorian censuses was highly problematic. Part-time and seasonal work and women working at home contributed to a pattern of consistent under-recording of females at work. Nevertheless, even if the record is incomplete, there are important clues in the census data.

Employment opportunities for women from the outset in Swindon were minimal, principally dressmaking or charring. The 1851 census reveals only one single young Irish girl in Swindon at this time, working at the railway superintendent's house as a servant.[36] As the town of Swindon had developed due to the engineering workshops and the building of the railway, it was a very male-orientated environment. The employment in the area was almost totally manual labouring work either within the railway buildings or building housing for the workers to live in. Therefore, being a 'new town' Swindon could not provide a ready supply of large old Georgian houses with wealthy occupants requiring maids and servants, as were found in other established towns. As a result, single Irish women, like their male counterparts, headed for towns of known employment opportunities.

It was not until 1872 that a few women were employed in Swindon within the railway works in the trimming shop. The formation of the sewing shop with the GWR to be worked only by the 'sterner sex'[37] was seen to be 'an important step, as it will afford occupation for a goodly number of unemployed wives and daughters of Mechanics and others in the town'.[38] However, women were not encouraged to work at the railway factory in any great numbers. By 1892, it was still only the trimming shop that engaged women, but still not to any great extent. This neglect of employment of women by the railways might stem from their apparent concern for the comfort of their female employees, as a separate entrance was provided, along with women being allowed to 'leave at somewhat different hours from the men'.[39] Within

Chart 3. Percentage of
Irish-born people living in
Swindon, 1841–1901. Source:
Census of Great Britain
(1841–1901)[40]

Irish in Swindon 1841 - 1901

the trimming shop the tasks of French polishing, sewing and net-making
were undertaken by 100 women.

In 1876, a large London clothier, J. Compton & Sons, built a sewing factory
alongside the railway works, with an Irishman as the manager. This factory
provided desperately needed employment for some 300 women initially. A
Clicker boot factory also appeared in Swindon about this time, again managed by an Irishman.

Throughout the nineteenth century, Irish people did settle in Swindon, as
can be seen from the above chart, but although the numbers of Irish-born
increased through the decades, so did the population of Swindon. The Irish
contingent of Swindon rose from 10 per cent to the relatively high figure of
22 per cent of the total population of the town,[41] although this may not seem
to be of any great importance as the Irish found employment and accommodation without causing any great problems within the town. These figures,
however, do reveal a very different pattern of Irish migration to records of
larger cities such as Liverpool. Colin Pooley noted that in 1851 the Irish made
up some 22.3 per cent of the population of Liverpool, but by 1871 this figure
had fallen to 15.6 per cent.[42] Frank Neal, in his study of principal urban areas
of the north-east of England, also records a pattern of a falling percentage of
Irish in areas such as Gateshead and Sunderland.[43] This pattern of Irish migration was not limited to the northern towns. Bristol also experienced a decline
of the Irish population from 1851 onwards as identified by David Large.[44] It
could indicate that these studies have been undertaken in areas of entry for
the Irish, some of whom stayed in these ports having found employment,
whereas many moved around the country until they found suitable regular
employment inland.

The numbers of Irish who settled in Swindon during this period was
comparatively small, but the pattern of increased percentage of Irish as the
century progressed shows a significant trend that the Irish moved inland into

towns where there was a supply of readily available work. A similar pattern
of increased Irish presence can be observed in Herson's study of Stafford,
where the percentage of Irish grew until 1871 and then subsided. This may be
linked with the dispersal of the Irish from the larger cities in search of gainful employment.[45] As Fitzpatrick observed, by 1871, two-thirds of the Irish
in Britain were to be found outside the major cities of London, Liverpool,
Manchester and Glasgow, indicating that the Irish were an increasingly
mobile people.[46] This pattern of settlement would appear to be borne out by
this study of the Irish in Swindon.

Swindon, with its modern industry, attracted the Irish to settle within the
town. Working and living alongside many other migrants from all over Britain,
the Irish were just another migrant minority within the new development. The
growth of the rail works along with the town during the second half of the
nineteenth century provided both employment and accommodation, albeit in
similar overcrowded conditions to those found in all large towns at this time.
However, the Irish were obviously keen to be employed and fend for themselves as very few applied for assistance in either outdoor relief or were taken
into the workhouse. The disbursement of Irish throughout the new town, along
with the lack of old courts and rookeries, did not allow for any Irish ghettos or
'little Irelands' to develop. Likewise, although the Greyhound public house was
adopted as an Irish gathering place, through using a back room as a Catholic
meeting point, the Irish in Swindon do not appear to have developed any
strong community ties and generally just assimilated into the local population.

Soldiers & Building Workers

Whilst the Irish population of Swindon increased throughout most of the
century, a different picture emerges when looking at the Irish-born in the
army located to the south of the county. Within the British army during
the first half of the nineteenth century, a large Irish presence was recorded,
often more than 25 per cent, and 'by 1830 there were more Irishmen than
Englishmen in the British army'.[47] The high proportion of Irishmen generally
within the armed services was recorded in the Westminster Review in 1835,
when it was observed: 'Irish men may freely man our navy, or serve in our
armies, because we do not desire that employment for ourselves. It is more
problematical whether they may officer them, because that is more genteel
and lucrative, and should therefore be reserved for ourselves.'[48]

Although this appears somewhat disdainful, Irish soldiers within Wiltshire
in 1841 made up some 37 per cent of the army based at the barracks in

Trowbridge, increasing by 1851 to 58 per cent, mostly of the rank of private. Of Irish men holding a higher rank there were only two in 1841 and six in 1851. These may have been from an Anglo-Irish background, having received the benefits of an English public-school education. These figures compare favourably with the national percentages of 37.2 per cent in 1840, and reducing to 30.8 per cent by 1868.[49]

Massive recruitment into the army resulted from the constant need to replace those invalided out of the army due to ill-health, along with those reaching the end of their term of service. During the early part of the nineteenth century, Ireland proved to be a good hunting ground for such recruits. However, as the century progressed and the famine and emigration took its toll on the population, recruiting officers found it harder to maintain recruiting levels from Ireland.[50]

Ireland's doubling population between 1780 and 1841 gave rise to a young nation, with a high percentage living in a rural environment. As Professor Hanham noted:'Ireland … was simply like good recruiting districts in England, where men were encouraged to enlist by want of alternative employment.'[51] Generally, recruits from a rural background were far healthier than those from the urban slum areas, therefore recruiting from Ireland decreased the rate of rejection. The rejection rate of English and Scottish recruits at this time was 34.7 per cent, whilst the rejection of Irish recruits was only 17.6 per cent.[52]

Whilst many Irish migrated to Britain or emigrated further afield, those who remained in Ireland experienced the advantages of education, primarily in learning to speak some English, which assisted entry into the army. Ireland, being largely rural with only limited industry, offered insufficient employment opportunities. The offer of accommodation, regular pay, and the chance for travel and adventure, encouraged many Irish to seriously consider the army. Enlisting in the British army appeared to be a 'practical alternative to utter poverty',[53] drawing from an immense reservoir of young, healthy men and boys. The Infantry and Royal Artillery regiments especially favoured Irish recruitment.

Certainly, enlistment into the army encouraged 'men in desperate circumstances, especially among those who frequented haunts of dissipation and inebriation where much of the recruiting was conducted', to sign up.[54] Frequenting local public houses, sergeants and recruiting officers received a 'Queens Shilling' for every boy or man accepted into the army. In such a locality, those wishing to escape from the rigours of rural life, the law or even sexual indiscretions, would willingly volunteer. The volunteers would then be subjected to a rigorous medical examination and a height check against a measuring bar before acceptance into the army. Recruits had to be basically fit and healthy and be a minimum height of 5ft 5in, this being the average

Fishers of Men – George Augustus Sala[55]

male height at that time. The commentator George Augustus Sala, in his work *Fishers of Men*, captured this moment.

Thomas Jordan, in his study of Irish recruits into the British army, recorded that the healthiest men came from the east of Ireland, whilst the least healthy came from the west. The Irish in the British army serving in Wiltshire during the 1851 census tended to come from County Cork, the most southern county, and in the south-western province of Munster, and produced some 14.7 per cent of the Irish recruits into the British army, second only to Dublin at 18.8 per cent.[56]

The average age for recruits was between 16 and 24 years; however, boys as young as 11 were enlisted, providing that they were tall enough, fit and healthy. Recruits also falsified their ages, ensuring an entitlement to a pension along with the start of active service abroad which began at 18. Older men would apply dye to their hair to give them a younger appearance in the hope that they would be accepted.[57] The 1851 Wiltshire census shows that the Irish-born in the army had an average age of 26.78 years, the youngest being aged 21, whilst the oldest was aged 47.

By 1861, many of the fittest and healthiest Irish had emigrated. Those in Ireland wishing to enlist were in such poor health that the army rejected them. The disappearance of the peasant soldier was observed by Lord Sandhurst, the commander-in-chief for Ireland (1870–75), who when recruiting sergeants found only the 'riffraff ... of Cork and Dublin'.[58] Sandhurst believed that 'The decent men who want to better their conditions do not now think of entering the Army, as was the case before the famine of 1846 and 47–48. This class now emigrates en masse to England, the United States, and the British Colonies, in search of work and high wages.'[59]

However, by 1861 the army seems to be absent from Trowbridge, possibly due to the Crimean War and the Indian Mutiny, and the only army personnel identified were in Salisbury at the Kings Arms public house, where a sergeant and an Irish corporal were trying to recruit.

This change can be observed in the 1881 census, as although the army generally had increased in Wiltshire, the Irish element had reduced to just 11 per cent. The ages of the men by 1881 also indicate a change in available recruits, as the average age of Irish soldiers had increased to 30.27, whilst the ages ranged from 14 to 46 years old. The following censuses indicate a large increase in the total army population within Wiltshire. Many more camps were built leaving the percentage of Irish-born to be totally insignificant, at less than 1 per cent.

Conditions within the British army were not good. The rate of pay for an infantry private in 1856 was only 1*s* 1*d* a day, although extra pay could be earned by working as officers' servants and mess waiters. Only with twenty-five years unblemished conduct under his belt could an infantry private expect to earn 1s 6d a day.[60] Out of this pay, stoppages of 8d a day, for 'messing expenses, clothing, equipment replacement, washing, hair cutting and barrack damages',[61] reduced significantly the actual level of pay. The low wage rates did, however, exceed those of an agricultural labourer in Wiltshire at this time, along with the advantage of having a regular income. The declining number of Irish recruits to the British army towards the end of the century may be related to the rise of Irish republicanism, but is more probably related to the availability of better-paid employment in other sectors of the British economy.

Whether enlistment into the British army was seen as a regular employment or just a different way to migrate is still cause for debate. The frequency of privates going absent without leave during the second half of the nineteenth century is borne out by the discontent felt at the deception of pay at enlistment. Certainly, by looking at the prison records for Devizes, it is apparent that not all recruits enjoyed the rigours of army life.[62] During 1880, there were twenty cases of fraudulent enlistment or desertion by Irish solders, all receiving between 112 and 672 days' hard labour, and they were often removed to Mill Bank. One such soldier, James Connolly, a 27-year-old widowed labourer from Limerick, was charged in December 1880 with fraudulent enlistment and insubordination, receiving 336 days' hard labour, having had two previous convictions. He had enlisted with his younger brother, Patrick, aged 25. By the 1881 census, both brothers were in Devizes: James in prison, due to be released on 13 November 1881, whilst Patrick was in the barracks.

The cavalry barracks, Trowbridge, built in 1796[63]

In Wiltshire, the cavalry barracks at Trowbridge, built in 1796 to suppress local riots, were not the most comfortable or healthy of places to live. The barracks, as pictured, comprised a long, low, two-storey building with stabling below the living quarters for the soldiers. Within these conditions some fifty-seven men were housed, just over half being Irish, comprising twenty-seven privates, three corporals, two sergeants and one captain.

The close confines endured by the soldiers were similar to levels of over-crowding and the associated health risks endured by most of the nation. Living in overcrowded conditions, with beds only 6in apart, these men must have been subject to a breeding ground for cholera, dysentery and tuberculosis, the three biggest killers of the day.[64] Neison reported in 1858 that of the 2,823 deaths of soldiers during peacetime, approximately 50 per cent were attributed to tuberculosis. The army's response to this report was to provide soldiers with a flannel cummerbund to wrap around their waists as a prophylaxis![65]

The barracks at Trowbridge also contained some married quarters in which two Irish families lived with their children. However, other married army personnel had to find accommodation elsewhere in the town for their wives and children. The size of the barracks at Trowbridge was minimal when com-pared to those of Aldershot, built in 1853. The population of the village of Aldershot grew from 875 in 1851 to 30,974 by 1901, as a direct result of the British army's presence in the area.[66]

The British army's period of rapid growth during the nineteenth century was not only in numbers of active soldiers but also of locations for their bar-racks. In Wiltshire, the barracks at Trowbridge were extended to include a tall, three-storey block[67] and new accommodation at Devizes was built. By 1878 the army headquarters had been transferred to the new barracks built at Devizes. However, the buildings at Trowbridge were still in use and housed some eighty-seven soldiers of the Royal Artillery in 1881, nine of which were Irish. The building at Trowbridge was finally closed in 1901.

The new militia barracks at Devizes were completed in 1859 and extended in 1863, when additional staff quarters were built. However, by 1878 this building had passed to the Wiltshire police on completion of the Le Marchant barracks in Devizes. This imposing building was named after Sir John Gaspard Le Marchant, the commander of the 99th Regiment of Foot, in 1839. The majority of the army personnel in Wiltshire were transferred to the new larger barracks, which housed some 278 people, nineteen of whom were Irish-born. The combination of barracks and married quarters allowed the total to include wives and children as well as serving officers. However, it would seem that the army either underestimated the accommodation requirements or had not totally completed the building works by 1881, as army wives and children

The imposing building of Le Marchant Barracks, Devizes, built in 1878[68]

could still be found living outside the barracks within Devizes. At the time
of the census four regiments were stationed in these barracks: the 99th and
62nd Foot Regiments and the 38th and 5th Brigades. Certainly, in July 1882,
the *Bristol Mercury* and *Daily Post* recorded the fact that the 750-strong 3rd
Battalion of the Wiltshire Regiment were living under canvas at Devizes.[69]

By the end of the nineteenth century, however, army camps were spring-
ing up throughout Wiltshire. The army training area around Aldershot was
proving too limited as it was surrounded by housing developments which
were pushing up the price of land. In Wiltshire the land was cheap, as a letter
written to the *Bristol Mercury* and *Daily Post* in 1881 indicated: 'The value of
pasture land in the West of England is sinking to zero ... an estate of nearly
15,000 acres in Wiltshire upon a term at 10s. an acre, the first year free.'[70] This
land was situated 5 miles outside Westbury and within easy reach of the railways. Additionally, the Military Lands Act of 1892 enabled the acquisition of
land for military purposes.

Salisbury Plain proved to be the ideal situation for a permanent army
training area and new barracks were built at Bulford and Tidworth to house
thirteen battalions following the Military Works Act of 1898.[71] Although
Tidworth barracks was not built until 1903, Bulford camp was used from
1899, where the troops were accommodated under canvas. During 1900 to
1901, the building of more permanent accommodation began, although
mostly made from corrugated iron. To speed up the process, 200 men from
the Monmouthshire Engineer Militia were drafted in to assist in the building
of the barracks.

Within the two census areas of Bulford in 1901, there was a total of 1,386 people within the camp, including serving officers, wives and children. The proportion of Irish-born was relatively low, at nearly 7 per cent. They were predominantly male, with only one army wife and her three children, all born in Ireland, accommodated in the barracks at this time. What is more interesting is the fact that the majority of these ninety-two Irish-born were being used on the construction of the barracks, with only twelve listed as army personnel. The census listed them as carpenters, joiners, builders, painters and labourers. This group of Irish workers all appeared to be living amongst the army privates, married couples and children, in the huts (or maybe tents) without discrimination.

Once discharged from the army, Irish pensioners often remained in Wiltshire. Although, in 1851, only five Irish-born pensioners were recorded as living in Wiltshire, many English soldiers had married Irish brides and they remained in the county with their children. According to the 1851 census for Wiltshire, there were over seventy people born in Ireland and associated with the army. This number, however, increased to almost 200 when including the non-Irish wives and the children associated with Irish army personnel. By 1881, the rise of the army in Wiltshire was apparent as over 200 Irish-born (nearly one-third of the total Irish in Wiltshire) had a direct link with the army. With the inclusion of non-Irish-born wives and children, this figure rises to nearly 350. Even by removing the forty Irish-born children of English parents in 1851, rising to nearly sixty in 1881, the number of Irish with an army connection was still quite considerable.

Having severed the ties with Ireland and married to English partners, they had no interest in returning to Ireland, where work and food were scarce. Once pensioned out of the army many obviously preferred to remain in Wiltshire, found work on the land as agricultural labourers and settled within the village associated with the birthplace of their English partner. This was doubtless to gain support from family whilst acquiring employment within a known environment.

A similar comparison to Wiltshire's army pensioners might be made with a retired sailor in London who, when interviewed by Robert Williams, admitted that he preferred to stay in London as 'it's a long time since I left Ireland and the old woman is here, and many old friends about'.[72] The 'old woman' referred to was his mother.

Within Wiltshire, the expansion of the army and the development of a police force during the early part of the nineteenth century, resulting from fears of Chartism and revolution, played a key role in providing an alternative method of migration for the Irish. Highly active recruiting regimes encouraged enlistment from over-populated and under-employed areas of Ireland.

Within the police force, Irish men were enlisted freely throughout Britain, primarily for their assumed knowledge of how to cope with violence on a scale known to exist in Ireland. For the Irish, this provided them with ready employment and a regular wage, whilst the British forces were able to call on a ready, willing and reasonably fit band of men to maintain law and order as decreed by the government.

Conclusions

Wiltshire's Irish community, although small in number and predominantly male, did play an important role in the development of the county during the nineteenth century. The possible under-recording of Irish in the north of the county within the early census returns may well mask their true number; however, they do provide a trend of Irish migrating into or passing through the county. This study of Irish migration into Wiltshire also serves to provide a useful contrast to other studies based on the large cities that highlight the peak period of movement in the period 1830 to 1860. In Swindon, a trend of increasing Irish-born settlers was evident from all the census returns, including those in the late part of the century.

Although minor pockets of disturbance have been observed, including Chartism and anti-Catholic tensions in Swindon, this did not pose any major problems of bias or exclusion within the host society. This was due, no doubt, to the fact that the percentage of Irish-born remained relatively small, whilst the wealth of employment opportunities for Irishmen, initially as navvies and latterly within the railway workshop, formed an important part of the national railway workforce.

Employment opportunities for women were scarce during the early part of the nineteenth century as Swindon, by the nature of its industrialised beginnings, was a male-dominated environment. However, by the end of the century, employment opportunities for Irish women became more readily available with the opening of the sewing shop.

The Irish who settled in the Swindon area integrated within the newly formed community, working and socialising with other migrants from throughout the country. The main difference between the Irish in this area and other studies was that Swindon was effectively a new town. There were no ghettos or rookeries for large numbers of Irish to congregate. This allowed the Irish to mix and integrate throughout the 'railway village'.

To the south of the county, the Irish-born were found in the army throughout this period. They formed an important part of the British army

in the barracks situated in Devizes and Trowbridge, providing military service at home and abroad throughout the British Empire. Their numbers at
the start of this period correlated with the national average, increasing to
some 58 per cent by 1851, albeit that they were nearly all of the rank of
private. By the end of the century, the numbers of Irish within the army in
Wiltshire had dwindled, in line with the national trend. Although enduring
sparse living conditions within the barracks, the Irish appeared to prefer
army life, with regular pay and accommodation, to that of remaining in
Ireland and poverty.

Whatever the reason for enlisting in the army, there were cases of desertion
or fraudulent enlistment. This might suggest that enlisting was regarded by
some as a ticket out of Ireland. Possibly, the overcrowded living conditions
and regime of army life were not to their liking. However, there was no indication that the Irish were causing disturbances within the barracks or even in
the local towns.

Only by the turn of the twentieth century were numbers of Irish found
at the barracks. However, these men were mostly engaged in the building of
the new barracks on Salisbury Plain and do not appear to be enlisted soldiers.
Therefore, these Irish builders, plumbers and painters were the latter-day
equivalent of the Irish navvies who built the town of Swindon, helped to
construct the railways and worked in the railway workshop. The Irish had
made a notable contribution to the building of Wiltshire.

Notes

1 J.H. Bettey, *Wessex from AD 1000* (London, 1986), p. 233.
2 E.P. Thompson, *The Making of the English Working Class* (London, 1991), p. 474.
3 1841 census for Wootton Bassett, HO107 1179/14.
4 *Bristol Mercury*, Saturday 1 August 1840, Issue 2630.
5 Ultan Cowley, *The Men who Built Britain* (Dublin, 2001), p. 45.
6 John Cattell & Keith Falconer, *Swindon, The Legacy of a Railway Town* (Swindon, 1995), p. 77.
7 Bettey, *Wessex From AD 1000*, p. 242.
8 Friedrich Engels, 'The Condition of the Working Class in England', in J.M. Golby (ed.), *Culture & Society in Britain 1850–1890* (Oxford, 1986), p. 281.
9 Cattell & Falconer, *Swindon*, p. 62.
10 Ibid.
11 E. Critall, K.H. Rogers & C. Shrimpton, *A History of Swindon to 1965*, p. 129.
12 Cattell & Falconer, *Swindon*, p. 63.
13 Ibid., p. 75.
14 Graham Davis, *The Irish in Britain 1815–1914* (Dublin, 1991), p. 62.

15 M.A. Busteed, R.I. Hodgson & T.F. Kennedy, 'The myth and reality of Irish migrants in mid-nineteenth century Manchester: a preliminary study', in Patrick O'Sullivan (ed.), *The Irish World Wide Vol. Two, The Irish in the New Communities* (Leicester: Leicester University Press, 1992), pp. 26–51.

16 Census Return for Swindon 1851, HO107, Piece 1833, Folio 603 609, pp. 16–28.

17 Critall, Rogers & Shrimpton, *A History of Swindon to 1965*, p. 128.

18 Cattell & Falconer, *Swindon*, p. 65.

19 John Chandler, *Swindon* (Stroud, 1992), p. 49.

20 Cattell & Falconer, *Swindon*, p. 77.

21 Ibid., p. 78.

22 *Bristol Mercury* and *Daily Post*, Saturday 28 October 1882, Issue 10, 751.

23 Cattell & Falconer, *Swindon*, p. 65.

24 Davis, *The Irish in Britain 1815–1914*, p. 153.

25 David Large, 'The Irish in Bristol: A Census Enumeration', in R. Swift & S. Gilley (eds), *The Irish in the Victorian City* (London, 1985), p. 55.

26 Highworth & Swindon Union Out Relief 1842–1875, transcribed by Beryl Hurley (Devizes, 1992), p. 25.

27 Census Return for Swindon 1851, HO107, Piece 1833, Folio 600, p. 10.

28 Census Return for Swindon 1881, RG11, Piece 2015, Folio 141, p. 6.

29 Census Return for Swindon 1851, HO107, Piece 1833, Folio 584, p. 58.

30 Chandler, *Swindon*, p. 49.

31 Richard Jefferies, *Landscape & Labour* (Bradford-on-Avon, 1979), p. 177.

32 Ibid., p. 176.

33 Ibid.

34 Ibid., p. 177.

35 Chandler, *Swindon*, p. 116.

36 Census Return for Swindon 1851, HO107, Piece 1833, Folio 613, p. 37.

37 Cattell & Falconer, *Swindon*, p. 91.

38 Ibid.

39 Ibid., p. 120.

40 Census Returns for Swindon 1841–1901.

41 Census Return for Swindon 1851.

42 Colin Pooley, 'Segregation or Integration? The Residential Experience of the Irish in mid-Victorian Britain', in R. Swift & S. Gilley (eds), *The Irish in Britain 1815–1939* (London, 1989), pp. 65 & 67.

43 Frank Neal, 'Irish settlement in the north-east and north-west of England in the mid-nineteenth century', in R. Swift & S. Gilley (eds), *The Irish in Victorian Britain: The Local Dimension* (Dublin, 1999), p. 83.

44 Large, 'The Irish in Bristol: A Census Enumeration', in Swift & Gilley (eds), *The Irish in the Victorian City*, p. 38.

45 J. Herson, 'Migration, "community" or integration? Irish families in Victorian Stafford', in R. Swift & S. Gilley (eds), *The Irish in Victorian Britain: The Local Dimension* (Dublin, 1999), pp. 156–89.

46 *The English Historical Review*, Vol. 108, No 427 (Apr. 1993), pp. 506–7.

47 Dan Harvey & Gerry White, *The Barracks, A History of Victoria/Collins Barracks* (Cork, 1997), p. 19.

48 J.A. Jackson, *The Irish in Britain* (1963), p. 92.

49 E.M. Spiers, 'Army organisation and society in the nineteenth century', in T. Bartlett & K. Jeffery (eds), *A Military History of Ireland* (Cambridge, 1996), p. 337.

50 Ibid., p. 336.

51 Ibid., p. 339.

52 Ibid.

53 Thomas E. Jordan, *Queen Victoria's Irish Soldiers: Quality of Life and Social Origins of the Thin Green Line* (Netherlands, 2002), p. 74.

54 Spiers, 'Army organisation and society in the nineteenth century', in Bartlett & Jeffery (eds), *A Military History of Ireland*, p. 340.

55 Jordan, *Queen Victoria's Irish Soldiers*, p. 77.

56 Ibid.

57 Ibid., p. 76.

58 Spiers, 'Army organisation and society in the nineteenth century', in Bartlett & Jeffery (eds), *A Military History of Ireland*, p. 340.

59 Ibid.

60 A.R. Skelley, *The Victorian Army at Home* (London, 1977), p. 182.

61 Ibid., p. 183.

62 Devizes Prison Records, Wiltshire Record Office, A1/517/9.

63 M. Lansdown, M. Marshman & K. Rogers (eds), *Trowbridge in Pictures 1812–1914* (Trowbridge, 1979), p. 69.

64 Jordan, *Queen Victoria's Irish Soldiers*, p. 82.

65 Ibid.

66 Bettey, *Wessex from AD 1000*, p. 231.

67 T.S. Crawford, *Wiltshire and the Great War* (Reading, 1999), p. 147.

68 Edward Bradby, *The Book of Devizes* (Oxford, 1985), p. 118.

69 *Bristol Mercury* and *Daily Post*, Thursday 13 July 1882.

70 *Bristol Mercury* and *Daily Post*, Saturday 23 April 1881.

71 Crawford, *Wiltshire and the Great War*, p. 100.

72 Jackson, *The Irish in Britain*, p. 92.

3

Politicians, Philanthropists & the People: Early Emigration from Somerset & Dorset to Australia

Celia Martin

Emigration played an important part during a time of great social change that occurred throughout the British Isles in the 1800s. This chapter uses evidence gathered for a dissertation on emigration, with additional material researched on families from the county of Dorset after the original task was completed. Since those early days my opinions on 'who went and why' have altered from my initial response to 'shovelling out paupers', and challenged the belief that the Irish were worse off than the farm workers of south-west England.

Reading secondary sources on emigration provided an essential academic context for my own study and also directed me to relevant primary sources. The writings of Frank Thistlethwaite and Charlotte Erickson[1] have encouraged family historians to look at the wider context of emigration. Their work was continued later by William Von Huyt. These three academics wrote mainly on migration to America from the British Isles. Eric Richards from Flinders University, Adelaide, has written a series of books and essays on migration to Australasia, followed by one of his pupils, Robin F. Haines.[2] These writers and many others concentrating on Irish emigration have made important inputs into the larger picture of world migration.

The British colonisation of America had begun in the 1600s, 200 years before the colonisation of Australia, and whereas America was settled by religious adventurers, Australia began as a convict settlement. Books published in the 1800s, when found, produce an intriguing insight into the way of thinking at the time; although most likely it was the thinking of the writer in England rather than that of the emigrants in Australia. Modern histories written by Manning Clark[3] and Robert Hughes[4] have history and myths moulded together; it is a fascinating story to tell.

The Politicians

The problem of where to send surplus prisoners had been discussed in parliament for some time and the decision was finally announced in 1787. There were several good reasons for choosing Australia: it was strategically useful as well as a good distance from home. When Captain Cook returned to England with the news of his discovery, his report made Australia sound ripe for development. Transportation had taken place since the 1600s to countries where the convicts could be put to work to the benefit of the mother country. After the failed Monmouth Rebellion in 1685, numbers of his followers, many coming from Dorset and Somerset, had been sent to the West Indies, where they were put to work on plantations owned by members of the British aristocracy. Later convicts were sent out to do similar work on plantations in America, but this had been curtailed by the American Revolution in 1776. When parliament made the decision to deport convicts to Australia, it was to be the first time that the original colonisers of a country, soon to be part of the British Empire, would be convicts and their guardians.

The politicians were not concerned with who were to be the first colonisers, rather that the colonisation of Australasia was seen as a possible method of dealing with the sudden increase in the population. There had been growing fear of a home-based revolution after the end of the American War of Independence in 1783, which was followed by the French Revolution and later the Irish Rebellion in 1798. The politicians were becoming nervous. Although only small localised riots had occurred in England, it was felt that a surge of social unrest could break into an uprising at any time.

In 1803 the problem of an expanding population was partly alleviated by large numbers going to fight in the Napoleonic Wars, but in 1815, when the surviving soldiers and sailors returned, the rural labour market was swamped in the post-war recession. From 1811–31, the population of England and Wales increased by 37 per cent.[5] The Industrial Revolution was gathering pace in urban areas but not fast enough to cope with the number of people needing employment, especially in the south of the country. The problem of surplus convicts was, therefore, followed by the problem of surplus people.

After the first fleet of eleven ships landed at Sydney Cove in January 1788, delivering more than 700 convicts and their guardians, the convicts were put to clearing the land and making settlements. By 1810 there were in the region of 400 free settlers in eastern Australia. They had been encouraged to take the risk by the promise of land, with the convicts providing free labour. Also in Australia, as in Canada, land grants were given to serving or retired soldiers, the number of acres granted being decided by their rank, and many of the soldiers who had been sent over to keep control decided to stay.

It was not until the 1820s that non-convict emigration was seriously envisaged. By 1821 the numbers of emigrants from the United Kingdom were recorded as 320 to Australasia, 12,955 to British North American colonies and 4,958 to the United States.[6] Clearly the pull of North America was stronger than anywhere else at this time, but the American Revolution had engendered pessimism in the minds of many British politicians. It was felt that a flourishing and successful colony would eventually want to cut ties with the motherland, and that the expense incurred by military protection, and that of the administration, would be wasted. The government's views on the countries most sustainable and beneficial for emigration had been formed by reports and inquiries. The funding of schemes to assist and organise emigration were also discussed with the same thoroughness. This was done in great detail by the Select Committee for Emigration in 1827, when the Rev. T.R. Malthus was among the people examined for their general views on emigration.[7] His analysis that there should be equilibrium between population numbers and the resources available was to be taken up by many politicians. His opinion was that labourers in a state of redundancy were operating as a tax upon the community, and that if the expense of exporting them to the colonies was less than financing them at home, there should be no doubt in the expediency of their removal. This argument was to be taken up by complainants of the excessive Poor Rates, as there were approximately 100,000 people on parish relief, with total Poor Law expenditure rising alarmingly.

Civil unrest, notoriously the Reform Riots of 1831, had to be quickly extinguished and order restored. By this time, politicians and philanthropists had realised that the transference, not just of convicts but also of possible future paupers, could be a remedy. As Frank Broeze wrote: 'During the whole period 1831–50 the Australasian interest married philanthropy, sociopolitical concern, and self interest. Its rationale was to utilize and hence to increase the economic value of the emigrants as well as their self-esteem and position in life.'[8]

Those more influenced by economics could see the advantages of a colony that would create another market for British goods. Others wanted Australasia peopled and protected since the fear of the French was still imminent, and a strong naval position was essential in the South Pacific.

Landowners and farmers were encouraged to believe that emigration would result in a reduction in the Poor Rates and could be achieved to everybody's advantage. Their sympathy for the poor was neither strong nor constant, and writers on pauperism discussed the subject in terms of 'cost to the tax-payer'. Complaints were constantly made about Poor Rates collected and relief paid out. As the modernisation of farming progressed with the use of machinery, the inevitable outcome was to be a reduction in the number of manual labourers needed.

The government was mainly interested in reducing pauperism and unrest. Some politicians cloaked their fears in philanthropy, as an alternative to the burden of taxes on property, with a hope of currying favour with landowners and farmers. Some farmers were against emigration as they were worried about their labour force being available during the periods of sowing, hay-making and harvesting. The fact that the workforce might have little or no income during the winter months did not concern them. Little consideration was given to the fact that the selection of emigrants by specific occupations and ages would remove the best workers at the prime of their working lives. When a group from a parish or village left to emigrate together, the effect on the area must have been considerable.

None of the imperialists who wanted colonisation could visualise that a country peopled by Englishmen could be anything less than a 'little England'. The same methods of disposing of Crown Lands were used in Australia as in the British North American provinces. The territory would be divided into counties, hundreds and parishes and then into plots of 640 acres, which were not to be sold at lower than 5s an acre. They also felt that there was an obvious difference between colonisation and emigration. Colonisation was the planting of settlers in a soil prepared to receive them, aided by a small portion of capital, to enable them to immediately take root and flourish. Emigrants were the labourers who would go out to nurture that growth. They were important because hitherto there were only the convicts in the vicinity of their penal colonies to clear the land. They had seemingly no idea of the vastness of the uncultivated land: their vision was of an England that could be transported and redeveloped anywhere. Their prime objective was to clear Britain of its surplus labour which could be put to better use settling colonial territory. This would turn paupers into men of property, through their own hard work, and they in turn would eventually need help of the same kind, developing a form of chain migration. Many government officials never visited the colonies they dealt with and their decisions were shaped by a colonialist philosophy.

The organisation of transporting large numbers of people from one continent to another would have to be regulated with great precision. The product of the 'all practice and no theory' method, described by Edward Gibbon Wakefield as the system used for the Atlantic crossing by the Irish, Scottish, Welsh and English, resulted in loss of life. If government and colonial money were to be expended on emigration, it was financially sound to transfer the cargo efficiently. A surgeon superintendent was to travel on each vessel, and they also had the responsibility of checking the applicants and choosing who would be allowed to go in the early days. It was thought that single women should sail together on single-sex ships, accompanied by matrons; although, of course, all the crew members were men. The occupations and the ages of the passengers would be checked with the 'free' travellers, whereas there were no such stipulations for those who went unassisted. Also, assisted passengers could not embark without proper clothing and luggage for the voyage.

By 1831 a temporary Emigration Commission was formed by the Colonial Office to promote, collate and disseminate information on emigration. Money acquired by sales of land in Van Diemen's Land and New South Wales was allocated towards defraying the expense of sending emigrants to the Antipodes. As New South Wales and Van Diemen's Land were dominated by convict settlements at this time, a substantial programme of assisted emigration was needed to introduce free settlers to redress the balance.

From the report of the commissioners on emigration, dated 15 March 1832, there were encouraging signs: 'We have reason to hope that the indifference, and the want of information, which have hitherto existed regarding these Colonies, are beginning to disappear.'[9] The numbers of applicants were increasing by the day. Initially, they intended to promote the emigration of mechanics and single women, as they were thought to be the most urgently needed groups of people. Single women were needed to correct the existing imbalance between the sexes, and, as some thought, to bring a civilising influence to settlements, as had been found in the Americas. A few years later the call was for agricultural labourers and their families.

The Poor Law Amendment Act of 1834 empowered individual parish vestries to raise loans against rates for the relief of the poor to assist any persons having settlement within the parish to immigrate to the British colonies.[10] At the parish level notices would be posted and ratepayers called to special vestry meetings: 'For the purpose of considering whether to raise or borrow a sum not exceeding half the average yearly Poor Rate for the past three years for a fund for defraying the expenses of the emigration of poor persons having settlement in this parish and being willing to emigrate.'[11]

The new law was to have a considerable influence on emigration. Legislation was passed to phase out outdoor relief, although it was not properly implemented. Boards of Guardians were formed to administer the newly created Poor Law Unions. The familiar parish workhouses would go and people forced to move from the area they knew to the new workhouse several miles away, where families would be segregated by gender. It is therefore not surprising that a rural labourer who had to survive by applying for parish relief, particularly in the winter months, and had seen the ignominy that the older generations of his family had suffered, viewed this as something to avoid. He wanted a better life for himself and his family, and when the opportunity arose to escape the inevitability of ending up in worse circumstances than his forebears, it is clear why the talk of freedom from restrictions through emigration caught the imagination.

In New South Wales, a circular was sent out from the Colonial Secretary's Office in Sydney, to magistrates and members of the Legislative Council within the colony, to enquire if settlers in their neighbourhoods wanted the services of free agricultural labourers (not convicts) or other workmen from England: how many might they employ, how much would they pay and would they have to contribute towards the labourers' passages. The reason given for these enquiries was to relieve the distress prevailing among the agricultural labourers of southern England. It had been suggested to the government that if the parishes were enabled to send to New South Wales those without employment, the colony might receive with advantage a considerable number of such emigrants.[12]

This resulted in a bounty system being introduced in 1835 for the benefit of settlers, which allowed farmers, landowners and merchants to purchase 'bounty orders' for the particular category of worker they required. Agents in England would find the appropriate people to fill the posts which meant they were assured of a job on arrival. By this time, land was being sold at 12s an acre and, with agricultural wages varying from £12–15 per annum, it was possible for the immigrant to save money and to acquire his own land. When this news reached home, others wanted to follow. Even with the strong pull towards North America, a number still chose the longer trip to Australasia. With the aid of active agents, reports in the press, books and pamphlets, the migration phenomenon to the South Pacific was created.

Between 1837 and 1838, the numbers immigrating to Australia and New Zealand rose from 5,054 to 14,021, whereas the numbers to the United States declined from 36,770 to 14,332 in the same period.[13] The government had achieved success in stemming the tide across the Atlantic, if only for a short time.

The Philanthropists

The harsh effects of the social changes produced by the Poor Law Amendment Act of 1834 were felt, not only by the people directly involved, but also by those who were concerned with the welfare of the poor. The radical journalist William Cobbett, recounting what he saw when riding through the English countryside in the 1820s, described the abundance of corn and food being produced on the farms by the agricultural labourers who were themselves half-starved.

Later, the Rector of Durweston, Sydney Godolphin Osborne (S.G.O.), attempted to rouse public concern over the appalling conditions of agricultural labourers and their families, with a series of letters that were published in *The Times*. This infuriated the Member of Parliament for Dorset, Mr G. Bankes, who brought the matter to the attention of the House of Commons, and wanted the bishop of S.G.O.'s diocese to rebuke him for his interference. After the failure of the potato crop in Dorset, the mainstay of the manual workers' diet, S.G.O. drew attention to parliament's preoccupation with the Irish dilemma which was taking up more time than the state of the poor in England. He was also concerned with the unhygienic and overcrowded living conditions in Dorset villages. The cause of rural poverty, he argued, was the result of low and irregular payment of wages.

Farmers from Ryme Intrinseca, near Sherborne, challenged S.G.O. to visit the village for a public inquiry, after his letter in *The Times* of 24 August 1846 described the methods of payment used by the tenant farmers of the Duchy of Cornwall in the village as being mainly of bad meat by the truck system. The labourers were lucky if they took home £2 during the year. In the same letter he also described the workhouse of Yetminster, the neighbouring village, where sixty inmates 'wallowed together at night on filthy rags, in rooms in which they are so packed, and yet so little sheltered'. *The Times* sent down a journalist to record the inquiry and, as S.G.O. had done his homework thoroughly, with the help of the local rector, a surgeon, local shopkeepers, the schoolmaster and a dozen members of farm workers' families, he was satisfied with the outcome. The county newspapers were not, and wrote dismissively of 'the exaggerations', while the farmers appeared to feel they had won the day. The leader in *The Times* of 5 October 1846 ended with: 'if Ryme is the seat of rural comfort and liberty, if the employers of that place are satisfied with this revelation, what must be the state of a county of which Ryme is a favourable specimen?'

This experience led S.G.O. to change his opinion on emigration. He felt there was little hope of wages increasing, and if there were to be improvements, the money would probably be absorbed by the increase of grist prices or rent. He became a founder member of the Dorset Colonisation Society and, in 1849, personally supervised the emigration of 135 people from the Blandford area to Australia on board the *Emigrant*.

Sydney Godolphin Osborne believed, as did Edward Gibbon Wakefield, that the best settlements in Australia would be made up of people from various backgrounds. Wakefield also wrote letters to the press. He started in 1829 with anonymous letters to *The Morning Chronicle*, which were later printed as a pamphlet. He was writing from Newgate Prison, where he was serving a sentence for abducting an heiress. There he met criminals awaiting transportation and felt that it was wrong just to populate the new colony of Australia with convicts, and that free men and women should be encouraged to emigrate and form new settlements. He deplored the lack of women of marriageable age in Australia, feeling this was an uncivilising factor. He viewed convict labour as a form of slavery, land should not be granted and he felt that the sale of large tracts of land to capitalists should be made prohibitively high to prevent the formation of big estates. Settlements formed with a more integrated style of life would create a more sustainable environment. He also addressed the acute shortage of labour and suggested that land should be sold to raise money to assist passengers financially, as the cost of the passage was prohibitive to most labourers. From a Quaker background, Wakefield had many radical ideas that were infused with the idealism of a perfect way of life. He was better on theory than practice and, having had a chequered past, he was not effective as a public figure, but could be extremely persuasive in the background. Having formed the New Zealand Company, he sailed in 1839 with the first party of settlers to Auckland.

The Macarthur family of Camden Park, Parramatta, was one of the largest landowners in New South Wales, with over 10,000 acres. They hired their own ships, with one of their family helping with recruitment and choice of emigrants in England. The workers were then contracted for three years, to receive £15 per annum, with rations of 7lb of meat and 11lb of flour, and were provided with a cottage. They signed an agreement that if they left before the end of their contract they would have to repay part of the cost of their passage. Robert Towns Esq., the commander of the ship the *Brothers*, that took out the first group of agricultural labourers from the Cranborne Chase area on the Dorset/Wiltshire borders to work at Camden Park in 1836, was examined for a report made by the Immigration Committee on the cost of sending out families to New South Wales.

The Macarthurs unintentionally followed in Wakefield's path with their vision of social balance. Having originally employed convicts to work on the

In corroboration of my statement as to the rate of passage-money which I think would remunerate the ship-owner, I beg to submit a statement of the sums paid to myself by Mr. Macarthur, for the emigrants whom I brought out for that gentleman in the ship "Brothers," viz.—

For 14 married couples, two single men and 18 children }	£.640; or

For say 15 couples, at 36 *l.* - - - - - - £.540

Bounty for the children, calculated according to the scale of ages; namely,—

Norris -	- One child above seven years -	- £.10	
	Three children under seven years	- 15	
Wright	- One child above seven years -	- 10	
	Three children under seven years	- 15	
J. Wicks	- Two children under seven years	- 10	
Cox -	- One child under seven years -	- 5	
Gumbleton -	- Two children under seven years	- 10	
Arnold -	- One child under seven years -	- 5	
R. Wicks	- Two children under seven years	- 10	
New -	- Two children under seven years	- 10	
		—— - 100	
		—— - - £.640	

Exclusive of the man Butts and his family, of whom I have spoken before, and whose passage, calculated according to the scale, would be 81 *l.*; viz.—

For himself and his wife - - - - - - -	- £.36
Three children above seven years - - - - -	- 30
Three ditto below seven years - - - - - -	- 15
	£. 81

Extract from a report given by Robert Towns (Parliamentary Papers, Vol. XIX, 1828–38)

land, when it became obvious that more labour was needed, they organised the recruitment and transportation of a workforce who were then able to take on tenancies of their own, after a recognised time, thus making the balance between capital and labour viable.

On the edge of the Dorset/Wiltshire border in the Cranborne Chase area, where many of the men involved with the Swing Riots originated, there was great hardship within the villages. A number of young men approached the Rector of Chettle, the Rev. John West, who was known for his involvement with religious work in Canada, for help and advice on emigrating. He made contact with Major Edward Macarthur, whose younger brothers had taken over the running of Camden Park after the death of their father. Major Macarthur was involved in the recruitment of labourers in England, and he arranged for them to sign contracts for three years' work. If, when they got to Camden Park, they stayed for five years, shepherds would be able to obtain a small flock of sheep on credit, and labourers a holding. In this way, he helped 235 people from the area to escape their hardships at home and find a new life with better prospects in Australia.[14]

A letter from West described the families gathering at Chettle on the morning of departure.[15] A peal of bells was rung at the church and Rev. West addressed the travellers. They then set off for Southampton in three covered wagons, where Major Macarthur awaited them. After boarding the vessel, Rev. West gave them an uplifting address before they set sail for New South Wales. Such was the success of this venture that seven more English families were sent out in October 1838 on the *John McLellan*, and in the following March, thirteen families and three single men were sent, partly from the same area and some from Benenden in Sussex. On this occasion, the Macarthurs chartered the *Royal George* for £2,000 and, as before, Rev. West and the major went on board the ship at Spithead. It was on the Sabbath and Rev. West was able to hold a divine service on the deck, where he addressed the passengers on the duty and privilege of prayer. This may have allayed their fears as they set off into the English Channel to sail halfway around the world.

The Press

The effect of the letters written to *The Times* by Rev. Sydney Godolphin Osborne in 1846, already described, increased after the *Illustrated London News* joined in the debate. The outrage expressed throughout the country was kept on the boil by a series of articles and illustrations entitled 'The Peasantry of Dorsetshire', in which part of *The Times* journalist's description of Dorset villages was reproduced. He described his arrival to the village of Stourpaine as:

> The first feature which attracts the attention of the stranger on entering the village is the total want of cleanliness which pervades it. A stream, composed of the matter which constantly escapes from pigsties and other receptacles of filth, meanders down each street, being here and there collected into standing pools, which lie festering and rotting in the sun so as to create wonder that the place is not a continual abode of pestilence. Indeed the worse malignant fevers have raged here at different times. It may be sufficient to add for the present that the inside of the cottages in every respect corresponds with the external appearance of the place. The wages here in very few instances exceed seven shillings per week.[16]

Poverty and emigration had become inextricably linked, and many of the county's philanthropists became personally involved when a new surge of interest in emigration began towards the end of the 1840s. By 1848, weekly meetings of the Dorset Colonisation Society were established at Dorchester, and in the following year branches met in Blandford and Sherborne. The newspapers were full of articles on emigration with advertisements placed by competitive agents. Posters were placed within parishes, but letters home from

Interior of a Dorset labourer's cottage, 1846 (*Illustrated London News*, 5 September 1846)

migrants turned out to be the most seductive form of advertising. Stories of good wages, good housing, good weather and a healthier way of life were the best agents for emigration and were sometimes manipulated by the press and the government in published letters of praise from those who had settled.

The Sherborne and Yeovil Mercury of 17 March 1849 reported, under the subheading of Wincanton, that many emigrants from the neighbourhood had taken their leave within the last month for Australia, and added their feelings on the present problems felt by its readership:

> The magnificent Island of Australia, part and parcel of the British dominions, is nearly as large as the whole of Europe, and has, at present, but one inhabitant to twelve square miles, while in England we have 260 inhabitants to every square mile, and this number is daily increasing, which adds to galling rivalry here, and, if this be not the true cause of the rapid increase of insanity, pauperism, mendicity, and crime, within this country, what is?

Emigrant guides, tracts and pamphlets were brought out by religious publishers and several periodicals were started. *The Emigrant* was a weekly publication that reported on meetings and events throughout the country. Letters were published from contented immigrants to Australia; nothing was ever included that was negative. Contemporary writers also showed an interest in the subject of emigration; Charles Dickens did his best to promote it while editor of the popular magazine *Household Words*. He also sent the impoverished character Micawber to Australia at the end of *David Copperfield*. There were several weekly articles written about emigration in *The Leisure Hour*, 'A Family Journal of Instruction and Recreation', although it was later discovered that many of the writers were not as familiar with Australia as they appeared to be. With a writer's imagination, and using the method of uplifting the reader with a happy ending, they aided the overall effect of 'Emigration Fever'. *The Sherborne and Yeovil Mercury* of 20 January 1849 joined in enthusiastically with this snippet of conversation:

'Ma', said a young lady to her mother the other day, 'What is emigrating?'

Mother: 'Emigrating, dear, is a young lady going to Australia.'

Daughter: 'What is colonising, ma?'

Mother: 'Colonising, dear, is marrying there and having a family.'

Daughter: 'I should like to go to Australia.'

Up to this point the news of emigration may have been read to men in the beer house or preached to the parish from the pulpit. Once news of the discovery of gold reached home the overall numbers immigrating to Australia and New Zealand rose to 21,532 in 1851 and to 87,881 in 1852.[17] In 1851, gold had been discovered at Bathurst, with larger amounts found later at Ballarat and Bendigo, boosting the number of independent ships from 68 in 1851 to 217 in 1852, and the number of independent immigrants from 8,143 to 44,796.[18] By 1853, the colony of Victoria had established five different immigrants' homes in different areas to help the new or homeless immigrant, thereby alleviating the problem of those who had not struck gold.

The People

From 1821–31, before the introduction of assisted passages, 10,469 people were recorded leaving the United Kingdom for the Australian and New Zealand Colonies.[19] They are not easily accounted for as they paid for their passages and there is limited archival evidence to tell us who they were or where they came from. Inquiries were held and names can be found in reports made by landowners and printed in parliamentary papers. There are individuals' letters and diaries deposited in County Record Offices, and a small amount of archival evidence can be found in deeds and transactions. Later, these same people would need a labour force to clear and cultivate the land, so that with land, labour and capital brought together, the colonisation of the Antipodes could be beneficial to all.

The earliest pioneers were capitalists who invested in land in Australia; others then followed. This early band of speculators was made up of sons who would not inherit the family estate but aspired to their own land, or young men who may have been fortunate in having a relative who wished to invest in the colony but not live there. Others rejected the modern world of the Industrial Revolution because they wished to retain a rural way of life. There were also spiritually minded individuals looking for the 'agrarian myth' and egalitarians who looked for a life away from the institutions and regimes of the Old World. Many hoped to be able to live somewhere where they were free from the fear of being snubbed by their superiors, and where the problems of the old form of society could be left behind.

Australian free settlement began in 1793, five years after the arrival of the first convicts. Amongst the initial settlers was the Rose family, who travelled on the *Bellona*: Thomas Rose, aged 40, a farmer from Blandford; his wife Jane Rose (*née* Topp), aged 33, from Sturminster Newton; their three children and a niece. The journey took 163 days and they travelled with four other settlers and seventeen women convicts, taking provisions for nine months and landing at Port Jackson on 15 January 1793. In February, Thomas was officially granted 120 acres at Hunters Hut in Liberty Plains, roughly 10 miles west of Sydney. This land was to be his for free for the first five years with the condition that it should be well cultivated, and in 1798 he was granted a further 70 acres.[20]

Although only six more free settlers arrived in the next seven years, the French Revolution being blamed for the disruption, the Roses settled successfully and had three more children. In 1802, they moved to Wilberforce

An emigrant ship being towed out of harbour, 1844 (*Illustrated London News*, 13 April 1844)

on the Hawkesbury River in New South Wales, in order to find better land, but this move was unsuccessful as they suffered losses during three successive floods. They moved to higher land in the same area which is where they built a wooden house named Rose Cottage. This cottage is still standing and is part of the Australiana Village at Wilberforce, where reunions of the now extensive Rose family have taken place.

There are several books published on the artist Thomas Roberts (1856–1931), who became known as the Father of Australian Landscape.[21] He went to Australia for different reasons. He was brought up in Dorchester, the county town of Dorset, where his father was the editor of the *Dorset County Chronicle*. This was a newspaper that covered both local and national events and had reported on all meetings of the Dorset Colonisation Society. After his father's early death, his mother, Matilda Roberts, took her two sons and daughter to Melbourne, where her brother was living. Thomas had been to the grammar school in Dorchester but when he arrived at Melbourne, aged 13, he went to work. He worked for a photographer before enrolling at the Artisans School of Design at Collingwood. Later, he won a scholarship to the National Gallery School of Victoria and, in 1881, he was accepted to study at the Royal Academy in London.

His style of painting was quintessentially English, similar to the Newlyn artists of Cornwall. He applied this style to Australian life and was asked to paint the opening of the first Australian parliament, which was seen as a great honour, but the work took him a considerable time to complete. He came back to England to enlist and served in the First World War. Sailing by steamship before the era of commercial airlines, he was a frequent traveller between the two continents.

John Diment Bagg was a return migrant who came back to Dorset after a long and fruitful period in Australia. He left Bridport, Dorset, in 1836 and travelled to South Australia in the *Africaine*. Little is known of his history before he went, but he made an impression with some of his fellow passengers when he and five others asked to be put on shore early so that they could walk overland to Nepean Bay. Only four of them survived the trip, including Bagg and a man called Fisher, whose life Bagg saved when crossing a swollen river. Soon after arrival, he was employed by a manufacturer of earthenware pipes, called John Hallett, who also came from Dorset. Three years after his arrival, Bagg was able to buy Plot 174 in Hindmarsh Town, where he established a brickworks and set up home with a girl who had come from London. By 1855 he had been granted twelve sections of land, totalling 1,339 acres, in the county of Stanley, for which he paid £1,761 5s, and 4,238 acres in the hundred of Kooringa, an area known as Spring Bank, where he built

LIVERPOOL & AUSTRALIAN NAVIGATION CO

STEAM FROM LIVERPOOL TO AUSTRALIA.

THE CELEBRATED AUXILIARY STEAM-SHIP

GREAT BRITAIN,

3209 Tons, and 500 Horse-power,

CHARLES CHAPMAN, Commander,

IS APPOINTED TO LEAVE THE RIVER MERSEY,

FOR MELBOURNE AND BRISBANE

(Landing Passengers and Cargo at Melbourne, and proceeding without delay);

TAKING PASSENGERS ALSO FOR

SYDNEY, ADELAIDE, AND NEW ZEALAND,

ON SATURDAY THE 25th OCTOBER, 1873.

THIS magnificent and far-famed Ship has made the passage out to Melbourne in the unprecedented short time of 53 days. She affords an opportunity for Passengers to reach Australia in almost as short a time as by the Overland Route, *viâ* Southampton, without incurring the very heavy expenses attendant thereon, and avoiding entirely the discomfort of frequent changes. Her Saloon arrangements are perfect, and combine every possible convenience, Ladies' Boudoir, Baths, etc.; and her noble passenger decks, lighted at intervals by sideports, afford unrivalled accommodation for all classes.

FARES,

Including Steward's Fees, the attendance of an experienced Surgeon, and all Provisions of the best quality.

		TO MELBOURNE.		TO BRISBANE.	
AFTER SALOON,- {POOP		60 and 70 Guineas		66 and 76 Guineas	
{BELOW		55 „ 60 „		61 „ 66 „
SECOND CLASS (on Deck)		25 „ 30 „		28 „ 33 „
THIRD CLASS		18 „ 20 „		21 „ 26 „
STEERAGE		15 „ 16 „		18 „ 19 „

Children under Twelve Years, Half-price. Infants under Twelve Months, Free.

In accordance with the Passengers Act, Wines, Spirits, and Malt Liquors will be supplied on board at very moderate prices. Passengers booked to be forwarded from MELBOURNE, by the first opportunity, to SYDNEY, ADELAIDE, and HOBART TOWN, also to HOKITIKA, OTAGO, and LYTTELTON, at an extra charge of 6 Guineas Saloon, 3 Guineas other Classes. To AUCKLAND and WELLINGTON, 8 Guineas Saloon, 4 Guineas other Classes. To LAUNCESTON, 4 Guineas Saloon, and 2 Guineas other Classes—for which separate Forwarding Tickets will be issued in Liverpool.

Beric Tempest Colourcard. Photographic reproduction of detail from poster dated 1873 a substantial stone house for his family. He later transferred all his property to his eldest son, charging him £13,854 for his inheritance, and invested in several properties in and around Adelaide. This meant he was able to retire to Dorset with a sizeable income, as a return migrant who had made a financial success of his life in Australia. He and his wife lived in obscurity in Bridport until his death at the age of 75, when a newspaper report described him as 'an early pioneer of South Australia where he had spent fifty six years of his life, a colony in which he owned a considerable number of estates'. His widow later became a repeat migrant by sailing back to Australia three years later.[22]

Like many others who decided to gamble on emigration, Thomas Hodder Berry must have seen the alternative as a life under the constraints of the workhouse. He had lived much of his life with his mother and brothers in Bridport Union workhouse in Dorset. Life had started well when his mother lived and worked as a servant for a farmer, who was most probably Thomas' father, but when John Hodder, the farmer, died, they were registered as paupers and had to go into the workhouse several miles away. The sea is within easy reach of Bridport workhouse and the harbour there had ships calling in from all over the world. Without money, Thomas at 16 had to work his passage to Australia, and like so many others, jumped ship on arrival. He must have worked in the gold fields for several years because he rose from miner to mine manager at Pleasant Creeks gold field.[23]

He married Sarah Hart, the daughter of a farmer, and had eight children. They made enough money to move to Longwood Creek in Victoria and started up a farm and a small tannery, and later Thomas started the first saw mill in the area. His history was typical of an early immigrant. He tried his hand at anything and changed his job or his location whenever necessary. He established his place within the community in Longwood and, by his death, had obtained a position he would have found difficult to match in Dorset.

The Roses and the Roberts' went out as families, but both John Diment Bagg and Thomas Hodder Berry left Dorset as single men going to seek their fortunes. The Macarthurs of Camden Park brought out forty-one families between April 1837 and March 1839, together with a small number of single men to work on the land. John Macarthur had originally arrived as a servicing officer in the newly formed New South Wales Corps, with his wife Elizabeth and a shipment of convicts. He introduced the merino sheep into Australia, and made his family's fortune and the fortune of many others. He had visions of creating a community of sober, industrious and moral labourers and their families. Once his sons grew up, they took over much of the work from their father. Many other families came from the Cranborne Chase area and were either related or known to each other. A judge had once described the people of Cranborne Chase as 'a wild and dissolute population of poach-ers, smugglers and deer stealers'. This may have meant a better than average diet, but little realistic hope of improving their lot legally.

On board the first of the Macarthurs' ships, the *Brothers*, were the Norris and Arnold families from Child Okeford, Dorset, the Butt family from Winterbourne Stickland, Dorset, the Cox family from Farnham, Dorset, the New and Weeks families from Sixpenny Handley, Dorset, the Gumbletons from Bishopstone, Wilts and the Wrights from Berwick St John, Wilts. Four Norris brothers were to take their families with them when they went to work at Camden. Sampson Norris went out on the *Royal George* in 1838. Isaac and William left later in 1849 and sailed on the *Emigrant*, although William had applied to leave at the same time as his older brother, Henry, but had not found a suitable wife in time for the voyage.[24] The second vessel leaving England with agricultural labourers bound for Camden was the *John McLellan*, arriving in Sydney in October 1838, and the third was the *Royal George*, bought for the purpose by the Macarthurs. John Macarthur had wanted to change the social structure influenced by the convict settlements and envisaged Camden Park as an estate of tenant farmers with groups of workers who knew each other, or were related, which would form a rural community.

The second ship, the *John McLellan*, took out Thomas Bugden, Henry Penny, Charles Read, William Talbot and their families, all from Donhead St Mary. Also on board were William Loader and his family, who came from Woodlands, and Stephen Kelloway and James Rideout and their families, from Tollard Royal. All were from villages on the Dorset/Wiltshire border and were related by marriage. The men were described as labourers. James Rideout, who was the son of a gamekeeper, was later recorded as one of the earliest tenant farmers at Menangle, which was part of the Camden Park estate.

When the *Royal George* arrived in Sydney on 10 March 1839, after 119 days at sea, the travellers may not have expected a further trip by steamer to Parramatta and 40 miles by cart before they reached their final destination. Each family was then assigned a small hut which had a kitchen, two bedrooms, a small pantry, a veranda and a quarter-acre of garden, which was far better than the homes they had left behind. William Macarthur would make daily inspec-tions of the huts, looking after those who were sick, inspecting their tongues and faeces, feeling pulses, making notes and providing what remedies he could. Each household was allowed to keep a milking cow, pigs and poultry 'on con-dition of getting into no mischief', and the women and children could earn extra money doing piecework. A school had been opened by the Macarthurs in 1838 which the younger Norris children attended. The schoolmaster was a prisoner who had been sent out for taking part in the Swing Riots.

Once they had become acclimatised to their new way of life, the families were able to have a far freer and happier existence, particularly the children whose lives improved with the change of climate and diet. Nevertheless, illnesses and accidents were inevitable. Henry Norris died a few weeks before his brother Sampson arrived at Camden, and Sampson later drowned in an accident. By 1849, when Isaac Norris arrived with his wife and three children, Josiah Wesley Walker had been employed by the Macarthurs to give medical attention to the people of the district. William Norris accompanied his brother and family on the *Emigrant* from England, still without a suitable wife. This was a situation he soon remedied by marrying Mary Anne Lucas three days after the ship's arrival; she had come from Tarrant Gunville, a nearby village to Child Okeford in Dorset, and had travelled out on the same ship. She was twelve years younger than William and, having borne him seven children in Australia, died at the early age of 35.

There were 326 people on board the *Emigrant* which sailed from Plymouth in March 1849. Apart from Captain Kemp and his crew, there were emigrants from Ireland, 25 from Wales, 19 from Wiltshire, 14 from Gloucestershire, 20 from Somerset, 18 from Maiden Newton in Dorset and 135 from the Blandford area. *The Plymouth, Devonport and Stonehouse Herald* reported that the Rev. S.G. Osborne had stayed on board to look after his charges until the pilot had left the ship.

The passenger list of travellers on board the *Emigrant* included the names of all the families and the unmarried single travellers, with details on their parentage, work, religion and age. Fifty-one of the emigrants from Dorset were born in the village of Stourpaine and twenty were from Child Okeford. Possibly many more of the people on board knew each other or were related.

Once at sea, a regular timetable would be enforced to keep an ordered existence on board. The master of the *Brothers*, Robert Towns, insisted that cleanliness was to be of great importance. All men had to rise at 6 a.m. and empty their slop pans and clean their berths. He found it a good rule to organise five or six of them each morning to help the crew in washing the decks. Major Macarthur had put a supply of bagging and twine on board the vessel for the men to make up into sacks and nets, and material for the women to make into shirts and shifts. Some printed material was supplied for the children to do dressmaking; some of the finished articles were kept by the women, who ended up with a better wardrobe than they started out with, and they received payment for their work when they reached Camden. Robert Towns attributed much of the quietness, regularity and discipline on board the *Brothers* to the fact that he did not allow spirits to be issued as rations to steerage passengers, and he did not allow gambling. A strict observance of the Sabbath was kept

TO SAIL ON THE 7th MARCH,

FOR SYDNEY DIRECT.

The fine fast sailing ship

EMIGRANT

A. 1. 733 Tons Register,

Has very desirable accommodation for Cabin and Interme-
diate Passengers.

Apply to   CAPT. KEMP, *on board; or to*
             LUSCOMBE, DRISCOLL, & Co.

Plymouth, 1st March, 1849.

An advertisement for passage to Australia, 1849 (*Plymouth, Devonport and Stonehouse Herald,*
3 March 1849)

and improper language prohibited. If there was not a clergyman among the
passengers, the surgeon or captain would take the Sunday service, as well as
the funerals of those that died at sea. There were separate services for different religions as there were Methodists, Wesleyans, Independents and Roman
Catholics, as well as members of the Church of England.

On the *Brothers*, the Macarthurs provided every family with a small cabin
6ft square, or two cabins in the case of large families; mattresses and blankets
were supplied. Every berth had its own slop pail, two or three pannikins,
tin plates, hook pots, a mess dish, a tea canister, a sugar box, wooden or iron
spoons and a keg for the daily allowance of water. All assisted passengers
travelled steerage and this area was divided. Single women had berths in the
stern of the vessel, separating them from married couples with children, who
were in the centre, with single men safely in the prow. Conditions on the
emigrant ships to Australia were generally far better than on those crossing
to the Americas. The British government tried to control standards through
the passing of New Passenger Acts from the 1820s, but these were sometimes
flouted by the entrepreneurs who were the main organisers of the Atlantic
crossing.

During the long voyage children attended school and books were provided for this, as well as Bibles and religious tracts. If there was an appointed
matron on board she took the classes, otherwise one of the passengers might
be given the task and either get a free passage or be paid later. Eventually
schoolmasters were introduced by the Colonial Land and Emigration
Committee, who were then able to leave the ship in Australia to find

employment. It was possible for the adults to attend lessons and classes were organised for them that included tailoring and cobbling. The assisted emigrants were found to have a high percentage of literacy when each person was tested for their reading and writing abilities, although more could read than write. The reason that they were found to be more literate than those crossing the Atlantic may have been that they had the opportunity to learn during the journey.

Those who did not have the choice of where they went or how they travelled were the men convicted for taking part in the Swing Riots. Many of the Dorset men found guilty and sentenced to death were from the Blackmoor Vale villages. This was an area known for some of the best grassland in Dorset, described by Thomas Hardy as the Vale of the Little Dairies in *Tess of the D'Urbervilles*. In November 1830, the tail end of the Swing Riots that had earlier ignited in Kent and Sussex swept through Hampshire and Wiltshire into Dorset and crossed over the Somerset border. In Somerset, forty cases were heard and only thirteen jailed; in Dorset there were sixty-two cases with fifteen jailed and thirteen transported to New South Wales. Three of the men convicted after the Blackmoor Vale Riots had their death sentence commuted to seven years' transportation. Of the nine sent to Australia on board the *Eleanor*, none of them were known to have returned home at the end of their sentences. Adam Thorne died in Bathurst Hospital and two others, who gained pardons, remained in Australia until they died.[25]

One of the villages these particular machine breakers came from was Hazelbury Bryan. The rector of the parish, Henry Walter, later gave evidence for the Royal Commission on the Poor Laws in 1834, where he stated that as early as 1821–22 the overseers had been in the habit of sharing out the pauper labourers amongst the farmers, including themselves, and paying them wholly out of the Poor Rates. The magistrates of the Blandford division had declined to check the abuse and pay was still being made up from the rates.[26]

It is easy to see why few made the return trip if they found out conditions had not improved since they had left. Five of the six Tolpuddle Martyrs transported to Australia chose to go to Canada after returning to England in 1836. They had been forced to return from Australia because of the public outcry after their deportation. The description of the agricultural workers' living conditions, given during a parliamentary inquiry in 1843 by Rachel Hayward of Stourpaine in Dorset, illustrates the poverty and deprivation she suffered with her husband and nine children.[27] They lived in a cottage with two rooms, one up and one downstairs. Most families lived with few utensils and often no stove, several to a bed, with holes in the walls for windows and open drainage, on an inadequate diet.

The punishment for poaching was transportation. Hobsbawn and Rudé measured the growing poverty and social tension of the period, before the Swing Riots, by the amount of poaching convictions per county.[28] They considered that the increase in poaching, rather than crime, illustrated the upsurge in rural resentment. As convicts in Australia discovered, conditions were tough, but opportunities on release were greater than in England. The riots may have unnerved the farmers and landowners, but wages would not be increased nor living conditions improved for years to come.

Conclusions

The parliamentarians who were politically disposed towards 'shovelling out paupers' must have been disappointed that the workhouses were not emptied and there was little effect on the Poor Rates. The threat of generations of parish relief claimants continued, but they had succeeded in sending a small proportion of the population to a distant colony from which there were few possibilities of returning; the same occurred with transported convicts, unless they became financially successful.

The philosophy of those who were involved in the practical support and encouragement of the assisted emigrants was not political. They preached the advantages of emigration and did their best to see that the translocation was made as efficiently as possible. Whether the actual landowners, who were often the patrons and the presidents of the societies formed to organise emigration, had the same philosophy is harder to establish.

The British have always been one of the most prolific colonising nations in the world. In the nineteenth century, as today, they appeared to have an ability to cope with a total change of location. Life at home receded with every day at sea and after crossing the equator they were able to stop looking backwards and prepare for their future. During a long sea voyage change becomes more easily accepted in the minds of passengers, as they settle into a routine and find their immediate surroundings more acceptable. Perhaps the length of the trip helped to make the transition to a new way of life in Australia.

An egalitarian society slowly grew into existence as it was not merely the independent travellers who prospered from the colonisation of Australia; the advantages for the assisted emigrant were numerous. They both had the opportunity of a better way of life and greater prospects for themselves and their families. So with some persuasive preaching from the pulpit, a small amount of spin doctoring from politicians and the press, they left the familiarity of their homes to sail halfway around the world.

Notes

1 Frank Thistlethwaite in *The Anglo-American Connection in the Early Nineteenth Century*, reprinted in *A Century of European Migrations, 1830–1930* (Illinois: University of Illinois Press, 1991). Charlotte Erickson in her introduction to *Leaving England* (Cornell University Press, 1972), footnotes on p. 32.

2 Robin F. Haines, *Emigration and the Labouring Poor: Australian Recruitment in Britain and Ireland, 1831–60* (UK: Macmillan Press, 1997).

3 Manning Clark, *History of Australia* (Chatto & Windus, 1993).

4 Robert Hughes, *The Fatal Shore* (UK: Collins Harvill, 1987).

5 B.R. Mitchell & P. Deane, *Abstract of British Vital Statistics* (Cambridge: Cambridge University Press, 1967), p. 7.

6 *British Parliamentary Papers Vol. XXII 1852–55* (Irish University Press), p. 61.

7 Taken from *British Parliamentary Papers Vol. 11 1826–7*, The Third Report, p. 38 and from questions put to Malthus, Nos 3244–8 (Irish University Press).

8 Frank Broeze, 'Private Enterprise and the Peopling of Australasia', in *Economic History Review*, Vol. 25, Part 2 (1982), p. 250.

9 *British Parliamentary Papers Vol. XIX 1828–1838, Report from the Commissioners of Emigration* (Irish University Press), p. 138.

10 Microfilm M362.5 ROY, Royal Commission on the Poor Laws, 1834, HMSO 1905, p. 357.

11 *British Parliamentary Papers Vol. XIX 1828–1838* (Irish University Press), p. 454.

12 *British Parliamentary Papers Vol. XIX 1828–1838*, p. 211, dated 18 July 1831.

13 *British Parliamentary Papers Vol. 11 1852–55, Appendix 1* (Irish University Press), p. 61.

14 Ian Stratton, *John West* (Dorset: Dorset County Museum), Dorset Worthies, Series 22 (1998).

15 Correspondence from the Reverend John West, dated 14 November 1838. Dorset History Centre PH 475/2.

16 'The Peasantry of Dorsetshire', *London Illustrated News*, 5 September 1846.

17 *British Parliamentary Papers Vol. XII 1852–55* (Irish University Press), Appendix to the 13th General Report, p. 72.

18 *British Parliamentary Papers Vol. XII 1852–55* (Irish University Press), p. 13. A further 8,731 passengers should be added to these numbers who did not travel on vessels under the protection of the Passengers Act, or from ports with emigration officers.

19 *British Parliamentary Papers Vol. XII 1852–55*, Appendix 1, p. 61.

20 *The Rose Family of the Bellona* (Thomas & Jane Rose Family Society), Dorset History Centre Library. Also article by Benjamin G. Cox, published in *Dorset Life* (Dec. 1988).

21 *Australian Dictionary of Biography* online. Also various publications held by Dorset History Centre Library, including 'Great Australians. Tom Roberts'. Part of a series written by Arnold Shore (Melbourne: Oxford University Press).

22 Compiled by Hugh McGrath, *John Diment Bagg and his descendants.* Typescript held by Bridport Library, Dorset.

23 Margaret Booth, *The Berry Family* (undated). Typescript deposited at Bridport Library, Dorset.

24 The Norris Family Research Group website, http://members.pcug.org. au/~athompso/family.htm.

25 Barbara House, *Machine Breakers* (Barbara Billings, 2000).

26 Royal Commission on the Poor Laws 1834, microfilm M362.5 ROY (HMSO 1905), p. 35.

27 J.H. Bettey, *Rural Life in Wessex* (Moonraker Press, 1977), p. 68.

28 E.J. Hobsbawn & George Rudé, *Captain Swing* (Lawrence & Wishart, 1970).

4

'Great Britain of the South': The Irish in Canterbury, New Zealand

Sara Moppett

Early movement from Britain and across Europe to New Zealand was largely in the guise of missionaries to 'Christianise the natives'.[1] In 1837, the New Zealand Association (later known as the New Zealand Company)[2] was formed with the intention to colonise this faraway place.[3] Indeed, a handbook for intending colonists to New Zealand considered that this society's 'zealous exertions … ultimately saved New Zealand from becoming a *French* penal colony'.[4]

As early as the 1780s, New Zealand was contemplated as a site for an English penal settlement. However, its natives were considered to be 'too dangerous and bloodthirsty',[5] a fact that was omitted from subsequent advertisements for immigration.

Nevertheless, it was not until the annexation in 1840 that larger numbers of immigrants or colonists began to settle in New Zealand, through a number of organised settlement schemes. Of the Canterbury settlement, W.J. Gardner writes that it 'represented the best in social and economic planning that Wakefield [Edward Gibbon Wakefield, a colonial reformer] and his colleagues could offer after a decade of experience'.[6]

According to W.A. Carrothers, Wakefield believed the subject of colonisation needed proper consideration, continuing that there were ultimately three objectives for colonisation: the extension of the market for disposing of surplus produce; relief from excessive number; and an enlargement of the field for employing capital.[7] Also to be taken into account was the land for disposal in the colonies. Land should no longer be given without charge; instead, a price 'should be determined by the needs of the colony for labour'.[8] The New Zealand Company and the subsequent provincial associations were therefore founded to put Wakefield's ideas for colonisation into effect.[9]

Regarding the selection of colonists for the Canterbury settlement, Wakefield's *HandBook for New Zealand* had this to say:

> So far as practicable, measures will be taken to send individuals of every class and profession, in those proportions in which they ought to exist in a prosperous colonial community.
>
> The Association retain, and will carefully exercise, a power of selection among all those who may apply for permission to emigrate to their Settlement, either as purchasers, or as emigrants requiring assistance. They will do so with the view of insuring, as far as possible, that none but persons of good character, as well as members of the Church of England, shall form part of the population, at least in its first stage; so that the Settlement may begin its existence in a healthy moral atmosphere.[10]

The settlement in Canterbury was to be established as an English settlement and as such it was important for the Church of England to be represented by the vast majority of immigrants. This was intentional, and therefore 'Irish' and 'Catholic' were not part of the equation. Social commentators of the time – including J.P. Kay and Friedrich Engels – were making observations on Irish immigrants in Britain, who were blamed for a number of social ills of the time.[11] The country of immigrants was often hoped to become the Greater Britain of the South, or as James Belich terms it, a 'Better Britain'; the encouragement of a predominantly English immigration and an establishment of Anglican foundations brought a distinctly English feel to Christchurch, which is still evident today in certain areas of the city.

The climate of New Zealand – particularly in the South Island and thus the Canterbury settlement – was not dissimilar to that of England and Ireland. As a consequence, the agricultural nature of this country was an integral part of its attraction to those willing to travel. Donald Akenson notes that, according to the *Dublin University Magazine* in 1858, New Zealand was favoured with a climate that shames that of Australia and with a soil exuberant in the highest degree, presenting many alluring young settlements with vast and fertile plains on their skirts; those islands are every year more largely engaging the attention of emigrants. This is a stock eulogy of all emigrant destinations – known as boosterism in America.[12]

The annexation of New Zealand in 1840 occurred for a number of reasons, according to W.J. Gardner – not as simply a matter of economics – although New South Wales saw New Zealand as a 'promising preserve for Sydney speculators', and the Wakefield group considered the territory as 'the fittest country in the world for colonization'. The annexation was also seen 'as a way of coping with distant but awkward social problems'.[13]

In order to colonise New Zealand, a series of schemes were adopted which were similar to other systems to promote emigration from the British Isles. Central to the majority of these immigration programmes was the fact that the colonisation of overseas countries advanced British interests. Quintessentially, as Donald Akenson comments, Irish migration was divided between America and Great Britain, and the nations attached to these Empires.[14] Through labour, industry, agriculture and population growth, many Irishmen and women would assist the development of a prosperous colony in New Zealand.

For Canterbury, the association which undertook its colonisation had a large number of important patrons with considerable financial or influential backgrounds; as the first volume of *A History of Canterbury* observes, 'the Association's first membership list testified to the popularity of the idea of overseas settlement and to the strength of Godley's connexion. Included in the fifty-nine members were two archbishops, seven bishops, fourteen peers, four baronets, and sixteen members of parliament.'[15] This association, and the committee who looked after the association's interests in England, maintained an important link with the mother country, a link which could be used to further the interests of the settlement. According to the *New Zealand Handbook* in 1875, John Robert Godly, a founder of the Canterbury Association, reported back to the friends of the colony in England that 'the Province of Canterbury alone, with a population at that time of 7,000, raised a revenue of £96,000: seven times as much, per head, as the revenue of England, and nearly twice as much, per head, as the revenue of the Colony of Victoria, "the richest community in the world up to this time".'[16] Thus the early profitability of the province was used to entice emigrants, particularly emigrants with money.

Nevertheless, it was not just the wealthy that were needed in the new settlement – all classes of the population were necessary to fulfil a whole range of jobs. As early as 1848, advertisements illustrating 'Here and There' or 'Home and Abroad' appeared in newspapers and magazines, including *Punch*, with exaggerated conditions of destitution, poverty and want in Great Britain as compared with comparative wealth, adequate accommodation and ample provisions in New Zealand. There were to be periodic concerns over the standards of emigrants and fears that there were too many of a destitute nature being sent to the colony, occasionally through the emptying of workhouses, thus relieving the burden on poor relief. W.D. Borrie has remarked that the British government in the 1850s rejected the assisted migration of English poor. The government believed that these poor would be superseded with other poor and therefore, the 'safest method was rather to continue to encourage emigration overseas from Ireland and Scotland than to lose English labourers only to have them replaced by Irish and Scots'.[17] So, paradoxically, immigration policy to New Zealand was partly driven by the wish to avoid an increase in pauperism at home.

Once a number of migrants had travelled to the colony, a new source of propaganda by way of emigrant letters became available; a source which would later be manipulated during the Vogel years (colonial treasurer in the government of 1869).[18] Not only did emigrant letters, more often than not, give an elaborate account of the colony, wages and improved standards of living, many implored family members and friends to follow them to the colony.

Once Canterbury (and also New Zealand) had established itself as a valid destination, through advertisement and promotion (some of which was deliberately misleading), potential emigrants were selected according to guidelines, which were at first restrictive, but became less stringent over time. *A History of Canterbury* details the early conditions for migrant selection for Canterbury:

> The intending emigrant was to be under forty years old, and preferably between twenty and thirty, and he was required to produce a medical certificate and a certificate from the minister of the parish 'that the applicant is sober, industrious and honest, and that he and all his family are amongst the most respectable of their class in the parish'. Preference was to be given to 'farm servants, shepherds, domestic servants, country mechanics and artisans', and young married couples would always be preferred to single persons.[19]

It further observes that particularly for the early arrivals, the age limit was fairly strictly followed, until a shortfall in emigrants occurred and the regulations were relaxed, 'except as to character and religion'.[20]

Even during the Vogel era of immigration, the provincial government maintained some control over emigration. In 1871, a document outlined a whole host of rules and regulations regarding immigration to Canterbury through the London office in Charing Cross. Nomination schemes were also used to encourage emigration. In 1873, 'the Canterbury Provincial Council therefore resolved to appoint another special agent, to allow settlers to nominate friends for free passage',[21] in an attempt to guarantee quality emigrants.

In the colonisation of Canterbury, Ulstermen and women were considered the ideal Irish migrants. The aspiration was for a Protestant and representative

British settlement in Canterbury during the late 1870s. The evidence from both this and Akenson's samples shows the Ulster Irish satisfied a very large proportion of the Irish contingent: 'Free and assisted passages are granted by the Government of New Zealand as under:- to Married Agricultural Labourers, Navvies, Ploughmen, Shepherds and a few Country Mechanics ... Free passages are given to single domestic servants.'[22]

New Zealand provided a perfect venue for Irish men, women and families wanting a better life. Irish men could work for wages in all manner of employment, follow the gold rush, and aspire for more than they were paid in Ireland. For Irish women, the free passage offered for single female domestic servants enabled them to break away from the family unit, without becoming dependent on somebody else. Ultimately, employment and wages could advance their expectations and improve their marriage prospects, thereby helping to populate the country.

Irish Migrants

Approximately 10,920 Irish travelled with assisted passage between 1858 and 1888 to the Canterbury province of New Zealand.[23] For the purposes of this study, persons of Irish origin were extracted from the *Assisted Passenger Lists*, and their numbers form the basis of this statistical analysis. These figures have been formulated with every person above the age of 12 constituting one statutory adult or one soul, and those below 12 counting as one-half of a statutory adult/soul. According to the fares charged for passage, those below the age of 1 were not included. However, in this study, because of the enormity of the numbers involved, this diminutive portion of the Irish population has been included as the others below 12 – as half a statutory adult, thus creating a small margin of error.

Shipping records for both New Zealand generally and Canterbury are problematical; as with many other resources they are often incomplete and faulty. One of the results of assisted immigration being subject to rules and conditions was that people were prepared to mislead the authorities – giving false ages and occupations and other inaccurate information in order to qualify for assisted passage. One example of this is related by Sean Brosnahan (author of *The Kerrytown Brosnahans*, 1992).[24] He tells how his great-great-grandparents, Hugh and Deborah Brosnahan (who sailed for New Zealand on the *Star of India* in 1873, with several other family members), gave their respective ages as 60 and 50, when they were in fact 80 and 60. Nobody appears to have questioned them. The statistics, therefore, being used cannot claim to be entirely reliable because of the inherent flaws of the material. However, the conclusions drawn nevertheless contribute towards a possible portrait of Irish immigration to Canterbury.

A general view of Irish immigration to Canterbury is first considered, exploring the actual numbers of Irish who ventured towards a new life across the world. The percentage of Irish on board the different ships is explored by relating the total number of statutory Irish adults from collected statistics and the complete passenger numbers as given in an inventory of *Passenger-Carrying Ships to Canterbury*, 1853–88.[25] In a small number of cases, no overall total was available for comparative purposes. Furthermore, the origins of the Irish immigrants are identified, paying particular attention to what will be termed, the 'north-south' divide. The 'desired' Irish were recruited from the Protestant north. A measure of the success or otherwise of the policy can be seen in a scrutiny of the counties of origin of all Irish immigrants. To clarify these definitions: 'north' or 'northern' encompasses the Irish who originated from the historic province of Ulster and its nine counties – Antrim, Armagh, Cavan, Donegal, Down, Fermanagh, Londonderry, Monaghan and Tyrone; 'south' or 'southern' incorporates the non-Ulster Irish – the rest of the country under the three provinces of Leinster, Munster and Connaught. In order to present a clear picture, the evidence will be broken down into five-year periods.

Under the initial provincial government schemes, Irish immigration to Canterbury before 1860 was little more than a trickle, never exceeding 14 per cent. Between the years 1858 and 1859, approximately 181 Irish travelled to Canterbury. The average percentage of Irish immigrants on board vessels bound for Canterbury was 7.54, since no assisted immigrants of Irish descent appeared in the records before the *Zealandia* in September 1858. The following period, continuing under the provincial schemes – 1860 to 1864 – saw Irish migration fluctuate.[26] During this period, approximately thirty-nine vessels travelled to Canterbury with the Irish forming an average proportion of 21.99 per cent of the total passengers carried. Irish immigration at this stage peaked through 1861 and 1862.

A more consistent Irish migration occurred in the years 1865 to 1869, rather than the haphazard peaks and troughs which were visible between 1860 and 1864. Of the twenty-five ships which travelled during these years, an average of 38.05 per cent Irish were present on each ship. However, when this is broken down, far higher figures are evident, particularly in 1866. Only one of the six ships which arrived in 1865 – the *Tudor*, arriving in September – contained less than 23 per cent, while the *Greyhound* in May and the *Indian Empire* in July both arrived with above 30 per cent on board.[27] The first boat containing nearly 100 per cent Irish was in 1866. The *Himalaya*, arriving in

Emigrants on board a ship

February, contained 94.12 per cent Irish (although only seventeen statutory adults were carried on board, sixteen of whom were Irish). Of the boats arriving in 1867, only the *Mermaid* which landed in January and the *Glenmark* in November carried less than 30 per cent Irish,[28] the other four ships during the year held above 40 per cent.

Immigration policies started to change during the period 1870 to 1874. While the provincial government in Canterbury continued to have some control over immigration into the province, the Public Works and Immigration Act of 1870 reasserted the control of the central government over immigration. This scheme increased the scale of immigration quite dramatically through the 1870s. Indeed, the bulk of Irish immigration to Canterbury occurred during this decade.[29] This was achieved through the extension of the programmes already in place, such as the nomination and assisted schemes. It was also at this stage that advertisements began to promote New Zealand with propagandist images of good living. Furthermore, even though New Zealand was still developing, both the country and Canterbury had now sufficiently evolved from the wasteland which had greeted the first settlers on their arrival. As Anna Rogers summarises about New Zealand more generally:

By the end of the 1860s New Zealand was a more attractive proposition as a place in which to begin a new life. There were schools to educate your children, banks to look after your money, newspapers to tell you what was happening in the rest of the world.[30]

Under the Public Works and Immigration Act, it was proposed that thousands of immigrants would assist in the building of new amenities, including roads, railways and telegraph lines to further improve the country.[31] They would also purchase land, thus expanding the colony and populating the land.

Of the fifty-two boats which travelled to the province within the first half of this decade, an average of only 21.61 per cent Irish were present on board. However, as ever, such percentages disguised the high proportions that Irish migration could reach: the *Siberia*, which arrived in January 1870, accommodated 58.21 per cent Irish, while the *Michael Angelo*, arriving in May 1873, comprised 51.71 per cent Irish. Nevertheless, the ratio of Irish during this time was relatively insignificant; only three boats contained more than 40 per cent, with a further nine boats holding above 30 per cent; forty boats carried less than 30 per cent Irish – twenty-two of which carried less than 20 per cent. Similarly to the flow of immigrants between 1860 and 1864, the flow during this time was generally inconsistent, although indicating a slight decline throughout the five years.

The period 1875 to 1879 saw a notable increase in the number of Irish travelling on board the forty-seven vessels bound for Canterbury. Although on average, 36.60 per cent of those carried to the province were Irish, a significantly larger contingent journeyed towards a new life on several of the boats. Two ships accommodated an Irish population of above 80 per cent: the *Rakaia*, which arrived in December 1877, held 80.04 per cent Irish, while the *Conflict*, which landed earlier in January 1876, had an Irish population of 93.32 per cent. One possible explanation for the size of the Irish community on board the *Conflict* was the fact that it was one of the few boats to depart directly from Ireland, which would have meant that Irish migrants could avoid the expense of first journeying to England to embark. Only ten boats held an Irish population of less than 30 per cent, while the majority of the boats set sail with a gathering of between 30 and 40 per cent. This would suggest that the second five-year period under the Vogel schemes of assisted and nominated passage was fully manipulated by earlier Irish immigrants to produce a comparatively stable flow of new Irish arrivals. The people themselves thus subverted official policy.

The periods 1880–84 and 1885–88 are more difficult to assess because the overall number of passengers was omitted for an increasing number of vessels, which thus rendered an Irish percentage incalculable. Between 1880 and 1884 an on-board Irish population averaged 33.05 per cent, while the proportion appeared to diminish significantly through the following five-year period. This was almost certainly as a consequence of the lack of information. There were a number of vessels on which at least half of the immigrants carried were Irish, while in contrast, only one boat held less than 20 per cent.[32]

Having examined the period 1855 to 1888 in five-year sections, the intention is to explore a more overall view of the period before breaking it down into a more specific analysis. In order to focus on a microcosm, Donald Akenson's sample year (1876) for Irish migration to New Zealand[33] has been set within a sample using two further years, 1866 and 1886,[34] to set immigration to Canterbury within its wider New Zealand context. The purpose of the sample is to investigate the exact numbers of Irish by county, thereby questioning what Akenson terms the 'geographic foci of Irish migration to New Zealand', with Ulster and Munster taking precedence as the primary exporters of immigrants,[35] and exploring whether this trend was also valid for Canterbury.

In examining the average percentage of Irish immigrants on board ships to Canterbury for the whole period of this study, the scale of migration is visible in the graph below.

Using this graph, with the exception of the middle years, there is a perceptible trend as Irish immigration increased through the provincial government period and early-to-middle Vogel period, before decreasing as assistance was withdrawn.

Immigration was not always wanted by those who were already established in Canterbury and New Zealand. Vogel's large-scale plans brought a great many into the country and continued to do so even in times of economic distress. Improvements in New Zealand (which were both desired and necessary, and which were to be addressed by Vogel's Immigration and Public Works Act) were popular. However, the immigrants who were assisted to the country in order to accomplish these improvements were not always appreciated and did not in all cases continue to fulfil the criteria under which they

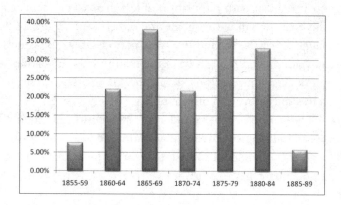

Graph 1. The average percentage of Irish immigrants on board ships bound for Canterbury, 1855–89[36]

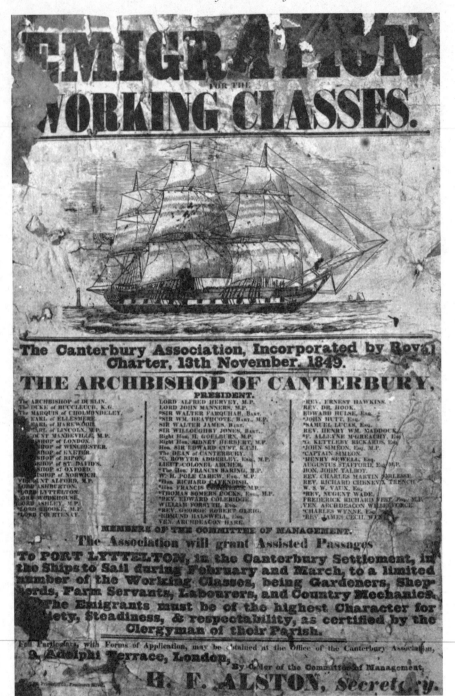

Poster: *Emigration for the Working Classes*, November 1849 (Canterbury Museum, New Zealand, ref. 19XX.2.952)

had been selected, as Anna Rogers writes: 'The men who had been employed on various public works were not always suited to their tasks and, rather than toiling on the land (agricultural jobs were still in demand), they tended to collect in the towns, putting pressure on urban employment and resources.'[37]

Although 'from 1877 the government began to cut back on immigration … [and] the flow of Irish migrants … remained steady',[38] the financial situation of a country which had taken on enormous loans to promote Vogel's scheme meant that the purse strings began to be tightened and the occupations which could benefit from free passage were restricted. Therefore, as is visible in Graph 1, as the assisted and free schemes for passage developed and increased through the provincial and government programmes, the number of Irish migrants expanded accordingly. As these schemes were withdrawn, Irish numbers contracted.

The table below illustrates the Ulster-South divide of Irish immigrants in the period 1858 to 1888:

Table 11: The Ulster-South Divide During the Period 1858–88 in Percentage[39]				
Year	Ulster	'South'	Ireland	Total %
1858–59	42.50	40.12	17.38	100
1860–64	59.86	39.61	0.51	99.98
1865–69	54.75	44.95	0.29	99.99
1870–74	57.05	42.66	0.28	99.99
1875–79	43.14	56.80	0.04	99.98
1880–84	38.49	61.50	0	99.99
1885–89	45.61	54.39	0	100
Total	48.77	48.57	2.64	99.98

'Ireland', instead of an Irish county, was given as the place of origin in the earliest period of Irish immigration to New Zealand. After 1860 the majority of immigrants gave a county rather than their country of origin. As we would expect, given that Canterbury was to be an Anglican province and the preferred Irish migrants were to be recruited from the largely Protestant north-east of the country, the nine counties of Ulster were well represented. Throughout the period 1858–88, the average percentage of Ulster Irish was 48.77 per cent, which was virtually identical with the average of 'Southern' Irish at 48.57 per cent. However, as is visible, Ulster Irish were more numerous before 1875, after which time their numbers were exceeded by 'Southern'

Irish. This confirms the view of the Canterbury Association that Protestantism was of particular importance in the early stages of the developing province. Hence there was a concentration of immigration agencies in the predominantly Protestant north-east of Ireland, and this resulted in a higher number of immigrants from Ulster in the early years of the settlement.

Donald Akenson observes of a study by David Fitzpatrick that, 'of New Zealand's immigrants who came directly from Ireland … the migrants were loaded towards an origin in the north of Ireland and, probably, slightly towards Protestantism', inferring that 'as a norm, a disproportionate number had those characteristics'.[40] Akenson further writes that the Irish in New Zealand largely came from the two provinces of Ulster and Munster (including its neighbouring Galway).[41] Akenson's assertions are drawn on as a base and the origins of Irish migrants to New Zealand are compared with the smaller Irish migration to Canterbury.

Table 12: The Number of Immigrants from the Province of Ulster during the Years 1866, 1876 and 1885/6[42]				
	1866	1876	1886	Total
Antrim	27½	87	3	117½
Armagh	9	73½	14	96½
Cavan	6	22	4	32
Donegal	17	51½	4	72½
Down	59½	76½	9½	145½
Fermanagh	10½	20	5	35½
Londonderry	2	41½	2	45½
Monaghan	0	15½	0	15½
Tyrone	18½	92	3	113½
Total	150	479½	44½	674

This table illustrates the total number of immigrants from the counties which made up the historical nine-county province of Ulster. During Donald Akenson's sample year of 1876, a larger number left Ulster for Canterbury than for the other years in this sample; the assisted and free-passage schemes were well established by 1876 which guaranteed a high level of immigration from all areas of British society.

Of the Ulster counties which appeared to promote a higher rate of immigration in the pre- and post-Vogel periods, Antrim, Armagh and Down led the way, followed closely by Tyrone and Donegal. However, all of the Ulster counties contributed to the flow of emigrants from Ulster, the sole exception being Monaghan. The numbers for which Table 12 was compiled reinforces the principal migrations (in order of size) from Down, Antrim, Tyrone, and to a lesser extent Armagh and then Donegal. Out of the 674 migrants who travelled from Ulster during this time, 55.86 per cent came from the three counties of Down, Antrim and Tyrone. Anna Rogers writes that 'the largest proportion of New Zealand's Irish migrants originated in County Antrim',[43] a fact which is supported by Akenson's figures.[44] In contrast to Rogers and Akenson, this sample would indicate that the largest proportion of Canterbury's Irish migrants in fact came from County Down; of which James Belich writes that it was 'the most New Zealand-prone County of all'.[45] Belich continues that the preponderance of Ulster migrants from Antrim and Down occurred as a result of their proximity to Belfast, 'a primary centre of crusader effort'.[46] However, it must be noted that the figures which Akenson has used focus on the Irish who left for New Zealand from Irish ports, whereas the figures which form this sample concentrate on the Irish who arrived in Canterbury.

Akenson observes that Ulster 'was the second main source of New Zealand migrants. It was not as large a supplier of migrants [during the Vogel period] as was Munster.'[47] Yet, as can be seen in Table 13, the results of this sample would imply that for migrants to Canterbury, the reverse was in fact true. Ulster was the primary source of migrants, accounting for 50.66 per cent of the sample as opposed to the 31.68 per cent who came from Munster. Even for the sample years separately, the numbers from Ulster exceeded the numbers from the other three provinces.

Table 13: The Total Number of Emigrants from the Provinces of Ireland during the Years 1866, 1876 and 1885/6					
	1866	1876	1886	Total	Percentage
Ulster	150	479½	44½	674	50.6
Leinster	29½	72½	8	110	8.3
Munster	51½	335½	34½	421½	31.7
Connaught	65	53½	6½	125	9.4
Total	296	941	93½	1330½	100

In Munster, many Irish had been displaced from the land in the post-famine era, as the consolidation of land signalled the decline in land subdivision and, for many, the emigrant ship became a valid option. James Belich discusses the Canterbury-prone English counties, which he divides into three groups:

The West Country counties of Cornwall, Devon and Somerset;
The South Midland counties of Oxford and Gloucester; and
The London hinterland counties of Surrey, Essex and Kent.[48]

He continues to write that 'high general emigration would also explain the high Canterbury migration of the two English counties outside the three main groups (Huntingdon and Cumberland), and of the Irish county of Kerry'.[49] As Table 14 shows, Kerry was by far the dominant county of origin from Munster after 1876. Of an earlier period, Ruth-Ann Harris comments that 'in 1841 persons from the province of Munster were the least likely to migrate elsewhere in Ireland, suggesting that reduced opportunity in the previous twenty to thirty years resulted in permanent out-migration from Munster earlier than from all the other counties except Ulster'.[50]

Table 14: The Number of Emigrants from the Province of Munster during the Years 1866, 1876 and 1885/6				
	1866	**1876**	**1886**	**Total**
Clare	10	15½	2	27½
Cork	12½	29½	9	51
Kerry	7	132	14	153
Limerick	6½	69½	1	77
Tipperary	11½	67	8½	87
Waterford	4	22	0	26
Total	51½	335½	34½	421½

In contrast with Ulster and Munster, emigration from Connaught and Leinster was significantly lower. The exception here is Galway. As shown in Table 15, Galway was the major contributor of immigrants to Canterbury, providing 73.6 per cent of the Connaught immigrants.

Table 15: The Number of Immigrants from the Province of Connaught during the Years 1866, 1876 and 1885/6				
	1866	1876	1886	Total
Galway	46	44½	1½	92
Leitrim	3	3	1	7
Mayo	12	1	1	14
Roscommon	4	3	3	10
Sligo	0	2	0	2
Total	65	53½	6½	125

These figures show a similar trend with those of Akenson.[51] Taking into account that Akenson's overall timescale was longer, a far higher proportion of Connaught immigrants originated in Galway than in other counties. The Galway Irish accounted for 53.69 per cent of Akenson's Connaught sample and 73.6 per cent of this sample. This shows that a significant majority of the Connaught migrants travelled to Canterbury.

Table 16: The Number of Emigrants from the Province of Leinster during the Years 1866, 1876 and 1885/6				
	1866	1876	1886	Total
Carlow	5	0	4	9
Dublin	6	9	0	15
Kildare	1	2	0	3
Kilkenny	0	21	0	21
Queens	4	6	0	10
Longford	0	4	0	4
Louth	2	0	0	2
Meath	0	2	0	2
Kings	2	7½	0	9½
Westmeath	0	8	0	8
Wexford	3	10	1	14
Wicklow	6½	3	3	12½
Total	29½	72½	8	110

Table 16 illustrates the findings of the Leinster sample. For the years 1866 and 1886 the numbers are relatively insignificant, while 1876 is little better in comparison with Ulster and Munster. James Belich observes that of the Leinster counties that were attracted to New Zealand, Carlow and Wicklow were 'New Zealand-prone' because of their proximity to a secondary centre of immigrant recruitment in Dublin. However, in this sample, Carlow and Wicklow were exceeded in numbers by Kilkenny and Dublin; this perhaps renders them more 'New Zealand-prone' counties, indicating a diversity of patterns within the region.

We know from a number of previous works[52] of the regional diversity of Irish migrants and their settlements in Britain. These resulted in a number of established routes, as Graham Davis details: 'The northern route linked Ulster and North Connacht to Scotland; the midland route connected Connacht and Leinster to the north of England and the midlands, and the southern route went from South Leinster and Munster, often via South Wales or Bristol to London.'[53]

The Irish in New Zealand would therefore appear to exhibit a similar trend in regional inclinations for settlement, although national tendencies are not always reflected in the smaller, regional patterns of colonisation. Even English migrants exhibited a propensity to migrate from specific counties to Canterbury.[54] The concentration of migrants from particular counties within Ulster and Munster are matched by the similar trends in English migration.

James Belich observes in his work *Making Peoples* that the desired emigrants for New Zealand were required to display a number of qualities in order to be eligible for assisted passage. Emigrants were to be 'moneyed, or else young, healthy and rural; with a balance of men and women ... decent working people ... to desire social promotion to respectability above all, but to be willing to serve a substantial apprenticeship as labourers and servants'.[55] Such high standards would not have been easy to maintain. Regardless of the standards set, the presence of the working classes was not just a necessity, it was essential to the development of the colony. In order to construct a settlement, people of all levels were of utmost importance, and the people who were prepared to undertake the most menial of the tasks would not always have met all the criteria laid down. Anna Rogers argues that for many of the Irish who travelled to New Zealand, prejudice was already present. It was transplanted from England and reinforced by unflattering images which were contrary to that of the ideal migrant.[56] However, Irish migrants had played their role during the Industrial Revolution in Britain by providing a mobile and adaptable labour force for a dynamic economy.

Having considered the origin of Irish emigrants, it is the intention now to explore the composition of the Irish emigrants who were Canterbury-bound during the period 1860 to 1884. A smaller sample of Irish immigrants has been collated by selecting approximately two representative vessels per year. Where it was possible, the two vessels have been taken from January and July to present equal spacing between vessels. Where this was not possible, the ships which were closest to this six-monthly spacing have been used.

In attempting to explore the character of the Irish emigrants within the sample, a number of features are addressed. Firstly, the travelling status of the emigrants is considered – whether they travelled alone or as part of a group. This is followed by the age distribution, to establish if certain ages were predominant. Finally, the given occupations of the migrants are examined, to explore a possible excessive concentration of Irish within the manual trades for men and within the domestic sphere for women. By using these categories, it is possible to assess whether or not they conformed to Donald Akenson's 'ideal types' – that is, 'mostly young, primarily unskilled … [with] a tincture of skilled and middle class migrants and indeed, a few capitalists and gentry'.[57]

In order to focus on the travelling status of the Irish immigrants within the sample, the immigrants are thus categorised:

Travelling individually
Single men
Single women
Travelling as part of a group
Family units with children and also sometimes incorporating extended family members, and on occasion non-family members (e.g. nephews and nieces etc.)
Married units without children
Siblings travelling together – of which the minority (if any) were married
Individuals travelling together – a number of individuals travelled with companions from the same county and, as with the siblings category, few (if any) appear to have been married

For single men and women, one person represents one unit, whereas for those travelling as part of a group, one unit represents any number of persons.[58]

Table 17: The Travelling Status of Irish Immigrants On Board Vessels Bound for Canterbury 1860–84			
Travelling Status	**Number**	**As Percentage of Total Souls on Board**	**As Percentage Travelling Alone or as Part of a Group**
Single Men	663	24.19	49.4 travelled individually
Single Women	681	24.85	
Family Units with Children	255	50.96 travelled as part of a group	
Married Units without Children	126		
Siblings Travelling Together	202		
Individuals Travelling Together	45		
Total	1972 'units'	2740 ½ Total souls	100

For the period 1860 to 1884, nearly half of all Irish who made the journey to Canterbury travelled individually, and of this figure, single Irish women were marginally a larger number. Approximately half of the Irish emigrants were unmarried and travelled halfway across the world without a companion.[59] This number of single individuals was further supplemented by unmarried siblings and individuals who, for whatever reason, chose not to face a journey which could take a number of months alone.

Many of these migrants best fulfilled the criteria set for immigration to the province of Canterbury, particularly the single female domestic servants who could take advantage of the free passage offered. However, terms were not always so favourable for single men. For married men, those with specific occupations were offered a better deal financially than single men generally.[60] Yet, this did not deter single Irishmen (and men of other origins) from travelling to the colony in search of a better life. Married couples, with or without children, were desirable immigrants. Those with children provided an instant increase in the population, while those without children would most probably at some stage contribute to an expansion of the population. Furthermore, married couples without children might have found both the decision to emigrate and the passage itself easier, given the length of the voyage and levels of infant mortality.

Donald Akenson observes:

In one sense, migrating with children was a handicap. Given the social prac-
tises of the time, only the man was available for full-time employment and the
woman for only casual jobs, such as taking in washing, doing mending and
the like. Thus, in the first year or two, the larger Irish families were inevitably
a handicap. With time, however, they turned to being a benefit. If the family
continued in wage labour, the children as they became adolescents, could be
sent out to earn money. And, if the family acquired a holding of land, then the
children became part of the economic unit, at first doing small jobs and eventually taking on adult farm tasks.[61]

The ratio of families with children to married couples without for the whole
period was 2.02:1, which would indicate that Canterbury, at this time, was a
more attractive option to families rather than married couples. Similarly, many
single Irish women had a strategy for migration. While filling an immediate
need for domestic servants, they would also have become potential wives for
the single men already in the province. For many of the single women who
chose to migrate, their opportunities of marriage in their homeland were
negligible. Therefore, as has previously been suggested, migration not only
provided an increased chance of marriage, but allowed for relative economic
freedom before marriage, and even a chance to marry for love rather than as
an economic union. The economic motives may have been as important as
romantic motives in the dire conditions for women in Ireland. We cannot be
certain. Certainly, the potential for expanding the population (whether or not
it was a contrived mechanism) was covered admirably by all eventualities.

Irish immigration to Canterbury was frequently dependent on the terms
offered to potential migrants. Canterbury only became a viable option for
settlement to the Irish when there were economic incentives, including free
passage for some, the deferment of payment for passage for those who were
required to pay, and carriage of children at reduced or free rates. When these
financial stimuli were removed or decreased, Irish immigration diminished
accordingly.

Of those Irish who travelled to New Zealand, those who Donald Akenson
termed 'ideal types' were 'mostly young'.[62] This is perhaps not surprising
when you consider that attempts were made to restrict immigrants over a
specified age. Anna Rogers comments upon the fact that 'if you were over 50
the New Zealand government would not help you emigrate, unless you were
a member of a large family'.[63] Very exact terms and conditions for passage
were laid down:

No assistance was given to a single man aged 40+.

No assistance was given to anyone above 50 except if they were part of a large
  family.
No assistance was given at all to anyone over the age of 60.

However, as Anna Rogers notes regarding the Brosnahan family, as an example, this age restriction was not always adhered to through deception or
omission.[64] Would-be migrants had an incentive to be economical with the
truth if it meant a free passage.

  To consider the ages of Irish migrants, the smaller sample is used, and Table
18 shows the results of this. It is interesting to note that for males and females,
a small number did not specify an age. Possibly, these were among those travelling as a family group.

Table 18: The Ages of Irish Immigrants On Board Vessels Bound for Canterbury, 1858–88			
Age	Male	Female	Sex Unspecified
0–11	267	245	2
12–19	247	454	0
20–29	847	923	0
30–39	148	113	0
40–49	49	41	0
50+	15	19	0
Age Unspecified	41	19	0
Total	1614	1814	2

The largest proportions of migrants were below the age of 30 – 84.3 per cent
for male and 89.4 per cent for females. In both cases, the major concentration
of numbers was within the 20–29 categories. The sexes of children aged 11 or
under were evenly distributed – a trend that did not continue beyond the age
of 15, where the number of females nearly doubled that of males. That difference can perhaps be explained, as from the age of 15, young women could
enter the realm of domestic service and free passage was offered to young single
women in the majority of domestic spheres. Therefore, the economic terms
were not as favourable for young single males. Furthermore, single young
women were a desired 'commodity' in the province and single Irish women
were more prone to migrate than single women of other nationalities.[65]

Consequently, it can be said that the great majority of Irish immigrants, being under 30, formed part of Akenson's 'ideal' Irish migrant.

In terms of occupation, the 'ideal' migrants were 'primarily unskilled, but there was a tincture of skilled and middle class migrants and, indeed a few capitalists and gentry'.[66] The *Assisted Passenger Lists* do not inform us as to the class of the migrant. Those with the means, including the middle classes, capitalists and gentry, would have paid for their own passages and, therefore, while they might have appeared in the lists as paying passengers, it is visible that they were not required to give a county of origin.[67] Also, while assisted migrants were required to give an occupation in order to qualify for passage, this was not always recorded in the lists. Furthermore, on examining the occupations of a small number of migrants when actually in the province, not all were employed in the trade for which they received assisted passage. All too often, Irish domestic servants (many of whom were untrained) were the subject of mockery and derision when they did not live up to the expectations of employers. Indeed, *The Christchurch Press* described them as 'Housemaids who have never handled a broom, cooks who scarcely know the difference between roast meals and boiled, and whose highest practical achievements in the art have been limited to preparing potatoes ... in the wilds of Connemara'.[68]

The final section determines whether the given occupations fulfilled Akenson's criteria for 'ideal' migrants; also, whether the migrants in Canterbury were representative of the Irish who settled elsewhere in New Zealand. And lastly, how representative were the New Zealand Irish in comparison with places of Irish settlement throughout the diaspora?

By far the largest proportion of men within the sample were classified as 'Farm Labourers', although 892 or 68.1 per cent of men were involved in agriculture in some form. This, without doubt, reflects the predominance of agriculture in the Canterbury area and indeed throughout New Zealand. Donald Akenson found, using his 1876 sample, that 76.7 per cent of men he classified as 'Heads of Household' and 82 per cent of single men were employed in agriculture.[69] Both sets of figures reinforce the view that the majority of Irish migrants came to New Zealand with an agricultural occupation.

This agricultural bias of labour is not unexpected considering that Ireland at that time was still recovering from the far-reaching effects of the famine. New Zealand may be the exception here. The Irish who went to Britain and the US mostly settled in urban communities, in search of better paid work. These jobs may not have been available in New Zealand. As has already been discussed, one social consequence of the famine was that the land, rather than being subdivided as had previously been the case, particularly in the west of

Ireland, was consolidated. This change of practice had implications for children and inheritances. It also had ramifications for other areas of Irish society, as Akenson observes:

> As the sub-division of farms sharply diminished, the landless agricultural labourers virtually ceased to exist as a class. They migrated to Dublin, Great Britain, and overseas. The band of single males that we observed in the 1876 data must have been the sons of small tenant farmers, young lads who, with no hope of acquiring enough land in Ireland to support a family, decided to chance life elsewhere.[70]

And so, those from an agricultural background had far more reason to migrate than did those of a non-agricultural background.

In contrast to the largely unskilled majority of migrants were the skilled or semi-skilled workers. These were a small and diverse group. At a time when the province was increasing in terms of population, consumers began to demand that goods were more readily available within the province rather than having to wait for them to be imported. This could be a lengthy process. Accordingly, those in certain occupations (including weavers for cloth, and sail makers to serve the all-important marine trade) could carve out a profitable niche for themselves by relocating to Canterbury. Moreover, with the expansion in population, more houses and accommodation were needed, putting a premium on the building trades in the colony. The great majority of houses in the early stages of settlement were simple buildings made of timber with brick fireplaces.[71] There were also more imposing, official buildings or larger houses for the wealthy. Hence the increasing need for sawyers and carpenters, masons and brick makers to build them.

Other occupations provided an obvious need: schoolmasters for education; tailors, bakers and shoemakers (for example) for consumer goods; carpenters, joiners, masons, bricklayers and tinsmiths for the building trade; millwrights, blacksmiths and carters for early transport and agricultural services; and a constable to police the community. The idea of Canterbury as a 'better Britain of the South' is endorsed by the selection of gardeners given assisted passage to the province. Hagley Park in Christchurch bears witness to the pleasure taken in beautiful gardens and the transplantation of English flora and fauna.

One would expect the inclusion of schoolmasters, although perhaps in higher numbers than actually occurred. Free second-class passage, under the Queen's Regulations, was provided for a schoolmaster on each voyage. He was responsible for checking on the cleanliness of the children each morning, to 'make a list or school register of those who are fitted to receive instruction between the ages of five and fourteen years' and deliver instruction for at least four hours daily, and to include religious instruction once a day. Schoolmasters could instruct an adult class as long as it did not interfere with the education of the children. They were also exempt from cleaning duties.[72] However, only three schoolmasters travelled to Canterbury during the entire sample, suggesting that they had less motivation than others to leave Ireland.

Table 19: The Total Occupations of Irish Men for the Sample Years, 1866, 1876 and 1886		
	Total	Percentage
Agricultural workers (including labourers, shepherds etc)	889	67.8
General servants	5	0.4
Building trades (including bricklayer, plumber etc.)	275	21
Equine occupations (including saddler, ostler, blacksmith etc.)	25	2
Schoolmasters	3	0.2
Clothing trades (including shoemaker, weaver etc.)	19	1.5
Miscellaneous (including mineral water maker, cabinet maker etc.)	27	2.1
Unspecified	67	5.1
Total	1310	100.1

For those women who were unmarried, it was predictable that the majority of them were involved in some sphere of domestic service, taking advantage of the free passage offered to them. For those women whose marital prospects had diminished in Ireland, Canterbury offered an opportunity of independence, employment and possibly even marriage. Excluding those who were married or with a family, domestic workers in varying guises accounted for the largest percentage (56.95 per cent).

The persistence of Irish women immigrating to Canterbury to find employment in a domestic sphere partially confirms the position of women in Irish society. While the pre-famine period was not entirely benevolent to Irish women, for those within a family, there was still a role for them to perform. Mary Cullen writes that 'folklore sources indicate that marriage in Ireland conferred status as a "full member of the community" on both men and women'.[73] One social consequence of the famine was that it saw the decline of a woman's economic contribution to a family unit. Joseph Lee discusses three ways in which this happened. Firstly, he argues, the domestic industry in Ireland, which he calls 'the main source of independent income' for women, went into a serious decline of about 75 per cent. Secondly, the change in agriculture from tillage to livestock meant that women were needed less on the farm. Finally, the number of smaller farmers fell, and since it was in the realm of the poorer farms that women 'enjoyed greater economic quality', their positions fell in importance.[74]

Table 20: The Total Occupations of Irish Women During the Period 1860–88		
	Total	**Percentage**
Domestic work	931	60.3
Farm labour/servant/dairymaid	133	8.6
Textile workers	31	2
Governess/teacher	4	0.2
Retail	3	0.19
Nurse/nursemaid/matron	19	1.2
Miscellaneous	4	0.2
Married/family	338	22
Unspecified	80	5.2
Total	1543	99.89

Ultimately, the experiences of the Irish emigrants altered with the destination and timing of their migration. In both the pre- and post-famine periods, those who went to Britain, America, British North America and Australasia satisfied vacancies within their host communities: as seasonal labourers and menial, industrial labourers in Britain; as labourers in America; and as agricultural workers in New Zealand. The underlying factor is that economic necessity often forced the Irish to undertake the most menial jobs in order to survive. It is perhaps fortunate that at the time when landless agricultural workers were finding it harder to survive, New Zealand and Canterbury offered opportunities for both survival and improvement. Similarly for women, while not all were trained (a point which was picked up on by Christchurch's press), domestic work was an area in which most women were capable. That Canterbury again provided scope for survival and improvement was often a chance which was too good to miss. Canterbury provided potential for Irish migrants to create a new life for themselves in a new country — a country that also provided them with the potential for a healthier and superior standard of living.

Irish migrants (both Catholic and Protestant) were able to take full advantage of the assisted passage schemes designed to create a better Britain of the South, based on allegedly English, Protestant virtues. British government policy, not for the first or last time, had unintended consequences. The individual actions of Irish migrants made a contribution to the making of New Zealand.

Notes

1 W.A. Carrothers, *Emigration from the British Isles* (Westminster, 1929), p. 122.

2 J.M.R. Owens, 'New Zealand Before Annexation', in W.H. Oliver (ed.) with B.R. Williams, *The Oxford History of New Zealand* (Oxford, 1987), p. 51.

3 A company had previously been formed in 1825, although many of the colonists had since moved to New South Wales, Australia, ibid.

4 E.G. Wakefield, *The Handbook for New Zealand: Consisting of the Most Recent Information for the Use of Intending Colonists* (London, 1848), p. 59. Wakefield did not put his name to this, rather signing himself 'A Late Magistrate of the Colony who resided there during four years'.

5 James Belich, *Making Peoples: A History of the New Zealanders* (Auckland, 1996), p. 129.

6 James Hight & C.R. Straubel (eds), *A History of Canterbury*, I, Section 3, as quoted by W.J. Gardner, 'A Colonial Economy', in W.H. Oliver (ed.) with B.R. Williams, op. cit., p. 62.

7 W.H. Oliver (ed.) with B.R. Williams, *The Oxford History of New Zealand*, p. 94.

8 Ibid., p. 95.

9 Ibid., pp. 123–4.

10 Wakefield, *The Handbook for New Zealand*, p. 14.

11 Graham Davis, 'The Irish in Britain, 1815–1939', in Andy Bielenberg (ed.) *The Irish Diaspora* (2000), p. 24.

12 Donald H. Akenson, *The Irish Diaspora* (Belfast, 1996), p. 14.

13 Gardner, 'A Colonial Economy', in *The Oxford History of New Zealand*, referring to Adams, *Fatal Necessity*, Part 1, p. 58.

14 Akenson, *The Irish Diaspora*, p. 150.

15 James Hight & C.R. Straubel, *A History of Canterbury. Volume 1 to 1854* (Christchurch, 1957), p. 150.

16 Julius Vogel (ed.), *The Official Handbook of New Zealand. A Collection of Papers by Experienced Colonists on the Colony as a Whole and on the Several Provinces* (London, 1875), p. 122.

17 W.D. Borrie, *Immigration to New Zealand 1854–1938*, p. 7; National Archives of New Zealand, 'Mrs Howard's Selection of Irish Emigrants', CH287 Item ICPS 1598/1874 Dept of Lands and Survey; Christchurch Office. This newspaper clipping detailed the selection of 200 Irish emigrants from a workhouse in Cork by a Mrs Caroline Howard, formerly of Dunedin.

18 Julius Vogel, *The Official Handbook of New Zealand*, pp. 77–80.

19 Hight & Straubel, *A History of Canterbury*, p. 170.

20 Hight & Straubel, quoting Canterbury Association Minutes, 5 August 1850.

21 W.J. Gardner (ed.), *A History of Canterbury Volume 2 1854–76 & Cultural Aspects 1850–1950* (1971), p. 314, quoting PPC, Sess XXXIX 1873, pp. 2, 45, 48.

22 Government emigration advertisement, October 1873, as quoted in Anna Rogers, *A Lucky Landing: The Story of the Irish in New Zealand* (Auckland, 1996), p. 57.

23 Canterbury Museum Library, *Assisted Passenger Lists*, 1850–88. These lists provide an alphabetical list of names of the people and families who travelled to Canterbury, their occupations and ages (where given), taken from the original shipping lists for every ship that travelled to Canterbury.

24 Rogers, *A Lucky Landing*, p. 34.

25 CML, *Passenger-Carrying Ships to Canterbury*, 1853–88. In recording the number of passengers carried on the majority of the ships, it illustrates the disparity with the actual numbers travelling to Canterbury.

26 CML, *Assisted Passenger Lists*, 1862–63. An example of this discrepancy of numbers was the *Zealandia* of 1862, which carried nearly 59 per cent Irish, as opposed to the *Lancashire Witch* of 1862 which carried less than 2 per cent Irish.

27 Ibid., 1865. The *Greyhound* carried 39.68 per cent Irish on board, while the *Indian Empire* carried 31.37 per cent.

28 Ibid. The percentages were 27.62 per cent and 27.74 per cent respectively.

29 Ibid. In 1860–69, 2,722½ Irish migrated to Canterbury. During the years 1870–79 the number rose to 6,690. In the years 1880–88 the number fell to 1,326½.

30 Rogers, *A Lucky Landing*, p. 56.

31 Ibid.

32 CML, op. cit. The *Opawa* arrived in October 1880 with 64.63 per cent Irish. The *Ionic* of June 1883 had 80.97 per cent Irish and the *Arawa* of December 1884 had 59.46 per cent Irish. The *Florida* of 22 October 1883 held 10.32 per cent Irish.

33 Akenson, *The Irish Diaspora*, Chapter 3, pp. 59–90; Section iv, p. 79.

34 Because 1886 saw few boats arriving in Canterbury, 1885 has been included with it in order to provide an adequate sample.

35 Akenson, *The Irish Diaspora*, p. 83; Akenson also included Galway with Ulster and Munster.

36 CML, op. cit. The figures have been calculated from the averages of the five-year periods which have already been discussed.

37 Rogers, *A Lucky Landing*, p. 61.

38 Ibid.

39 CML, op. cit. The averages have been calculated from the Ulster-South percentages already used.

40 Donald H. Akenson, *Half the World from Home* (Wellington, 1990), p. 69, quoting David Fitzpatrick, 'Irish Emigration in the Later Nineteenth Century', *Irish Historical Studies*, Vol. 22 (Sept. 1980), pp. 133, 138–9.

41 Akenson, *The Irish Diaspora*, pp. 69–72. Angela McCarthy, *The Desired Haven*, citing Sean Brosnahan, 'The Greening of Otago: Irish [Catholic] Immigration to Otago and Southland 1840–88', unpublished paper delivered at the New Zealand Historical Association Conference, February 1993, p. 8 & fig. 7. More than half (53.2%) of Canterbury's Irish population originated from Ulster, with Munster supplying 20.8 per cent. See table 1:50, p. 222 in Keith Anthony Pickens, 'Canterbury 1851–1881: Demography and Mobility. A Comparative Study', unpublished PhD Thesis (Washington University, 1976).

42 CML, op. cit. Relatively few vessels sailed during 1886, and to provide an adequate sample for comparative purposes, 1885 has been incorporated.

43 Rogers, *A Lucky Landing*, p. 66.

44 Akenson, *Half the World from Home*, pp. 70–1, Table 22: Geographic Origin of Natives of Ireland who immigrated to New Zealand from Irish Ports, 1876–1920.

45 Belich, *Making Peoples*, p. 319.

46 Ibid.

47 Akenson, *Half the World from Home*, p. 72.

48 Belich, *Making Peoples*, p. 319.

49 Ibid.

50 Ruth-Ann M. Harris, *The Nearest Place that Wasn't Ireland* (Iowa, 1994), p. 39. She further notes: 'The migration of Scots settlers from the province of Ulster to America had been underway since the first of their leases began coming due around 1715. In the following decades increasing numbers of Scots-Irish preferred to sell-up and use the accumulated capital for emigration rather than pay the increased cost of leases for their land.'

51 Akenson, *The Irish Diaspora*, p. 86.

52 Including two works edited by Roger Swift & Sheridan Gilley, *The Irish in the Victorian City* (London: Croom Helm, 1985), and *The Irish in Britain 1815–1939* (London: Pinter Publishers, 1989); and also Graham Davis, *The Irish in Britain 1815–1914* (Dublin: Gill & Macmillan, 1991).

53 Davis, 'The Irish in Britain, 1815–1939', in Bielenberg (ed.), *The Irish Diaspora* (2000), p. 24.

54 Belich, *Making Peoples*, p. 319. Canterbury-prone English counties included Cornwall, Devon and Somerset; Oxford and Gloucester; Surrey, Essex and Kent.

55 Ibid., p. 313.

56 Rogers, *A Lucky Landing*, p. 59.

57 Akenson, *The Irish Diaspora*, p. 61.

58 In choosing to arrange the travelling status in this way, slightly different to Donald Akenson, the results still present relatively similar information.

59 N.B. Relationships, very possibly, were formed during the long journey south.

60 Government emigration advertisement, October 1873, as quoted in Rogers, op. cit. p. 57: For married men in certain trades, 'a Promissory Note for £10, payable in the Colony by instalments; or by giving £5 in cash' were all which was required, whereas for single men, 'are taken on payment (before sailing) of the sum of £8; or on payment of £4 in cash, and giving a Promissory Note for £8'.

61 Akenson, *The Irish Diaspora*, pp. 80–1.

62 Ibid., p. 61.

63 Rogers, *A Lucky Landing*, p. 57.

64 Ibid., p. 34.

65 Akenson, *The Irish Diaspora*, p. 65.

66 Ibid., p. 61.

67 The original lists from which both samples are taken contain the names of paying passengers, of whom none appear to have given the county of origin.

68 Stevan Eldred-Grigg, *A New History of Canterbury* (1982), p. 24.

69 Akenson, *The Irish Diaspora*, p. 82, Table 18: Occupation of Adult Male Assisted Migrants from Ireland, 1876. Source: derived from NANZ, IM/15, pp. 260–86. Akenson listed the categories individually, but I have added them together to give an overall figure.

70 Akenson, *The Irish Diaspora*, p. 83.

71 Warren Jacobs, *The Birth of New Zealand* (Christchurch, 1995), pp. 59–61.

72 National Archives of New Zealand. Abstract of the Queen's Order in Council of 25 February 1856, for preserving Order, promoting health, and Securing Cleanliness and Ventilation on board of 'Passenger Ships' proceeding from the United Kingdom to any of Her Majesty's Possessions, points 11, 12, 13, 14 and 17.

73 Mary Cullen, 'Breadwinners and Providers: Women in the Household Economy of Labouring Families 1835–6', quoting Poor Inquiry, H.C. 1836 (42) xxxiv, p. 19, in Maria Luddy & Cliona Murphy (eds), *Women Surviving: Studies in Irish Women's History in the 19th and 20th Centuries* (Ireland, 1989, 1990 edn), p. 112.

74 J.J. Lee, *The Modernisation of Irish Society 1848–1918* (Dublin, 1973, 1989 edn), pp. 3–4.

5

From Sligo to St John's: The Gore-Booth Assisted Emigration Scheme, 1847

Emily Slinger

A retrospective look at the famine in Ireland (1845–52), might identify victims not only among the 2 million who died or emigrated, but also among the leaders of Irish society, the landlords. Before the famine, landlords enjoyed a privileged status as MPs, magistrates and employers in their localities. After the famine, many suffered from a long process of decline and were forced into selling off at least part of their estates in the face of unmanageable debts. This financial plight was accompanied by a slow erosion of support from the British government, which bowed to political pressure from the growing nationalist movement. Irish landlords were blamed for the famine deaths and were compared unfavourably with their English counterparts, who were regarded as more paternalistic towards their tenants.

This is the context for the controversial role of those landlords who devised schemes of assisted emigration for their tenants. What was viewed at the time as a positive step in alleviating poverty and distress, financed at the expense of landlords, was later denounced as enforced 'exile', oppressive and unjust, and providing financial relief to landlords in ridding themselves of surplus tenants.

Sir Robert Gore-Booth (1805–76) succeeded to the Lissadell Estate in 1826. He also succeeded to the prosperous Booth estates in Salford and Manchester. The Lissadell estate, 10 miles from Sligo, totalled in excess of 30,000 acres and spread across forty townlands in the parishes of Drumcliff,

Sir Robert Gore-Booth (Courtesy of Joe McGowan, from his book *Constance Markievicz: The People's Countess*, www.sligoheritage.com/books.htm)

Rossinver and Ahamlish. Gore-Booth's first wife, the Hon. Caroline King, second daughter of Robert King, Lord Lorton, brought with her a dowry of £10,000 but died in childbirth. Gore-Booth's second marriage in 1830 was to Caroline Goold, the daughter of Thomas Goold of Dublin. She too brought a dowry, although not as substantial, of £2,000.[1]

Clearly Gore-Booth was intent on establishing himself and his family in Ireland. In 1830 he commissioned Francis Goodwin to build him a new home. Neo-classical in style, Lissadell House cost him £11,701 and was completed in 1833.[2] By the time of its completion, Gore-Booth had spent £130,000, increasing the size of his estate through the purchase of Ballymote, which in turn increased his Sligo rental threefold. The funds for this were raised by a mortgage of £20,000 against his Salford and Manchester estate in England, and an additional £79,000 was raised as a result of sales of lucrative English rents. In 1845 he assigned the mortgage, increasing it to £30,000, and in 1853 he repeated the process, raising the mortgage to £50,000. Documents relating to the Salford and Manchester estate show that in 1807 the annual rent from the estate was £6,240 and that by 1834, a year after his purchase of Ballymote, the rental was reduced to £2,140. By 1880, forty-six years later, this figure was £2,868.[3]

Gore-Booth believed that the land was unable to support its population. This was based upon his own experience as a landowner and from his association with local relief committees. An active landlord, personally involved in the administration of his estate, he held various public positions within the local community, including member of the Board of Guardians, former Chairman of the Central Finance Committee, Chairman of the Grand Jury and Chairman of four relief committees. He would later become a Member of Parliament. He was not an absentee landlord, having been resident in Ireland for all but three of the previous eighteen years.[4]

Lissadell House (Courtesy of Emily Slinger)

Aware of an excessive population in Connaught since he was 18, Gore-Booth believed that smallholdings could not provide 'any Degree of comparative Comfort', and to this end he endeavoured to increase the size of farms on his estate through the removal of entire families, a policy advocated by the Devon Commission. Therefore, when a lease expired, Gore-Booth offered relocation to land elsewhere on his estate or assistance to immigrate to America.[5]

The relationship between landlords and tenants in the nineteenth century was very much a public affair. Estates, visible centres of both employment and expenditure, provided a social, economic and political focus in the form of power, capital and patronage, whilst the landlords, by virtue of their position and status, were often the local Poor Law guardians, magistrates and justices of the peace.[6] They were not, though, one homogeneous group. How they administered their duties varied from total involvement at one extreme to complete apathy at the other. Thus various elements would determine attitudes towards a landlord and thereby establish the 'tone of the estate'.[7] Similarly, emigration, itself a highly emotive issue, was also propelled into the public arena where perception and reality became blurred. David Fitzpatrick established that between 1833 and 1855 it was the efforts of a group of ten landlords, of which Gore-Booth was one, who were responsible for the assistance of one of the largest groups of emigrants. Examination of records relating to eight of these by Fitzpatrick help to provide us with an understanding of the nature of landlord-assisted emigration. Here, we can establish

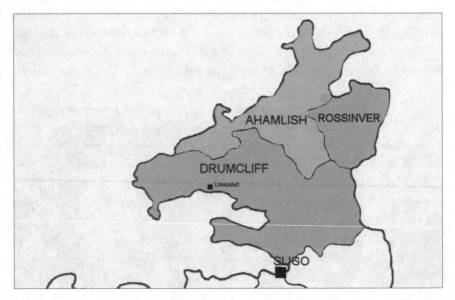

Location of the Lissadell Estate, County Sligo

that emigration from the Lissadell estate took place between 1835 and 1842 and again between 1847 and 1848.

This first period of emigration occurred over seven years and assisted only 262 people at a cost per capita of £3. The figures for the second period show that the total number of emigrants assisted was 1,122, at an overall cost of £5,936 over the one year, and that the price per capita had increased to a little over £5. Assistance usually included clothing and provisions, as well as a small monetary contribution to help them continue their journey beyond the port of arrival. Assistance beyond this was limited, although some landlords did offer additional help. Colonel George Wyndham is cited by David Fitzpatrick who refers ambiguously to Wyndham's 'shiploads' of tenants being 'shepherded inland'.[8] Gore-Booth also provided some assistance, albeit limited, for his tenants upon arrival in Canada. In return for his passage, he arranged for his tenants to be accompanied by Mr Yeats, the son of the late rector of the local parish who, upon arrival in St John's, assisted the captain of the *Yeoman* in finding employment for the passengers.[9] He was able to help many of the women find employment as servants with wages of between 15s and £1 per month. Interestingly, Yeats also noted that it was the women and not the men who were successful in finding work, commenting that 'there appears to be a great Facility in Girls getting Employment'.[10] In contrast to the men, the female emigrants appear to have had less trouble in adapting to their new life. This would support studies in America by Hasia Diner and Janet Nolan, which have acknowledged the success of female emigrants over males in settling into a new life.[11] Yeats further believed that employment would not have been so difficult to find had it not been for the 'way in which the Passengers of the former Ship conducted themselves'.[12] In August, two months after its arrival, some of the emigrants from this ship still remained in the old poor house, begging on the streets. Many had been sent to the alms house and the infirmary, but it was now expected that the state would provide for them.[13] From his evidence, it would seem that Gore-Booth did attempt to provide assistance beyond the emigrants' arrival in St John's. In addition to the assistance of Mr Yeats, Gore-Booth also arranged for the ships agent in St John's, John Robertson, to aid the emigrants upon their arrival, ensuring that they had what they needed and helping them find employment. Prior to sending out emigrants, he also applied to the government through Lord Besborough for land in any area of Canada based upon 100 acres per family he sent out. If it could not be given then he suggested it could be purchased with payment being made in instalments. Furthermore, Gore-Booth would himself provide the services of an agent not just to accompany them, but stay for a year so that they could be assisted in clearing the land. As requested, he submitted his application in writing but never heard anything back. His plan, he pointed out, was one he intended to implement himself and was never meant to be part of a plan for 'Colonization and Emigration'.[14]

Emigration in 1847 was not a new concept to Gore-Booth, or indeed to Sligo, where it had been recorded as far back as 1728. Generally, though, eighteenth-century emigration had been small-scale involving people with some capital who wished to improve their prospects.[15] However, following the Napoleonic Wars, emigration levels rose, especially during the 1830s. The *Sligo Journal* in 1830 commented on the increased numbers arriving in Sligo:

> Never at any former period have we known the spirit of emigration to be carried out to a greater extent than during the present year. For the last few weeks whole families of comfortable looking persons, having passed daily thro' our streets, seated on cars containing their luggage and provisions for the voyage, make their way to take their place in the long lines waiting patiently at the Quays. Our town actually swarms with men, women and children from the surrounding counties waiting for sailings, and all are big with hope and expectation of future prosperity.[16]

Levels of emigration continued throughout 1841 and 1842, easing off by 1844. However, this was short-lived and by 1846 emigration was once again occurring on a larger scale. In July 1847, the local paper, the *Sligo Champion*, reported that the total number was at least 13,000.[17] Emigration from Sligo was renewed when the mass exodus of 1847 took place.

Prior to the famine, Gore-Booth had implemented an organised programme of emigration from his estate which would come into effect upon the falling in of the lease. If the numbers upon the farm were considered to be in excess of what could reasonably be supported, then the tenants would be offered the choice of removal to another farm or payment for their house and improvements, as well as paid passage to America. Such a programme had been carried out in the townlands of Ballygilgan and Cartron Willinmogue, for which Gore-Booth submitted details in his evidence to a parliamentary inquiry. Ballygilgan, part of 800 acres which Gore-Booth had purchased from his father-in-law, Lord Lorton, had become over-populated, with many holdings less than 4 acres per family and so unable to support their occupants. The emigration of tenants occurred over a period of seven years, involved forty-two families and cost £784 0s 5d. Those who remained were given holdings (albeit on 'inferior' ground) elsewhere, some of which had houses and offered employment on the estate. The total cost to Gore-Booth of providing for all the tenants from Ballygilgan would finally amount to £4,271 11s 2½d.[18]

Gore-Booth admitted that he wanted to increase the land around his newly built house,[19] but in doing so he did not want to throw the people off the land immediately, allowing them to remain until they came to a decision. He was aware that many had a 'very strong Affection for the Ground they have resided upon' and that they would prefer to remain. However, the appeal of emigration ultimately won out over an 'indifferent farm'.[20] Kincaid, agent for Gore-Booth's neighbour, Lord Palmerston, summed up the predicament of the tenants: 'The poor creatures are going they scarcely know where and of

An Account of Expenses attending the Emigration of sundry Families from the Townlands of Ballygilgan and Cartron Willinmogue on the Estate of Sir Robert Gore Booth Bart., Lissadell.

	£	s.	d.
1835. Paid as Compensation to the Tenants of Ballygilgan for giving up Possession	166	5	1
1837. Paid same for same	39	13	4
1839. Paid Passages to America for Eighteen Families, comprising 131 Individuals, at 2*l.* per Individual	262	0	0
„ Paid for Twelve Individuals, for same as Charity	10	12	0
„ Paid for Four Families, comprising Thirty-three Individuals for Cartron Willinmogue, at their own Request	62	0	0
1841. Paid for Nineteen Families, comprising Sixty-three Individuals	126	5	0
1842. Paid for Five Families, comprising Twenty-three Individuals	67	5	0
„ Money distributed by Lady Gore among the Emigrants from Ballygilgan	50	0	0
Total	784	0	5

In addition to the above Forty-two Families who emigrated from Ballygilgan, Twenty-one Families got Land, and some of them Residences, as follows :

James M'Clean, House and Land, in Lissadell.
Thady Currid, Land, in Lissadell.
Michael Burns, Land, in Lissadell.
Martin Feeny, House and Land, Cloonachine.
Terence M'Shany, Land, in Ballintullick.
James M'Shany, Land, in Ballintullick.
Anthony Mullarky, Land, in Ballintullick.
Michael M'Glone, Land, in Cartron Willinmogue.
Patrick Feeny, Land, in Cartron Willinmogue.
Michael M'Gowan, Land, in Cartron Willinmogue.
John Coney, Land, in Cartron Willinmogue.
William Lindsey, Land, in Coola Drummond.
Thomas Ewing, Land, in Cullaghmore.
James Currey, Land, in Cullaghmore.
Patrick O'Brien, Land, in Ballinafull.
Reverend Malachi Brennan, House and Land, in Cullaghmore.
Patrick M'O'Brien, House and Land, in Ballygilgan.
Jack O'Brien, House and Land, in Ballygilgan.
James Armstrong, House and Land, in Ballygilgan.
Francis Feeny, remains in Ballygilgan.
Barth Gillen, House and Land, in Clonacool, which he sold for 80*l.*

The Amount expended in Labour on the Demesne, &c. from March 1834 up to the Period when the last of the Ballygilgan Tenants were provided for, was upwards of 4,000*l.*, in which Labour the Ballygilgan Tenants largely participated, in fact always getting a Preference.

An account of expenses relating to the emigration of tenants from Ballygilgan between 1835 and 1843 (Evidence of Sir Robert Gore-Booth, Second Report on Colonisation: Further Minutes of Evidence, 1848 Session Vol.V [2639], p. 259)

course cannot see what is before them but they see nothing but misery and starvation before them if they stay where they are and anything is better than that.'[21] The emigration of these Ballygilgan tenants proved to be controversial and would come back to haunt Gore-Booth.

Gore-Booth vehemently denied that emigration was forced and, in support of his actions, submitted a letter from the local Catholic parish priest of Drumcliff, the Rev. O'Gara. He openly supported the Gore-Booths, comparing them with other less proactive landlords, referring to the 'unremitting Anxiety thus manifested for the Well-being of the Emigrants as well as the feverish Sympathy' towards the poor and concluding that their actions would mean that they were 'deeply rooted in the Affections of a grateful Peasantry'.[22] However, within a few years, Gore-Booth's reputation was to face fierce criticism as his conduct as a landlord during 1847 became the focus of much public attention. In the campaign leading up to the 1852 election, Rev. O'Gara's earlier support for Gore-Booth had disappeared. Now, in the editorial concerning the recent elections, the *Sligo Chronicle* reported that O'Gara had given the 'most strenuous opposition to Sir Robert Gore-Booth'. O'Gara, it continued, was 'an eye witness of Sir Robert's munificence … he strained every nerve to procure his defeat'.[23] One explanation for this change in attitude was a consequence of recent political events and the alliance between the Tenant League and the Catholic Defence Association. These two groups represented an increasingly powerful middle class of farmers now empowered to vote, which resulted in animosity towards their landlords. This alliance, with its strong nationalist outlook, became prominent during these elections, attacking landlord nominees like Gore-Booth. The *Sligo Journal*, in support of Gore-Booth, reminded its readers of the assistance he had provided during the famine, whilst the *Sligo Champion* summoned Catholics to support the independent nominee, Mr Swift, who had the backing of Archbishop McHale and the Church.[24] The campaign, reported in the local press, see-sawed between attack (from the *Champion*) and support (from the *Journal*). On Gore-Booth's appointment to Chairman of the Board of Guardians in March 1851, the *Champion* voiced their concern at his lack of knowledge regarding the Poor Law.[25] In view of his involvement between 1846 and 1847, as Chairman of the Finance Committee and four relief committees, this would appear to be somewhat unfounded.[26] At the centre of the campaign was Gore-Booth's famine record. He was either praised for his benevolence or damned for driving the people from their land. The emigration of tenants from Ballygilgan had indeed come back to haunt him. The parish priest of Ahamlish, Rev. Noon, referred to this in a speech in which he declared: 'Ballygilgan made destitute with 350 houses of the most comfortable, honest and religious men tumbled to the ground. They were promised farms but never got them. They died along the ditches like vermin, many of them got a watery grave in rotten ships which sank at the bottom.'[27]

This account would appear to be quite different to the evidence offered up by Gore-Booth. It is therefore important to remember that this was a public speech in support of a candidate for the election, and its purpose was to discredit one candidate over another. An emotive and dramatic account is far more likely to be remembered than a clear statement of fact. Noon's reference to the sinking ship is in all probability referring to the ship *Pomona* which was, according to folklore, alleged to have sunk off the Irish coast with the loss of all on board. There is no evidence to support this. Although a ship with the same or similar name was used to transport tenants from Ballygilgan in 1839, it arrived safely in Quebec having had a routine crossing.[28]

Ships taking the Atlantic crossing like the *Pomona* were popularly referred to as 'coffin ships', because they transported the starving in overcrowded, poorly built, unseaworthy vessels with little or no access to food and water and a high risk of death. Gore-Booth responded to the criticisms levelled against him during the campaign in a poster directed to the electors of Sligo. In it he asked the people to remember his past conduct which he hoped would 'protect him from slander, got up by interested and designing parties and with no other object than to render me unpopular'.[29] Attempts to discredit Gore-Booth failed and he won the seat, which he would hold for the next twenty-six years, until his death in 1876.

Gore-Booth considered emigration as part of a long-term investment programme which he felt should be carried out as economically and as humanely as possible. In return, he expected to get his rents paid more regularly as a result of the consolidation of farms into larger areas. Experience had taught him that on these bigger holdings, payment was more likely to be forthcoming compared to the smaller farms, from which he could expect nothing. To support his argument, he submitted details from Vernon Davys, of the Rent Office in Sligo, concerning the townland of Ardtarmon. Of the 145 acres, only 40 were arable, the remainder consisting of loamy sand, blowing sand, marsh and water, and upon which it was recorded there were located thirty-one families, making a total population of between 185 and 200 people. Up to March 1847, the arrears amounted to a total of £1,130 5s 4d, compared to the yearly rent of £102 13s 2d. It was also recorded that since 1840, the amount received totalled only £196 5s 6d. This was derived from only two receipts, no one else having paid since that date. At the bottom of the statement there is an additional note which states that there had been a lease but that much of the good ground had been buried beneath the blowing sand.[30] These blowing sands were referred to by Johnathan Binns, in 1837, when he described Ardtarmon as being covered by blowing sands to a depth of up to 10ft, in which 'all houses embedded as high as the eaves – many of them entirely covered', their roofs broken by the weight; and 'has affected an area of in excess of 500 acres, the greater part of which was fine and cultivated land'.[31]

Although the majority of the 1847–48 emigrants were 'direct tenants', a few were not. Demand outstripped supply and as such Gore-Booth assisted more people than he had originally intended.[32] Gore-Booth stated that he would 'not send out any but those who were direct Tenants', but when pressed added that perhaps 'to fill the vessel I may have sent a few, but they were almost all direct Tenants'.[33] Indeed, sixteen stowaways were found on the *Yeoman* upon arrival at St John's in New Brunswick, despite Gore-Booth having already personally removed three or four whilst still in the bay back in Ireland.[34] Likewise, on the estate of Francis Spaight, as a consequence of more than twice as many applicants, the number of emigrants had exceeded the number of ships available.[35] This would confirm that emigration was voluntary and that they were not 'forced' to leave by their landlords.

Believing that emigration could bring an end to suffering, Gore-Booth corresponded with Lord Palmerston to enquire whether they might collaborate on a scheme to send tenants to America. There is, though, some confusion as to whether the idea of emigration originated with Gore-Booth or Palmerston. Whilst Tyler Anbinder suggests that it was Gore-Booth, Desmond Norton maintains that it had already been recommended to Palmerston by his attendant, Dr West, and by John Lynch. Ships were sent out as a result of this partnership, although both landlords also hired additional vessels. Despite Gore-Booth initially being the more enthusiastic of the two to implement emigration, it was Lord Palmerston who removed the greater number of emigrants, even though it was the Gore-Booth estate that contained the greater population.[36]

Correspondence in 1846–47, regarding Lord Palmerston's estate and his land at Ahamlish, compares the actions of these two neighbouring landlords. Reporting back to Stewart and Kincaid, their agent John Lynch wrote:

> Sir Robert is giving employment to all his own Poor and Providing them with Indian Meal [corn], and has it given out in three or four places on his Estate. He is paid by all who are able. The Rev. Jeffcot … says he takes notes from some who are not able to pay at present, and gives a good deal away to poor Widows etc.[37]

An examination of the Gore-Booth accounts,[38] submitted with his evidence before parliament, gives us a clear indication of the extent of his importation of food from America via Liverpool, Glasgow and Greenock. Between

August 1846 and July 1847, the total expenditure was £34,822 5s 10d.[39] The accounts are interesting because they also reveal that over the course of time, any profit which he had originally made was increasingly whittled down, culminating in a total, final loss of £4,212. It would seem from correspondence between Gore-Booth and General Dobree, the Deputy Commissary General, that Gore-Booth wrote to the government seeking assistance for the cost of transporting goods from Liverpool. Initially refused, approval was later given following favourable reports from Captain O'Brien to Lt Col Jones on Gore-Booth's good work.[40] Relief Commission records refer to Gore-Booth's generosity. One example was the assistance he provided to the tenants on the neighbouring estate of Lord Palmerston.[41]

The proactive involvement of Gore-Booth was in contrast to the seemingly inactive Palmerston, causing Lynch to comment that 'we are in the background altogether'.[42] Despite pleas to Stewart and Kincaid from the local Catholic priest in Drumcliff, and another local landowner, John Wynne, Palmerston's tenants in Ahamlish appear to have received little help. It turned out, though, that Kincaid had ordered supplies of maize from America the previous October, but by January they had still not arrived. Gore-Booth was to write to Stewart and Kincaid, concerned that they were not aware of the situation. Kincaid was. He had applied for loans and was proposing to set up soup kitchens. Coming six months after Gore-Booth, the actions of the Palmerston estate were considered to be 'too little, too late'.[43] This lack of involvement was increasingly seen as abandonment and his reputation which had previously been favourable was now lost.[44]

Humane considerations apart, it is clear that Gore-Booth expected a return on his investment. This was based upon previous experience which had taught him that once the farms had been increased in size he could fully expect to receive his rents more regularly. In his evidence he stated: 'In all Cases where they are large Farms one is sure to get paid; in Cases of small farms we do not get anything.'[45] He also believed that the land could be improved to the benefit of both landlord and tenant: 'The Greatest proof I have had of the Improvement upon the property is that those Tenants did not require Relief in the Districts where my system of Emigration has been longer established, unless where the Farms were left too small originally.'[46] Gore-Booth had a responsibility to his estate as well as to his tenants. Economic survival was fundamental but would only be possible through a cessation of subdivision and a reduction in population.

There is no doubt that emigration itself was likely to be unpleasant. The journey could be perilous, especially during 1847–48, when unscrupulous shipping companies strove to capitalise on the situation and increase their profit levels at the expense of their passengers. Winter sailings, overcrowding, poor conditions and inclement weather combined to form a disastrous combination.[47] Mortality on ships crossing the Atlantic varied, but during 1847 the rate was unusually high. During that year figures presented by the government emigration office in Quebec indicated that just over 5 per cent died at sea, with 3.46 per cent dying in quarantine on Grosse Isle and a further 8.3 per cent in hospitals, which puts the total mortality rate for this year at 17 per cent, compared to the next year's recorded rate of 1.11 per cent.[48]

Landlords were accused of cruelty and negligence in sending out their 'coffin' ships, but enquiries into these accusations failed to support the charge and landlords such as Gore-Booth, Palmerston, Wandesforde, Fitzwilliam and Desci were officially absolved from blame. After all, the poor physical condition of the tenants prior to leaving would inevitably have made them more susceptible to the effects of the journey and more vulnerable to disease. Bitter criticism also came from Canada regarding the 'worthless and unprincipled hirelings', but information from passengers committees that were published illustrates a degree of appreciation. Those who travelled on Gore-Booth's vessel, the *Aeolus*, thanked their 'ever to be remembered landlord' for his kindness towards his tenants: 'he was always kind to his tenants; it was not tyranny which forced us to emigrate – it was the loss of our crops for two years past.'[49] Gratitude, in the form of similar 'committees of passengers', were frequently published in the press.

Like that of landlords, the subject of emigration has also suffered from the popular image handed down through folklore. Assisted emigration, in particular, was denounced as yet further evidence of the cruel landed classes who imposed 'exile' upon their tenants through a policy of expulsion. Emigration and its association with eviction and house tumbling made it an issue that aroused intense feeling, gathering momentum in the 1840s. As David Fitzpatrick suggests, those who remained manufactured this popular image. They were most likely to object and cry 'tyranny' and they were also most likely to be the ones who had been refused assistance.[50] Yet, whilst landlords were accused of selfish behaviour, it was also a reality that emigration provided a less expensive alternative to maintaining them at home. Furthermore, in the wake of new legislation whereby landowners were required to pay all expenses through extended tax, assisted emigration became increasingly considered as an alternative. For some, though, this alternative was as a consequence of legislation which had 'almost forced the landlords to get rid of their poorer tenantry; in order that they should not have to pay for these small holdings'.[51] Landlords became damned whatever they did. Lord Palmerston's agent Kincaid summed this up when he defended the landlords:

If they keep the surplus population of their estate at home, the property will not be sufficient to maintain them, and they are exposed to the charge of either neglecting them or obtaining support for them out of public funds; if they make extraordinary exertions in the hopes of benefiting the people and relieving their properties by providing free passages to the British Colonies in North America, they are abused by the colonists for sending out paupers to them, although every account we receive from the emigrants themselves proves that their condition is much improved by the change, and that there is ample demand for their labour at remunerative wages.[52]

Kerby Miller, a leading American historian on emigration, recognised that famine emigration was different because it now involved a greater number of family groups than previously. He calculated that 49 per cent of emigrants to New York in 1846 were in family groups.[53] With landlords seeking to

COST AND FAMILY GROUPING OF LANDLORD-ASSISTED EMIGRATION, *c.*1835–55

landlords	period of assisted emigration	cost (£)	number	cost per capita	family groups number	families	mean size of family group
Fitzwilliam[1]	1842–6	–	–	–	560	124	4.5
Fitzwilliam[2]	1847–56	19,018	5,903	3.2	5,924	889	6.7
Wandesforde[3]	to 1847	14,525	4,854	3.0	–	–	–
Wandesforde[4]	1847–53	–	–	–	2,844	668	4.3
Lansdowne[5]	from 1851	17,059	4,616	3.7	–	–	–
Bath[5]	from 1851	7,988	2,459	3.2	–	–	–
Wyndham[6]	1839–47	7,634	1,582	4.8	1,582	238	6.6
Gore-Booth[7]	1835–42	784	262	3.0	262	42	6.2
Gore-Booth[7]	1847–8	5,936	1,122*	5.3*	–	–	–
Spaight[8]	from 1846	6,000	1,400	4.3	–	–	–
Mahon[9]	1847	3,571	883*	4.0*	883*	217	4.1*

Asterisked figures refer not to individuals but to 'statute adults' (children under 12 years counted as half units; infants omitted). In some cases the reported cost of emigration probably excludes ancillary expenses. 'Family groups' often include kinsmen or friends not immediately related to the head of the emigrating household. The Fitzwilliam emigration registers are inflated slightly by inclusion of persons approved for emigration who did not embark.

[1] N.L.I., MSS 18429.
[2] N.L.I., MSS 4974–5; Finlay Dun, *Landlords and tenants in Ireland* (London, 1881), p. 32.
[3] *Report of the select committee of the house of lords on colonization from Ireland; together with the minutes of evidence . . .*, p. 193, H.C. 1847 (737), vi, 209.
[4] N.L.I., MS 4178.
[5] *Report from the select committee of the house of lords on the Tenure (Ireland) Bill [H.L.], together with the proceedings of the committee, minutes of evidence, and index*, pp 18–19, H.C. 1867 (518), xiv, 458–9.
[6] As in note 3 (p. 140).
[7] *Second report from the select committee of the house of lords on colonization from Ireland; together with the further minutes of evidence . . .*, pp 258–9, 260–61, H.C. 1847–8 (593), xvii, 266–7, 268–9.
[8] *Report from the select committee on law of rating (Ireland); together with the proceedings of the committee, minutes of evidence, appendix, and index*, p. 436, H.C. 1871 (423), x, 448.
[9] N.L.I., MS 10138; *First report from the select committee of the house of lords on colonization from Ireland; together with the minutes of evidence*, p. 201, H.C. 1847–8 (415), xvii, 205.

Cost and Family Grouping of Landlord-Assisted Emigration between *c.* 1835–55 (David Fitzpatrick, 'Emigration 1801–1870', in W.E.Vaughan (ed.), *A History of Ireland, Volume V: Ireland Under the Union 1801–1870* (Oxford, 1989), p. 615)

clear their properties, percentages for landlord-assisted emigration could be expected to be higher. Landlords such as Spaight would only assist families: 'I take the whole family or none', thus enabling him to level the properties, the *raison d'être* was that this was crucial to the recovery of capital outlay.[54] That the majority of emigrants left in family groups would, as suggested by Deirdre Ryan, appear to concur with the findings of Kerby Miller.[55] Indeed, in percentage terms, the number sent out by Gore-Booth on the *Aeolus* was higher, with figures of 63 per cent of two-parent family groups and 15 per cent one-parent groups. The number of two-parent families on the *Yeoman* was considerably lower at 41 per cent, with 14 per cent one-parent families; whilst those for the *Lady Sale* record 51 per cent two-parent families with 13 per cent one-parent families. In addition to couples/siblings or cousins, records indicate that 7 per cent travelled as singles on the *Aeolus*, 27 per cent on the *Yeoman* and 16 per cent on the *Lady Sale*.[56] David Fitzpatrick in his investigation of the Coolatin emigration[57] establishes the number of single emigrants as 1.5 per cent, whilst groups of unmarried people represented 5.6 per cent.[58] This compares with figures derived from the Quit Rent Office which suggest this was 3 per cent.[59] As Ryan suggests, and within the context of other landlord schemes, this demonstrates that within his scheme a 'much greater flexibility was shown in the number of single people sent out'.[60] Miller established that the average age of the tenants to New York was 24 and that this was also in line with pre-famine emigration. This compares to an average age of 21.3 (*Aeolus*), 20.3 (*Yeoman*) and just 17.7 (*Lady Sale*), giving a combined total of the three vessels as 20.5. Taking into consideration actual numbers as opposed to statute adults, Ryan was able to establish that dependency on board the *Aeolus* was high, with 38 per cent children and 9 per cent over-fifties, prompting condemnation from the emigration agent in St John's, Moses Perley. By comparison, the *Yeoman* was lower with a rate of 28 per cent children and 5 per cent over-fifties, whilst the third vessel, the *Lady Sale*, had the lowest dependency with 26 per cent of children and 7 per cent of over-fifties.[61]

Despite a paucity of surviving records, and based upon only twenty-one cases, Deirdre Ryan has been able to indicate the farm size of the Gore-Booth emigrants. From this small sample, Ryan established that most emigrants had come from holdings of between 5 and 15 acres.[62] Here, then, it would appear that these emigrants did not come from the 'lowest' group. Indeed, the 1841 census, in classifying types of families, put farmers with between 5 and 15 acres in the second-class category.[63] Interestingly, Cousens maintains that evidence of the poorer classes' inability to emigrate was based upon changes in land holdings. He identified four main causes of this decline: the death of the holder, the tenant leaving, eviction and emigration, and concluded that in the west, the decline in holdings of between 5 and 15 acres was often more than that in holdings of 1–5 acres.[64] That they were poor and distressed there is no doubt, but they also had the ability to bargain or negotiate their land in return for assistance.

When the government agent, Moses Perley, submitted his annual report on emigration at the end of December 1847, he noted that 'thousands' of the emigrants were either tenants who had held less than 5 acres of land, or cottiers who had had no land at all and who had been 'sent out at the expense of their landlords, or proprietors'.[65] Based on this, the Gore-Booth tenants did not represent this majority. The first ship to leave with tenants from the Gore-Booth estate at Lissadell was the *Aeolus*. A new ship, it was fitted out 'for the convenience of the poor of his estate in Sligo to our colonies in North America'.[66] A committee from the *Aeolus* was so grateful for the assistance provided that they wrote to thank Gore-Booth and his brother. The ship's captain, Michael Driscoll, also wrote to Gore-Booth in praise of his efforts.[67]

However, this contrasts with the response of the Canadian press which was more damning, criticising Gore-Booth for ridding himself of his 'useless paupers' whom it feared would become 'a permanent charge upon this community'.[68] The 500 emigrants on board the *Aeolus* had cost Gore-Booth £1,600, a figure which did not include the supply of clothes and money. Despite this, the condition of the emigrants who arrived on the *Aeolus* is unclear. In a dispatch from the lieutenant governor, S. W. Colebrooke, to Earl Grey, in June 1847, the passengers were described as having generally been 'satisfied with their treatment on voyage, and have arrived in good health, which may be attributed to the attention paid to their comfort, and especially to cleanliness and ventilation, with a due supply of wholesome food and water'.[69] This is substantiated by John Saunders, from the secretary's office, who in writing to the government emigration agent, Moses Perley, confirms that they 'appear to have come out in good health', although he goes on to add that they have 'since suffered from destitution and sickness'.[70] However, nineteen days later, in correspondence to the emigration office, Perley gave an altogether different account:

> The passengers by this vessel, 500 in number, state that they were 'exported' by their landlord, Sir Robert Gore-Booth, who paid their passage money, in order to disencumber his estate. Several of these people will, in all probability, become a permanent charge on the public funds; and this 'shovelling out' of helpless paupers, without any provision for them here, if continued, will inflict very serious injury on this colony.[71]

Unlike the earlier account, blame for the poor condition of the emigrants was laid at the feet of Gore-Booth. This discrepancy raises further questions, and might even suggest that these emigrants were attempting to court sympathy from the Canadian officials and thus obtain free assistance. Deception amongst emigrants was not impossible and is even suggested by Gore-Booth when asked to comment on the miserable condition of the emigrants on board the second voyage of the *Aeolus*, which had been 'obtained by the kindness' of Gore-Booth, who had fitted out the ship, supplied provisions and inspected it. He would, therefore, have been well placed to comment.[72] Gore-Booth had advised Palmerston's agent to remove the old clothes from the emigrants because 'they would put them on again to make themselves look as miserable as possible on the other side'.[73] In a letter to Henry Gore-Booth at the end of June, John Robertson (Gore-Booth's agent in St John's) also commented on the emigrants from the *Aeolus* whom he considered to be 'a difficult people to manage for their own good'. Those who had been sent on to Fredericktown had secured work unlike those who remained: 'others who will not take advice are suffering for their folly. There is plenty of work for them if they would only take reasonable wages.'[74] Although there is no specific reference to Gore-Booth, the chief emigrant agent, A.B. Hawke, also commented on the duplicitous nature of some of the emigrants who appeared to make little effort to adapt to their new circumstances:

> The few who possess any money invariably secrete it, and will submit to any amount of suffering, or to have recourse to begging in the streets, and the most humiliating and pertinacious supplications to obtain a loaf of bread from boards of health or the emigrant agents, rather than part with a shilling.[75]

He also noted that this behaviour had become much more widespread than in previous years.

In August, Gore-Booth's second ship, the *Yeoman*, arrived in New Brunswick with a further 500 emigrants. Moses Perley was much more complimentary towards this second group, who had been 'amply provided with provisions of the best description ... and no pains have been spared to render them comfortable'. Indeed, the facilities on board were so plentiful that the discovery of sixteen stowaways had made no difference. He further commented that he considered them to be 'superior' to those who came from the same estate on the *Aeolus* and who had remained in the city poor house, 'a permanent charge upon this community'.[76] There was no obvious sign of fever and only three deaths had occurred during the voyage, although after arrival this number rose whilst in quarantine on Partridge Island.

As well as the usual provisions, Gore-Booth donated a cow so that they could have fresh milk. He also gave all emigrants two medical inspections prior to departure, supervised by his own doctor, Dr Hamelton. Furthermore, the master of the ship, a qualified surgeon, was accompanied by his wife who looked after the women and children. Whilst there appears to be little doubt that ample provision and care was taken on the voyage, criticism was made about the lack of provision upon their arrival, although Capt. Purdon and Mr Robertson, Gore-Booth's agent in St John's, did help them to find employment. With a small supply of provisions and a little money, arrangements were made for the transfer of 150 emigrants to Fredericktown, where the demand for employment was greater. Yet despite his favourable report on the condition of these emigrants, Perley remained cautious at the prospect of the imminent arrival of Gore-Booth's third ship, the *Lady Sale*.

The *Lady Sale* arrived in St John's in September and spent eight days in quarantine, twenty-one people having died en route. Whilst this was not an unusually high number, it was their condition which brought about strong criticism. The emigrants on board were not all from the Gore-Booth estate, as indicated by Perley, but included some of Lord Palmerston's tenants. It is unclear how many emigrants on board the *Lady Sale* were from the Gore-Booth estate, but in his evidence, Gore-Booth referred to 340 adult passengers, and he made no reference to any of them being from Lord Palmerston's estate. In his dispatch to J.S. Saunders, of 24 August 1847, Perley had anticipated 500, whereas Messrs Stewart and Kincaid, agents for Lord Palmerston, had stated that there were about 400 passengers, of which half were from the Palmerston estate.[77] Perley was appalled not just at their condition but at the high volume of widows, orphans and old people, 'the helpless and infirm', which he took as evidence that the landlords were ridding themselves of their most insignificant tenants whom the colony would now have to support.[78] Appalled by their pathetic state, even though many had had to be supplied with clothes in order to make them decent to leave, he further exclaimed: 'I have never yet seen such abject misery, destitution and helplessness as was exhibited yesterday on the decks of the *Lady Sale*.'[79] Stewart and Kincaid defended themselves and Gore-Booth by maintaining that 'every attention' had been given to the emigrants before departure and that 'large sums had been expended' in providing for them.[80] Figures suggested by Ryan indicate that the proportion of women was 1.6 females per male emigrant. Interestingly, though, she also established that the ratio for the *Yeoman* was higher than that of the *Lady Sale*, at 1.8 females per male. As Ryan has noted, a comparison with emigrants to New York in 1846 by Kerby Miller indicates that the ratio was 1.75.[81] Nonetheless, it was the *Lady Sale* which was criticised for its predominance of female emigrants.

The cost to Gore-Booth in sending out these ships was approximately £6,000, a figure which represented £4 15s per head. The annual figure suggested for maintaining the emigrants at home in the workhouse was £2 12s.[82] Accounts were submitted before the parliamentary committee which illustrated the assistance he had given during the famine in supplying bread, oats and other goods. His total expenditure, which included the cost of emigration, was £15,499 16s 6d. It was one he could not have met, he maintained, had he not borrowed against his estates in England.[83]

In November 1847, totally overwhelmed by the number of destitute Irish, the Common Council of St John's attacked the actions of landlords such as Gore-Booth. In an angry response, it passed a resolution which announced that there was no more space available in the almshouses, warning that the emigrants would be returned to Ireland.[84] This threat, however, was never implemented. The response by local communities, like that in St John's, was mixed. Whilst sympathies lay with the emigrants, landlords, including Gore-Booth, Palmerston and Fitzwilliam, were criticised for their actions.

There has been much criticism against the British government for their lack of assistance. Yet the government recognised that substantial numbers were emigrating successfully as a result of their own efforts and was perhaps understandably reluctant to upset the 'status quo', as the following comment from Lord Grey illustrates:

> the government cannot undertake to convey Emigrants to Canada if it were to do so, if we were even to undertake to pay part of the cost, an enormous expense would be thrown upon the treasury, and after all more harm than good would be done … some £150,000 would have to be spent in doing that which if we do not interfere will be done for nothing.[85]

The government was reluctant to intervene upon a system which was both spontaneous and very successful; after all, private backing formed the bulk of assistance to emigrants. Furthermore, any expenditure on its part, if such intervention had taken place, would have involved unprecedented levels of public expense. If the status quo were to be upset, then the whole process of emigration might itself have become threatened, resulting in an even bigger problem. The alternative, the reclamation of wastelands and boglands, advocated by the Devon Commission in 1843 who estimated that it would produce additional farmland to aid half a million people, was not in reality such a practical idea. Gore-Booth himself had considered it on his estate but found it to be very expensive and a much less profitable investment than improvements in the land.[86] The question rather than the principle of funding was therefore crucial to any form of state assistance. Thus, any financial outlay would have been on a massive scale, but no agreement could be reached about how or from where these funds should be raised. Voluntary emigration had become so successful that it diminished the prospect for state assistance.

Support for state assistance was further hampered by the landlords themselves, who were seeking help from the government for something that they were already doing. The government, by shifting the burden of responsibility upon the landowners through the imposition of taxes, had artificially introduced a programme of emigration. This in turn would be self-perpetuating as a consequence of chain migration. Emigration was an already established part of Irish life; to a greater extent it was both self-funding and self-perpetuating. Government interference would then be at a cost – economically, socially and psychologically.

A further part of the story is establishing what happened to these emigrants. Surviving letters sent back from Gore-Booth emigrants are scarce but indicate that there was little regret despite the hardships endured. While most letters are from St John's and written in 1847, there are other slightly later letters from emigrants who had travelled on to New York, Maine and Massachusetts. One emigrant, Thomas Garry, wrote to his wife in March 1848, telling her of the 8s a day he earned on the railway and his intention to send the money for her passage the following August. Garry was, according to the evidence of Gore-Booth, a professional beggar who had stowed away on one of his ships.[87] Eliza Quinn, writing to her parents from New York in 1848, was grateful to 'Lady Gore', whom she asked her mother to thank: 'this is the best country in the world it is easy to make money … but hard to save it.' A second letter, two months later, enclosing £2, sent messages back to Ireland and commented on the suitability of young people rather than the old whom she felt would be better off back home, finally adding: 'I would not encurrage no body to come here unless there are inclined themselfs.' Catherine Hennagan was unable to put into words the distress suffered by everyone; she thought of the thousands now buried on the island, whilst those unable to go to the States were either in the poor house or begging on the streets of St John's. Yet despite this, she looked forward to the future, believing that 'times will mend here'. Writing in October 1847, Ference McGowan wrote of the distress and of those 'dieing in Dozens' as all the ships arrive with fever on board, but added that it remained a good place for young people. He also looked forward to the future, and the following spring he intended to move on to the States. Indeed, the majority of emigrants proceeded on from St John's to various destinations in the US. Although no official records exist of the numbers involved, it has been suggested that in excess of 30 per cent of those who arrived made this journey.[88]

Peter Douglas Murphy's study of the St John's Emigrant Orphan Asylum Admittance Ledger provides an interesting source of information. It reveals that many emigrant children were left behind whilst their parents made their way on to the United States in search of work. Of the 310 children who were admitted over a two-year period, 47 per cent were born in County Sligo, the majority of which were emigrants of 1847. Furthermore, it contains details of where they had come from and in some cases where they went, and establishes that half of the children who 'were sent to, or claimed by, one or both of their parents or by other relatives, almost all of whom were residing in the United States'.[89] Whilst further research is needed to answer this more fully, it is known that some emigrants ended up in New York's notorious slum Five Points, where between 1830 and 1845 the immigrant population rose from 9 to 36 per cent, increasing by a further 15 per cent in the following ten years.[90] Here, inhabitants lived in overcrowded slum tenements where the streets were full of rubbish, sewage and destitution. The notoriety of the Irish immigrants in Five Points was immortalised in the Martin Scorcese film, *Gangs of New York*, a drama based on Manhattan's infamous Five Points slum, where mobs ruled the streets and murder hid at every corner. Whilst emigrants from all over Ireland settled there, it was those from counties Sligo, Cork and Kerry who accounted for 44 per cent of Irish Catholics in Five Points, and it was those from Sligo which represented the largest proportion. This was because by the time of the famine there was already an established population of Sligo natives who, in turn, were able to send money back to those remaining in Ireland, and when the new immigrants arrived they preferred to settle with their fellow countrymen. Furthermore, half of all Sligo immigrants had originated from just two parishes, having been assisted by their landlords, Gore-Booth and Lord Palmerston.[91] For many of these, work involved the lowest paying occupations, but despite this, their work was more consistent and better paid than it had been in Ireland.[92]

Today, no longer called Five Points, the neighbourhood bears little resemblance to its nineteenth-century counterpart, although it continues to serve a large immigrant population where problems of overcrowding and gang warfare remain. The Irish population relocated to the suburbs and Queen's County, and today can be found in the neighbourhoods of Rockaway Beach and Woodside. Descendants of these earlier immigrants now work in the police department and district attorney's offices in Centre and Pearl Streets, formerly part of Five Points.[93]

Gore-Booth's scheme of emigration only occurred on parts of his estate. Other areas continued to witness hardship and destitution. An example of this was in an area on the northern side of Sligo bay, known as the Sands, where

The Five Points in 1859 (D.T. Valentine, comp., *Manual of the Corporation of the City of New York for 1860* (New York, 1860), Old York Library)

between 250 and 300 people were recorded as living in sixty huts during March 1847.[94] Emigration was crucial in establishing Gore-Booth's Lissadell estate on a better footing and therefore the potential for the estate, and ultimately for his tenants, was far-reaching.

Gore-Booth was criticised for not supplying enough provisions for his emigrants. Yet the accounts from the Gore-Booth estate show that all three ships were supplied with bread, Indian meal, whole meal and flour, in addition to clothes, bedding and tickets, and there were medical inspections prior to departure. As well, any supplies which remained upon arrival in North America were to be distributed amongst the passengers. The accounts also show that Gore-Booth was mindful of distress among his tenants during the famine period. He spent £34,000 on the importation of food, which he supplied to other owners as well as freely distributing amongst his own tenants and those on adjacent properties. Furthermore, they show that he also incurred a loss of over £6,000.[95] Clearly, Gore-Booth did supply provisions, but the appalling physical appearance of his tenants upon arrival in Canada led the authorities to believe that landlords were clearing their estates of their destitute and pauper tenants.[96] To what extent the blame for the condition of these tenants can be laid upon Gore-Booth is difficult to establish. As Oliver MacDonagh has indicated, the consequences of the famine contributed to levels of mortality on board ships, especially during 1847 and 1848, when the already weakened physical state of the emigrants left them particularly vulnerable to disease.[97] The arrival of huge numbers of emigrants inevitably brought with it distress, but when they brought disease as well, the situation deteriorated even further. The Canadian authorities criticised the poor standards on ships which helped to spread disease, condemning the ships' masters for being 'unable to maintain the simplest rules of cleanliness amongst the passengers'.[98] Also, despite assistance from John Robertson, finding employment was not always possible because emigrants lacked the skills necessary for the jobs available. Furthermore, they would not work for wages less than those available in Ireland, nor were they prepared to get that experience, preferring instead to send out their wives and children to beg.[99] Influenced by letters sent home, perhaps their expectation did not match up with reality.

Assistance offered by Gore-Booth had not been carried out in sudden response to the situation which prevailed in 1847, but had been in use before. Emigration was part of a long-term remedy into which a large amount of capital had been invested and from which Gore-Booth expected a return. Previous experience had taught him that once farms had been increased in size, he could finally expect to receive rents more regularly.[100] Although substantial costs were incurred, Gore-Booth knew from experience that the land could be improved to the benefit of both the tenant and the landlord.

With the practice of landlord-assisted emigration varying from estate to estate, it would be unwise to consider the actions of Sir Robert Gore-Booth as exceptional. His programme of emigration was carried out in response to socio-economic conditions that prevailed at the time. There is no doubt that Gore-Booth used emigration to clear his estate of its excess population, which, in doing so, allowed him to increase the size of the holdings upon it. Thus, emigration was not a stand alone solution but a part of it that had to be combined with a policy of consolidation, which would in turn reduce levels of poverty and congestion. Evictions did take place and an alternative was offered, albeit a limited one.

The story of the Gore-Booth assisted emigration scheme can be interpreted in two ways. In a narrative that identifies landlords as villains and assisted emigrants as victims, Gore-Booth has been depicted as characteristic of his class in removing 'surplus' tenants from his estate and enlarging holdings to ensure his rents were paid in full. The alternative version depicts Gore-Booth as a humane landlord who provided a voluntary escape route to the New World for some of his impoverished Sligo tenants. His assisted emigration scheme was not a matter of taking money out of Ireland, as absentee landlords did, but was financed by the mortgaging of his English estates for the benefit of strengthening his estate in Ireland. The first narrative has endured longer as part of a broader version of the famine and the role of landlords in nineteenth-century Ireland. The second was believed at the time before the role of landlords became enmeshed in the political battles between landlords and tenants. What remains central to an understanding of the scheme is the pressure of the commercial reality of estate management in mid-nineteenth-century Ireland.

Notes

1 Thomas Goold, Sergeant at Law and later Master in Chancery. Dermot James, *The Gore Booths of Lissadell* (Dublin, 2004), p. 11.

2 PRONI Lissadell Papers, D/4131/H/3. Dermot James, *The Gore Booths of Lissadell* (Dublin, 2004), p. 14.

3 A.P.W. Malcomson, Michael Goodall & Sephen Scarth, Notes for the Lissadell Papers (D/4131/B/16), Public Record Office Northern Ireland; and Dermot James, *The Gore Booths of Lissadell* (Dublin, 2004).

4 Evidence of Sir Robert Gore-Booth, Second Report on Colonisation from Ireland: Further Minutes of Evidence, 1848 Session Vol. V [2593–2612], pp. 255–6.

5 Ibid. [2638], p. 258.

6 The collection of rents, for example, was a public process; so too were evictions and debt collections, see W.E. Vaughan, *Landlords and Tenants in Mid-Victorian Ireland* (Oxford, 1994), pp. 1–2.

7 Examples of these two extremes cited by Vaughan are Lord Leitrim and Thomas Staples, which also includes Lord Fitzwilliam, William Wann, John Hamilton, Sir John Benn-Walsh and Lord Mountcashell's agent, Mr Joy: 'rent increases, evictions and the character of the agent and the landlord' were all identified as 'the most definable ingredients in the mixture which made good or bad landlords', W.E. Vaughan, *Landlords and Tenants in Mid-Victorian Ireland*, pp. 104–5.

8 David Fitzpatrick, 'Emigration 1801–1870', in W.E. Vaughan, *History of Ireland Volume V: Under the Union 1801–70* (Oxford, 1989), p. 593.

9 Evidence of Sir Robert Gore-Booth, Second Report on Colonisation from Ireland: Further Minutes of Evidence, 1848 Session Vol. V [2653], p. 264.

10 Letter from Mr Yeats presented in evidence of Sir Robert Gore-Booth, Second Report on Colonisation from Ireland: Further Minutes of Evidence, 1848 Session Vol. V [2671], p. 264.

11 Hasia Diner, *Erin's Daughters in America* (London, 1983); and Janet Nolan, *Ourselves Alone* (Lexington, Kentucky, 1989).

12 Letter from Mr Yeats presented in evidence of Sir Robert Gore-Booth, Second Report on Colonisation from Ireland: Further Minutes of Evidence, 1848 Session Vol. V [2671], p. 264.

13 J. Elizabeth Cushing, Teresa Casey, Monica Robertson, *A Chronicle of Irish Emigration to Saint John, New Brunswick 1847* (New Brunswick, 1979), p. 35.

14 Evidence of Sir Robert Gore-Booth, Second Report on Colonisation from Ireland: Further Minutes of Evidence, 1848 Session Vol. V [2756], p. 272.

15 In 1822 the number of arrivals in Quebec broke all previous records. Of the 8,000, 600 had departed from Sligo. Other instances of early emigration from Sligo can be found in the evidence of John Irwin of Tanrego, High Sheriff of Co. Sligo in 1822, before a Select Committee. Ibid., pp. 1–5.

16 30 April 1830 and cited by John C. McTernan, 'Strangers on a Foreign Shore: Emigration through the Port of Sligo in the Nineteenth Century', Part 2, in *Memory Harbour: The Port of Sligo* (1992), p. 6.

17 Ibid., p. 26.

18 Extract from the evidence of Sir Robert Gore-Booth, Bart No 1095, in reply to evidence of Mr Edward Howard Verdon, No 367. Devon Commission Digest of Evidence Supplement to Part II, pp. 87–8.

19 This point was put forward during a conversation with Sir Josslyn Gore-Booth, November 2005.

20 Evidence of Sir Robert Gore-Booth, Second Report on Colonisation from Ireland: Further Minutes of Evidence, 1848 Session Vol. V [2641–2], pp. 259–60.

21 Kincaid to Palmerston, cited by Tyler Anbinder in 'Lord Palmerston and the Irish Famine Emigration', *Historical Journal*, Vol. 44 No 2 (2001), p. 456.

22 Evidence of Sir Robert Gore-Booth, Second Report on Colonisation of Ireland: Further Minutes of Evidence, 1848 Session Vol. V [2786], p. 275.

23 *Sligo Chronicle*, 31 July 1852 and cited by Deirdre Ryan, 'The Lissadell Estate of Sir Robert Gore-Booth: Famine and Emigration, 1845–1847', p. 80.

24 Ibid., pp. 75–6.

25 Ibid., p. 77.

26 Evidence of Sir Robert Gore-Booth, Second Report on Colonisation of Ireland: Further Minutes of Evidence, 1848 Session Vol. V [2604, 2605], p. 255.

27 Referred to by Ryan, 'The Lissadell Estate of Sir Robert Gore-Booth: Famine and Emigration, 1845–1847', p. 78.

28 John C. McTernan, *Memory Harbour*, p. 14.

29 Cited by Dermot James, but no specific reference is given in *The Gore-Booths of Lissadell*, p. 46.

30 Evidence of Sir Robert Gore-Booth, Second Report on Colonisation from Ireland: Further Minutes of Evidence, 1848 Session Vol. V [2724–5], p. 269.

31 Johnathan Binns, extract from *The Miseries and Beauties of Ireland*, Vol. I (London, 1837), pp. 347–8.

32 Evidence of Sir Robert Gore-Booth, Second Report on Colonisation from Ireland: Further Minutes of Evidence, 1848 Session Vol. V [2649], p. 260.

33 Evidence of Sir Robert Gore-Booth, Second Report on Colonisation from Ireland: Further Minutes of Evidence, 1848 Session Vol. V [2653], p. 261.

34 Evidence of Sir Robert Gore-Booth, Second Report on Colonisation from Ireland: Further Minutes of Evidence, 1848 Session Vol. V [2655], p. 261.

35 Evidence of Francis Spaight, Second Report on Colonisation from Ireland: Further Minutes of Evidence, 1848 Session Vol. V [3233], p. 334.

36 Tyler Anbinder, 'Lord Palmerston and the Irish Famine Emigration', p. 454; and Desmond Norton, *Lord Palmerston and the Irish Famine Emigration: A Rejoinder*, pp. 159–60 & 454.

37 Stewart and Kincaid were one of the principal land agents in the 1840s and were appointed to manage Lord Palmerston's estate. Captain O'Brien to Lt Col Jones, 2 March 1847 in 'Correspondence Relating to the Measures Adopted for the Relief of Distress in Ireland', Board of Works series, second part (1847) (797) LII, p. 182, in British Parliamentary Papers, 'Famine' VII, p. 204; and referred to by Tyler Anbinder, 'Lord Palmerston and the Irish Famine Emigration', *The Historical Journal*, 44, 2 (2001), p. 451.

38 These accounts related to Gore-Booth's importation of grain, the cost of gratuitous relief and private subscriptions entrusted to Gore-Booth. Evidence of Sir Robert Gore-Booth, Second Report on Colonisation from Ireland: Further Minutes of Evidence, 1848 Session Vol. V, p. 276.

39 Ryan, 'The Lissadell Estate of Sir Robert Gore-Booth: Famine and Emigration, 1845–1847', unpublished MA Thesis (Dublin, 1996), p. 26.

40 Ibid., pp. 28–9.

41 Rev. Jeffcott to Relief Commission, 2 December 1846, Ref. RLFC3/2/7935. Ibid.

42 Lynch to Messrs Steward and Kincaid, 12 September 1846, Norton Manuscript, cited by Tyler Anbinder, 'Lord Palmerston and the Irish Famine Emigration', p. 451.

43 Desmond Norton also disagrees with Anbinder, maintaining that Malachi Brennan was the parish priest of Ahamlish and not Drumcliff. Desmond Norton, *Lord Palmerston and the Irish Famine Emigration: A Rejoinder*, p. 158. Malachi Brennan to Palmerston, 24 October 1846, BR 148/3/15, Broadlands papers. Wynne to Kincaid, 7 December 1846, Norton Manuscript. Kincaid to Sir Robert Gore-Booth, 3 February 1847, reel 1, microfilm 590 series H/8/1, Lissadell papers, Public Records Office Northern Ireland (PRONI), referred to by Tyler Anbinder, 'Lord Palmerston and the Irish Famine Emigration', p. 452.

44 Tyler Anbinder, 'Lord Palmerston and the Irish Famine Emigration', p. 452.

45 Evidence of Sir Robert Gore-Booth, Second Report on Colonisation from Ireland: Further Minutes of Evidence, 1848 Session Vol. V [2787–8], p. 275; and Gerald Moran, *Sending Out Ireland's Poor: Assisted Emigration to North America in the Nineteenth Century*, p. 58.

46 Evidence of Sir Robert Gore-Booth, Second Report on Colonisation from Ireland: Further Minutes of Evidence, 1848 Session Vol. V [2692], p. 267.

47 Christine Kinealy, *This Great Calamity: The Irish Famine, 1845–52* (Dublin, 1994), pp. 301–2.

48 Joel Mokyr, *Why Ireland Starved: A Quantitative and Analytical History of the Irish Economy, 1800–1850* (London, 1985 edn), pp. 267–8.

49 *New Brunswick Courier*, 5 June 1847, reproduced in Cushing, Casey & Robertson, *A Chronicle of Irish Emigration to St John's, New Brunswick, 1847* (New Brunswick, 1979), p. 18.

50 Fitzpatrick, 'Emigration 1801–1870', in Vaughan (ed.), *A History of Ireland, Volume V: Ireland Under the Union 1801–1870*, p. 597.

51 Sir Denham Jephson-Norreys, Marrow Parish, Co. Cork, referred to by Tyler Anbinder, 'Lord Palmerston and the Irish Famine Emigration', *The Historical Journal*, 44, 2 (2001), p. 455.

52 Stewart and Kincaid to Palmerston, 16 December 1847 in Commons, Papers Relative to Emigration, 18,478 (50), XLVII, pp. 161–2, in British Parliamentary Papers, Colonies, Canada, XVII, pp. 351–2, and cited by Tyler Anbinder, 'Lord Palmerston and the Irish Famine Emigration', p. 466.

53 Kerby Miller, *Emigrants and Exiles: Ireland and the Irish Exodus to North America* (New York and Oxford, 1985), p. 296.

54 Fitzpatrick, 'Emigration 1801–1870', in Vaughan (ed.), *A History of Ireland, Volume V: Ireland Under the Union 1801–1870*, p. 594.

55 Miller, *Emigrants and Exiles: Ireland and the Irish Exodus to North America*, p. 296, and cited by Ryan, 'The Lissadell estate of Sir Robert Gore-Booth: Famine and Emigration, 1845–1847', p. 43.

56 The figures for couples, siblings or cousins account for 15 per cent for the *Aeolus*, 18 per cent for the *Yeoman* and 20 per cent for the *Lady Sale*. Ibid., p. 44.

57 Fitzpatrick, 'Emigration 1801–1870', in Vaughan (ed.), *A History of Ireland, Volume V: Ireland Under the Union 1801–1870*, p. 594.

58 Deirdre Ryan further points out that any direct comparison with David Fitzpatrick cannot be made as it was not possible to establish couples without children amongst the Gore-Booth emigrants; however, her comparison is based upon combining the figures for singles and groups of unmarried people. Ryan, 'The Lissadell Estate of Sir Robert Gore-Booth: Famine and Emigration', p. 44.

59 Eilish Ellis, *Emigrants from Ireland 1847–52: State-Aided Emigration Schemes from Crown Estates in Ireland* (Baltimore, 1997), pp. 13–59, referred to by Ryan, 'The Lissadell Estate of Sir Robert Gore-Booth: Famine and Emigration', p. 44.

60 Ryan, 'The Lissadell Estate of Sir Robert Gore-Booth: Famine and Emigration', p. 43.

61 Ibid., pp. 46–7.

62 Miller, *Emigrants and Exiles: Ireland and the Irish Exodus to North America*, p. 296, and cited by Ibid., p. 45.

63 Census of Ireland, 1841, p. xviii.

64 S.H. Cousens, 'The Regional Pattern of Emigration during the Great Irish Famine, 1846–51', *Transactions and Papers* (Institute of British Geographers), No 28 (1960), pp. 119–34.

65 M.H. Perley to Sir William M.G. Colebrook, 31 December 1847, 'Papers Relative to Emigration', British Parliamentary Papers, Colonies Canada, Vol. 17 (1847–48), p. 431.

66 *Sligo Journal*, 23 April 1847.

67 Third Report of Select Committee of the House of Lords on Colonisation from Ireland, with Minutes of Evidence, Appendix and Index, 1847–49, Vol. V, Appendix X, pp. 122–2.

68 Taken from the *New Brunswick Courier* and cited in the *Sligo Journal*, 15 October 1847.

69 Dispatch from Lt Governor S.W. Colebrooke to Earl Grey, Fredicton, New Brunswick, 11 June 1847, *Correspondence and Papers Relating to Canada*, Vol. 17 (1847–48), p. 251.

70 Dispatch from the Hon. J.S. Saunders, Provincial Secretary to M.H. Perley, Emigration Agent, 9 July 1847, *Correspondence and Papers Relating to Canada*, Vol. 17 (1847–48), p. 265.

71 M.H. Perley to the Hon. J.S. Saunders, 28 July 1847, *Correspondence and Papers Relating to Canada*, Vol. 17 (1847–48), p. 285.

72 Palmerston's agents had been unable to secure a vessel themselves. Gore-Booth, however, was able to obtain the *Aeolus* through his brother's business in Scotland. Gore-Booth had the ship fitted up and provisioned for the crossing.

73 Evidence of Sir Robert Gore-Booth, Second Report on Colonisation from Ireland: Further Minutes of Evidence, 1848 Session Vol. V [2785], p. 275.

74 John Robertson to Henry Gore-Booth, Third Report of Select Committee of the House of Lords on Colonisation from Ireland, with Minutes of Evidence, Appendix and Index, 1847–49 Vol. II (29 June 1847), Appendix X, pp. 122–3.

75 A.B. Hawke, Chief Emigrant Agent to T.E. Campbell, Civil Secretary, 16 October 1847, *Correspondence and Papers Relating to Canada*, Vol. 17 (1847–48), p. 217.

76 Perley to Saunders, 24 August 1847, *Correspondence and Papers Relating to Canada*, Vol. 17 (1847–48), p. 296.

77 Evidence of Sir Robert Gore-Booth, Second Report on Colonisation from Ireland: Further Minutes of Evidence, 1848 Session Vol. V [2651], p. 261. Perley to Saunders, 24 August 1847, *Correspondence and Papers Relating to Canada*, Vol. 17 (1847–48), p. 296. In a later dispatch, Perley specifically refers to the total number of 414, of which there were 176 women and 57 children, Enclosure 1, in No 25.

Perley to Saunders, 2 September 1847, *Correspondence and Papers Relating to Canada*, Vol. 17 (1847–48), p. 300. Enclosure 2, in No 37, Messrs Stewart and Kincaid to Viscount Palmerston, 3 December 1847, *Correspondence and Papers Relating to Canada*, Vol. 17 (1847–48), p. 353.

78 Donald MacKay, *Flight from Famine. The Coming of the Irish to Canada* (Toronto and London, 1990), p. 286. See also Perley to Saunders, 2 & 18 September 1847, *Correspondence and Papers Relating to Canada*, Vol. 17 (1847–48), p. 321.

79 Perley to Saunders, 2 & 18 September 1847, *Correspondence and Papers Relating to Canada*, Vol. 17 (1847–48), p. 321.

80 Messrs Stewart and Kincaid to Viscount Palmerston, 18 December 1847, Enclosure 2, in No 37, *Correspondence and Papers Relating to Canada*, Vol. 17 (1847–48), p. 163.

81 Ryan, 'The Lissadell Estate of Sir Robert Gore-Booth: Famine and Emigration, 1845–1847', p. 47, from Miller, *Emigrants and Exiles: Ireland and the Irish Exodus to North America*, p. 296.

82 Evidence of Sir Robert Gore-Booth, Second Report on Colonisation from Ireland: Further Minutes of Evidence, 1848 Session Vol. V [2732], p. 270.

83 Accounts showing importation of grain, cost of relief given by Sir Robert Gore-Booth, private subscriptions and submitted in the evidence of Sir Robert Gore-Booth, Second Report on Colonisation from Ireland: Further Minutes of Evidence, 1848 Session Vol. V, pp. 276–82 & [2787–9], p. 275.

84 Gerard Moran, *Sending Out Ireland's Poor: Assisted Emigration to North America in the Nineteenth Century* (Dublin, 2004), p. 109.

85 Extract of a letter from Lord Grey to Sir George Grey, November 1846, Grey Emigration Papers, 1823–1850 and cited by Gilbert Tucker, 'Famine Emigration to Canada, 1847', *The American Historical Review*, Vol. 36, No 3 (April, 1931), p. 535.

86 Evidence of Sir Robert Gore-Booth, Second Report on Colonisation from Ireland: Further Minutes of Evidence, 1848 Session Vol. V [2708–15], p. 268.

87 Thomas Garry to his wife, 8 March 1848, in Third Report of Select Committee of the House of Lords on Colonisation from Ireland, with Minutes of Evidence, Appendix and Index, 1847–49 Vol. V, Appendix X, p. 129; evidence of Sir Robert Gore-Booth [2674–6], p. 265.

88 British Parliamentary Papers: Emigration Part 1. British provinces in North America, ordered by the House of Commons to be printed, 20 December 1847, Enclosure 5, No 30. Perley to Saunders, 16 October 1847, p. 143, and cited by Cushing, Casey & Robertson, *A Chronicle of Irish Emigration to Saint John, New Brunswick 1847*, Introduction.

89 This figure excludes thirty-eight children who died, as well as five who ran away. Peter Douglas Murphy, 'Poor, "Ignorant Children": "A Great Resource"', the Saint John Emigrant Orphan Asylum Admittance Ledger in Context, unpublished MA Thesis (Halifax, Nova Scotia, September 1977), p. 7.

90 Tyler Anbinder, *Five Points* (New York: Free Press, 2001), p. 42.

91 Anbinder suggests that by 1855 these two landlords, together with the Marquis of Lansdowne (Kerry), were responsible for one in five Roman Catholic emigrants, in ibid., pp. 48–9.

92 Anbinder gives a detailed analysis of the occupations of Five Pointers, in ibid., Chapter 4, pp. 111–40.

93 Ibid., pp. 439–41. A survey in 2005 recorded an immigrant population of 47.6 per cent in Queen's Co. American Community Survey Factsheet for Queen's County, New York, United States Census Bureau, accessed 24 February 2007.

94 Moran, *Sending Out Ireland's Poor: Assisted Emigration to North America in the Nineteenth Century*, p. 68f.

95 Evidence of Sir Robert Gore-Booth, Second Report on Colonisation from Ireland: Further Minutes of Evidence, 1848 Session Vol. V, pp. 276–82.

96 Moran, *Sending Out Ireland's Poor: Assisted Emigration to North America in the Nineteenth Century*, p. 106.

97 Oliver MacDonagh, 'Irish Emigration to the United States of America and the British Colonies During the Famine', in R. Dudley Edwards & T. Desmond Williams (eds), *The Great Famine: Studies in Irish History 1845–52*, (Dublin, 1994), p. 366.

98 Annual Report of the Chief Emigration Agent, 1847, in *Papers Relative to Emigration to the British Provinces in North America* (1847–48) (964), xlvii, p. 17, and cited by Moran, *Sending Out Ireland's Poor: Assisted Emigration to North America in the Nineteenth Century*, p. 92.

99 Evidence of Sir Robert Gore-Booth, Second Report on Colonisation from Ireland: Further Minutes of Evidence, 1848 Session Vol. V [2678], p. 265.

100 Ibid. [2787–8], p. 275, and Moran, *Sending Out Ireland's Poor: Assisted Emigration to North America in the Nineteenth Century*, p. 58.

6

James Hack Tuke & Assisted Emigration from the West of Ireland in the 1880s

Tessa English

On the evening of Thursday 18 May 1882, an Englishman, Mr James Tuke, arrived in Galway City at the head of a motley procession of men, women and children. These were eighty-six Connemara families, many of them recent victims of evicting landlords. Early next morning, the families were taken by the City of the Tribes tugboat to the steamship *Winnipeg*, anchored in Galway Bay, to leave the country of their birth for a new life in America. The scene was graphically described in *The Galway Vindicator*:

> Yesterday Mr Tuke, the indefatigable philanthropist … departed no less than eighty-six families to the Western World … The emigrants seemed delighted with the arrangements of the vessel, and were most demonstrative in their expressions of gratitude to Mr Tuke for having taken them from their old homes – or rather … for having picked them up from being homeless outcasts in Connemara.[1]

This scene is far from the images of the starving, skeletal, wailing men and women who boarded the 'coffin ships' for America during the Great Famine.

What is their story? Between 1882 and 1884, some thirty years after the mass exodus during the years of the Great Famine, 9,500 men, women and children were to leave poverty and starvation on the west coast of Ireland for

the greater opportunities in the New World. That they were able to do so
was largely the work of one man, James Hack Tuke. To 'his' emigrants he was
something of a hero and a saviour. Who was he and why did he concern himself with the fate of the Irish poor? What was the fate of those families who
entrusted themselves to his emigration scheme? Were they victims of exile or
willing men and women who wished to forge better lives for themselves and
their children? It is a many-faceted story that has largely figured only in the
margins of nineteenth-century history in Ireland, yet it engages with significant political, economic and social themes in the period: themes of famine,
emigration and the interventions of the state and individuals.

The Indefatigable Philanthropist

James Hack Tuke was born in York in 1819 into a leading family of Quakers.
His father was Samuel Tuke, a successful tea and coffee merchant who was
closely involved in charitable works and took an active interest in the plight
of Irish immigrants. From a very early age, James was deeply imbued with the
Quaker humanitarian ideals of service and duty to God. He became a successful banker, yet all his life he devoted himself to numerous charitable projects.
It was, however, his work for the relief of the poor of the west of Ireland
which was to consume his passion and energy, and to which he devoted more
than forty years of his life.

He first became involved in Ireland during the Great Famine and its aftermath, from 1845 to 1852. Tuke travelled across Ireland with William Forster
and his son, W.E. Forster, later to become Chief Secretary of State for Ireland
in Gladstone's government, in order to organise and distribute Quaker relief
funds. Tuke wrote of his experiences in the first of many pamphlets, 'Distress
in Ireland'.[2] Following his second visit, he published 'A Visit to Connaught in
the Autumn of 1847'.[3] Tuke's observations, revealing as they did the huge scale
of the catastrophe that was unfolding, also exposed the inadequacy of the government's response. His pamphlets found immediate circulation amongst the
Quaker relief committees in both Ireland and England. What he witnessed
on those harrowing journeys, particularly in the west, a region he described
as 'by far the poorest and most destitute in Ireland', led to his conviction that
emigration was the key to helping the starving people he encountered.

Tuke's opinions on the economic condition of the remote west were per-
ceptive. He recognised that a uniform economic policy for the country as a
whole would not be successful; a policy that worked for the more prosperous

James Hack Tuke

eastern counties, with their indigenous industry and arable lands, could not benefit the smallholding tenant farmers of Connaught. He saw a two-fold benefit in assisting emigration: firstly, by offering to those who emigrated a new life with greater opportunities for work in Canada and North America, and secondly, by relieving the plight of those who did not leave through the consolidation of emigrants' plots into larger and more productive farms.

He had to be persuasive and persistent if he was to convince English politicians of his views. They, and the wider population, were suspicious of the reports of distress that came from the Irish nationalists and clergy, believing it to be part of a propaganda campaign to further their political aspirations. In the prevailing climate of anti-Irish prejudice, some believed that the Irish, as usual, 'were merely consummate actors and impostors pulling a fast one' to deceive 'good' Mr Tuke by dressing in rags and hiding their food stocks.

The second and major phase of his work for Ireland took place between 1880 and 1885, during a recurrence of famine in the west of Ireland. On revisiting Ireland in 1880, at the request of the Quakers, Tuke discovered that although conditions in the majority of the country, especially the north and east, had improved since the Great Famine, for those in the west living conditions appeared little improved. He concluded that radical and immediate measures were needed to help remedy the destitution. A cornerstone of his proposals was the assistance of those families who wished to settle in the New World to seek to build a better life for themselves. First, he set himself the task of bringing the plight of these remote districts to the attention of the British government, and the public at large, writing extensively and persuasively of his observations and proposals. He wrote letters for circulation among his friends, letters to *The Times* and articles. His published pamphlet 'Irish Distress and its Remedies'[4] caught the imagination of the times and proved a popular success. Tuke's graphic and persistent descriptions of 'the stealthy tread of hunger'[5] of a people living on the verge of starvation, his first-hand experience of the country and the conditions, and his proposals for relief measures, were to result in a seminal meeting. This took place at the home of the Duke of Bedford in Eaton Square on Friday 31 March 1882, and it was to be the birth of 'Mr Tuke's Fund'.

This meeting of men of influence and standing in London's political circles was called to 'consider the expediency of assisting those who desire to emigrate from certain districts in the West of Ireland'.[6] Tuke set out his ideas of assisted emigration and recommended a scheme which could open the way for an approach to the government for support for emigration on a larger scale. His efforts paid off. Those present resolved to set up a fund to provide assisted emigration for smallholders in the west. They agreed that the work, to be overseen by Tuke himself, should be supported by private subscription, be well organised, should avoid unnecessary controversy in pursuing its objectives and confine its operations to a limited area in the first instance. Before the group departed, £8,000, a large sum for those times, was raised from those present for the work to begin.[7]

So began the most concentrated and arduous phase of his efforts to relieve the distress. He continued to lobby for support and personally superintended most of the work. By the end of 1884, some 9,500 people from the west coast unions of Belmullet, Newport and Swineford in County Mayo, and Clifden, Oughterard and the Aran Islands in County Galway, had received help to emigrate and resettle successfully, through both private and government funds. However, the end of the scheme was then in sight. Increasingly, powerful and negative pressures from the Catholic Church, the British government, the Irish nationalists and, crucially, the receiving countries, all pointed to one inevitable conclusion. The scheme was wound up and Mr Tuke's Fund for Assisted Emigration ended. It was a great disappointment to him believing, as he did, that there was so much more work to be done. The Duke of Bedford expressed the measure of Tuke's achievement: 'I have learnt what religious feeling and a sense of duty can do, when men so animated, undertake to lessen human suffering.'[8] Although he continued to advocate the merits of assisted emigration, and, indeed, paid from his own pocket to assist many, Tuke's energies turned towards alternative initiatives.

The third and final phase of Tuke's involvement arose from the reputation he had gained during his emigration work. In 1886, following another failure of the potato crop, he was influential in raising, again through private subscription, over £5,000 to help alleviate distress on Achill Island and the west coast of Mayo through the distribution of seed potatoes to improve a weakened stock. His reports and persistent letters to *The Times* proposing permanent improvements through alternative initiatives, such as the development of light industries, fisheries and the railways, brought him to the attention of Arthur Balfour, Conservative Chief Secretary for Ireland, 1887–91. His continuing efforts bore fruit with the establishment, by the Irish Land Act of 1891, of the Congested Districts Board. A key instigating factor was the reports and pamphlets written by Tuke 'that heightened public awareness of Irish poverty and forced the government to deal with it'.[9] Tuke, the only Englishman appointed, remained on the board until his death on 13 January 1896. Typically, he had turned down the honour of a knighthood bestowed upon him in 1889 in recognition of his lifetime's achievement to better the lives of the Irish poor.[10]

To twenty-first-century eyes, Tuke appears a colonialist and imperialist. He was a man of his times. In the late nineteenth century the British Empire

covered over a quarter of the land surface of the earth and Tuke was undoubtedly caught up in the prevailing fever of optimism for bringing progress and
civilisation to new lands. He aligned his Quaker duty to fashion a vision of
Empire which was 'one of justice, peace, freedom and equality, of the Pax
Britannia and of the fulfilment by Britain of its trusteeship mission'.[11] Tuke
had faith in British imperialism, embracing a vision of migrants not as refu-
gees but as heroic builders of nations. He appears to have given little thought
to the indigenous peoples who were losing their lands to them. Tuke was
vigorously opposed to Home Rule. He wholeheartedly supported English
Unionism, or Constructive Unionism, as it became known. He ardently
believed, and indeed all his endeavours rested on, the premise that the Union
was capable of promoting assistance and reform without conceding Home
Rule. For Tuke, the Union, and its maintenance, was the foundation on which
hinged his efforts to pursue his initiatives for Ireland.

Mr Tuke's Fund for Assisted Emigration

Tuke decided that, initially, the scheme would operate in the Clifden region
of Connemara. This decision rested on four major factors. The first was the
endemic poverty of an area where the majority of the holdings (69 per cent)
were less than 15 acres and, therefore, classed as unviable. The second was the
remoteness of the place, which gave rise to lack of outside assistance. The
third was support for assisted emigration by the local Board of Guardians. In
February 1881, the guardians had passed the following resolution:

> That taking into consideration the poverty and destitute conditions of the
> poorer classes of tenantry of this union, particularly those evicted for non-pay-
> ment of rent, and those along the sea-shore holding miserable patches of land
> caused by the sub-division of holdings, and who for three-fourths of the year
> are in a state of semi-starvation, we respectfully request the interference of the
> government to assist in the way of emigration.[12]

Furthermore, they also decided to request a grant from the Local Government
Board for Ireland to support emigration. The fourth, and key reason, was the
support of the local Catholic clergy. The power of the Catholic Church at
this time cannot be underestimated. The higher echelons, the bishops and
archbishops, vigorously opposed assisted emigration on the grounds that they
feared for the moral welfare of their people in a foreign land, and the deple-
tion in numbers and strength of Catholics in Ireland. They argued that the

morals and spiritual welfare of Catholics overseas were in jeopardy due to a lack of Catholic priests. They feared, too, that emigration was a way of undermining Catholic beliefs and practice, and indeed a way for Protestants to gain converts. The local priests on the ground, however, working hard to support their flocks and knowing the desperate conditions in which they lived, saw emigration as a way of providing much-needed relief: 'The holdings are so small, the land so sterile, that these people will always be steeped in poverty … I wish to God half the people of this barren territory would emigrate somewhere, for penal servitude would be a paradise … compared to their present condition.'[13] Tuke capitalised on support from local priests, and also ensured that priests accompanied his emigrants on their voyages. Indeed, some stayed on with the emigrants in places of settlement.

'Solving the Western Difficulty'? The Organisation of Emigration

A key reason for the perceived success of the Tuke Committee's operation was the efficiency of its planning and organisation. Tuke established systems and structures, and mobilised support from a close-knit group of Quaker colleagues.[14] He secured the services of key agents, such as the relieving officers Major Gaskell and Major Ruttledge-Fair, who had an intimate knowledge of their regions, and were well known and respected by the local people. Pre-planning was particularly important to Tuke, informed as he was by Quaker principles and practice. He and his supporters did not stint on preparatory visits to the receiving countries. According to the Canadian Immigration Report of 1883, Major Gaskell and other members of the Tuke Committee went to Manitoba and to Toronto to 'make arrangements with the Ontario Government, assisted by the Catholic authorities, for the settlement of Irish families'. Major Gaskell asked for an Irish-speaking agent to be on each train to help families passing through, and for a female Irish-speaking agent to see to the 'special needs of the women'.[15] In his Annual Report of Halifax, Nova Scotia, the immigration agent Edwin Clay welcomed this level of personal attention. 'The fact,' he wrote, 'that a few cases of distress only have arisen is in my opinion, strong evidence of the success of the arrangements that were made.'[16]

Tuke was involved in every detail of the operation, from selecting the emigrants, to clothing them, to helping transport them to the point of embarkation. As the scheme progressed, he insisted that the structures and guidelines laid down at the outset be adhered to. Any applicant looking to bypass the strict selection criteria was struck off the list. He insisted that only families

In Search of a Better Life

People gathered at stone wall (National Library of Ireland)

Galway Bay from Spiddal (National Library of Ireland)[17]

would be helped, as, he argued, it was only in this way that holdings in the west would be consolidated to the benefit of the whole community.

Tuke was encouraged by the evident demand for emigration from the people themselves. Within a few days of his arrival, which happened to coincide with an unprecedented high level of evictions from neighbouring estates, 222 families (one-fifth of the population of Clifden) had come forward. This response confirmed Tuke's opinion of the need for emigration, as did a positive response from authorities in Canada, as well as from John Lynch, Catholic Archbishop of Toronto.

The argument, as propounded by the nationalists, for relief schemes to support the people at home in Ireland was strongly supported. Yet amongst the people, demand for emigration was growing.

Tuke became convinced that this demand, and the scale and expense of the scheme as he envisaged it, was so great that it was beyond the power of any private organisation to accomplish. The committee sent a memorandum to the government in April 1882 arguing that while the desire for emigration was strong (it estimated that 100,000 people would require assistance over a five-year period), government support was required. Partly as a result of the evident success of Tuke in Clifden and frustration with alternative schemes to alleviate poverty, such as providing funding for potato seed schemes or grants to Poor Law Unions, parliament decided to support Tuke's scheme. Through the Arrears of Rent Act, £10,000 was to be provided for state-aided emigration, and forty-two unions in the west were scheduled for support. The Tuke Committee, in view of its considerable experience in the administration of emigration, was invited to oversee the poorest of the unions: Clifden, Oughterard, Newport and Belmullet. The government would provide £5 for each emigrant, with any shortfall made up by the committee.

Tuke worked tirelessly throughout 1883 to promote his scheme. He wrote numerous letters to *The Times*, which included excerpts from glowing letters received from satisfied emigrants.[18] In England these letters stimulated lively debate, both for and against the work of Tuke. Edward W.O. Brien, former assistant commissioner under the Land Act, stated that while the generous motives of Tuke and his committee could not be doubted, and while their actions undoubtedly were of great benefit to individuals, 'we must look the facts in the face. Emigration cannot, in our time at least, solve the western difficulty.'[19]

In spite of the continuing debate, 1883 proved a successful year for the emigration scheme. There was no shortage of demand for assistance for emigration in the areas administered by the Tuke Committee. In Clifden alone 1,589 applicants were successful. From Belmullet, 3,500 people, 14 per cent of

the population, were helped to emigrate in 1883 and 1884. Demands started
to be received from single men and women eager for assistance. These requests
were largely rejected. Family emigration only was part of the Tuke plan.

A series of unique photographs form part of an album, recently donated
to the National Photographic Archive, Dublin.[20] They illustrate both an emigrant ship and its likely passengers. The dedication in the album reads: 'These
were taken for Mr Tuke by Major Ruttledge-Fair on their Emigration Work
in the West.'

'No Meal Whatever, Children in Rags': The Tuke Emigrants

Tuke, frequently on hand to bid the emigrants farewell, described the departure of assisted emigrants from Clifden: 'I did not hear a single "wail"[21] as
we left the ship; but before we steamed out a multitude of hand-shakings
and blessings were showered upon me, and three cheers rang out across the
bay.'[22] Similar descriptions and the overwhelming number of applicants do
not paint a picture of the emigrants as 'victims of exile' of nationalist narrative
of emigration, but rather, willing people who saw their departure as a means
of escape from poverty. Emigration from the west was fast becoming, as it had
done earlier in the century, 'a fact of life, a fashion, a fever'.[23] This was recognised by a Catholic priest, Father Sheehan:

> the crowds on shore look with envy at the fortunate friends who are escaping.
> They no longer shout an everlasting farewell, but a ringing cheer, which is
> strengthened by the hope that when the letter and the passage money arrive,
> they too, will be able to leave this land of bondage.[24]

Who were the 'fortunate' emigrants and how did they come to be selected?
One of the principal features of the private emigration schemes was that
those who financed them reserved the right to choose who should go and
who should stay. With the numbers applying for emigration greatly exceeding expectation and places available, Tuke adopted clear guidelines as to who
was to be assisted. In order to minimise distress and the effect on local communities, only families would be assisted. Further, to be eligible most of the
family members were to be over the age of 12. This was to ensure a sufficient
number of breadwinners to support each family. Only families employed in
agriculture would be considered, and then only those thought likely to suc-
ceed. There were to be no workhouse inmates. (Tuke wanted the highest
calibre of emigrant to take up the role of pioneer in the new lands.) At least

one member of the family had to be able to speak English in order to maxim-
ise their prospects at their destination.[25] Emigrants should, in theory, provide
some money themselves towards their costs, or at least pay back a proportion
of the fare over time. In practice, this share of costs was often not forthcoming; many emigrants were indebted to landlords and shopkeepers and had no
clothes or shoes, let alone money for their fare. Nor did repayment always
materialise once the emigrant was safely in America.[26] Tuke described a 'typical' and successful applicant to the scheme:

> H.B, aged thirty-five; wife thirty; five children … Rent £15 a year, jointly with
> another. Twelve years ago had several head of cattle and sheep; was then worth
> £200 or more. Had sold his last cow for £6 10s, and had now no milk to give
> his children … no meal whatever, children in rags.[27]

The 1882 Arrears of Rent Act directed that successful applicants were only
informed ten days before the date of sailing. In this way they would be
encouraged to sow an annual crop which would feed them in case of failure
of their application. In common with the Irish talent for getting themselves
on advantageous schemes, many tenants were quick to sell off all their possessions and present themselves as destitute. The selectors would then have no
option but to send them in order to prevent a further drain on the charity of
the Poor Law Union. On occasion, selectors were faced with a family whose
ranks of children had suddenly and inexplicably grown. This, too, was a way to
take advantage of the 'free ride' and to send out children to friends and family
in the Americas, thus relieving the need to feed them from scarce food stocks.
The Irish in the west were, as ever, nothing if not resourceful.

'This is a Good Country': Places of Settlement

Where should the emigrants be encouraged to settle? Tuke saw this as key to
the success of the scheme. He made numerous visits to North America, as did
his Quaker friend and supporter, Howard Hodgkin, in order to explore the
options and to secure support of the receiving authorities. Tuke understood
that meticulous planning and preparation was essential for the successful
settlement of the Irish. Lessons had been learnt from the earlier emigration
during the years of the Great Famine, when the Irish had tended to congregate in the large towns and cities. In 1881 the Richmond Commission had
reported:

The greatest misfortune that fell to the lot of Catholic immigrants coming to America forty or fifty years ago was that they were allowed to be huddled in cities where, as a rule, nothing was possible to them but to be made hewers of wood and drawers of water, instead of being induced to occupy the fertile lands of the Western States, where independent homes were to be won with little cost and little labour.[28]

This was not part of Tuke's vision. He believed in the ideal of colonising land waiting to be opened up. Of all the possible destinations, Tuke favoured Canada, and it was to Canada that the majority of the Tuke emigrants in 1882 and 1883 were sent, unless they could provide evidence of ready support from friends or family in the United States. For Tuke and his political supporters, with their dreams of cementing the Empire, Canada provided an ideal place. Unlike the United States, it was a colony of the British Empire, the closest British colony to Ireland. With their need for agricultural labour for the new lands that were opening up in the west, the Canadian authorities were well disposed to the scheme, promising material support to the emigrants. The Canadian-Pacific Railway, at the same time as opening up large tracts of virgin land for agricultural labourers, would provide well-paid work for others.

Initially, the Connemara emigrants had to be persuaded to opt for Canada rather than the United States. Canada at that time was a country largely unknown to those on the remote western shores of Ireland. However, the situation changed as positive letters from successful emigrants gave glowing descriptions of the work to be found and the money to be made. With these letters, and the remittances that started to flow back home, the reluctance for Canada as a final destination rapidly diminished.

We are happy that we are all working for the same man for 8 dols. a month each 3 of us and board, and the rest of the family live in a house across the road ... This is a good country we like it good any man can earn money in it. Tell Jim Cauley he can earn lots of money, any young man that can plough or bind can get 25 dollars a month in harvest time tell the rest of the boys this ... Anthony if you were here you would do well this is a better place for young men than America ... Canada is a great place if all the people in Ireland would come here there would be lots of room for them.[29]

The following was sent from Toronto by a former inhabitant of Belmullet on 8 July 1883: 'If you give me a present of a house and farm in Tipp I would not go back to it ... I could not describe it to you, its more like a Paradise, the very smell of the trees growing all along the footpath here would do you good.'[30]

For these same reasons in support of colonisation, Tuke proposed emigration to the agricultural Midwestern states of the United States. He was supported in his conviction by Bishop John Ireland of St Paul, Minnesota, an Irishman himself, who led the largely successful Minnesota emigration scheme and was a key supporter of Tuke's scheme. Tuke emigrants did settle successfully in the rapidly developing cities such as Minneapolis and St Paul, filling the demand for unskilled labour. Ever adept at taking advantage of any opportunity, a number of the emigrants initially sent to Canada found their way over the border and into the larger cities of the United States. While this was acknowledged by the Tuke Committee, there was little they could do to prevent them.

Australia, also a colony, was a more remote destination and therefore a more expensive option. Regulation of emigration to Australia was tightly controlled by the colonial authorities. They looked for particular skills and were strict in the selection of those who they deemed would contribute to the development of the country. Largely on account of the cost and distance, fewer than 250 Tuke emigrants were sent there.

It is interesting to note that in 1883 and 1884 more than double the number of Tuke emigrants were sent to the United States rather than the preferred destination of Canada. This can be accounted for by the fact that, while initially supportive of the scheme, by 1884 the Canadian authorities had started to withdraw support, for reasons discussed in later pages. It is also of interest that the Tuke emigrants were indeed well provided for, with the average cost per head approximately £2 more than for government-aided emigrants.

'We Like this Country First Rate': The Emigrant Experience

The letters of the Tuke emigrants, and the reports of those charged with their support, indicate that the majority appear to have fared well in their new lives. They describe the support given, both during the voyage out and on arrival at their destinations; jobs are found, wages are good and opportunities abound for those who are willing to work hard and keep off the drink. Importantly, many refer to the possibility of owning a home of their own as well as the plentiful food available, enough for some to even report a growing stoutness – important considerations for evicted tenants who had left Ireland on the point of starvation. They also refer to opportunities for their children to become ladies and gentlemen. Significantly, nearly all letters back to Ireland refer to the amounts they are sending home, either to pay off debts or to assist relatives to follow their example: 'I am sending you the sum of £4 which I am glad to have the gladness to send. This money is from me and Martin. We like this country first rate.'[31]

Few, if any, express homesickness, but then they had their immediate family with them. They were not slow to avail themselves of social and material opportunities for advancement. In this, the Tuke emigrants were little different from the mass of emigrants leaving Ireland in the nineteenth century.

From Mrs T—, Ontario, Canada, 16 July 1883:

I will write to you again when T is paid and send you something ... that will release your clothes. How happy I will be when you come out here and my dear sister. I am sure they will do well for Harry can work everyday and get 6s a day. T— ... is greatly improved he takes no drink to signify, he feels so delighted at you and Harry coming and we will have a nice place before you please God. We are all well and fat.

From T—L, St Paul, Minnesota, 21 May 1883:

I wish my father and mother were all out here. This is a fine country. All the children and myself are to work. Pat is at the plumbing trade Maria and Delia at Tailors trade – so that in a short time we will be all right we will have a property of our own please God! This is the country that everyman is a gentleman and everywoman a lady if they conduct themselves.

Other favourable reports were received. Bishop John Ireland reported favourably on the safe arrival and settlement of the emigrants in Minnesota: 'All able to work have found employment and are doing well. The emigrants sent out this spring are of a superior class, and must be looked upon as a benefit to the community among which they may cast their lot.'[32] But these letters were carefully selected and published by the very officials and philanthropists who had a vested interest in reporting the success of the scheme. One letter in a manuscript collection at the London Library of the Religious Society of Friends, not unsurprisingly omitted from the collected letters for public consumption, strikes a more pessimistic note. William Rathbone, visiting the Tuke emigrants in the United States, writes that he is sorry he is:

unable to give a more hopeful account of matters but I trust our Committee will be no way discouraged for though undoubtedly the Irish emigrants give trouble at first, they seem after twelve months or so (if we can get them away from New York) to become merged with the rest of the population, and with all their faults, they will add to the wealth and prosperity of America.[33]

Historian Kerby Miller has argued that efforts to locate original letters written by assisted emigrants have failed. He interprets this failure as 'a function of the social stigma experienced, or the personal shame felt by assisted emigrants and/or their offspring'.[34] I would argue that this theory, neatly fitting as it does his 'emigrant as exile' thesis, is unsubstantiated. His failure to locate such letters may equally be attributable to the fact that these emigrants integrated quickly and easily with their host countries; they very quickly became Canadians or Americans. In other words, they were more in the mould of the 'fortunate escapers' and 'eager entrepreneurs' of revisionist historians.

'Getting Rid of the Irish Difficulty by Getting Rid of the Irish People': Obstacles & Opposition

In spite of the initial successes of the Tuke Scheme, it was dealt a series of blows as its third year of operation progressed. The first of these was the growing strength of the nationalists. The Irish Parliamentary Party and the National League, under the leadership of Parnell, was opposed to emigration, deeming it unpatriotic. Parnell publicly denounced the Tuke Scheme at the Parnell Banquet at the Rotunda Hospital, Dublin, in December 1883. He claimed that he had proof that three out of four of the emigrants ended up destitute in the cities, and that however well-intentioned Tuke was:

> the committee stand exposed as an indecent attempt to assist the government to get rid of the Irish difficulty by getting rid of the Irish people and shield that government from the responsibility which rightly belongs to it of providing for the inhabitants of this country as long as it insists on the right to govern us.[35]

Tuke, in turn, was openly hostile to 'Dictator Parnell'. He saw him as willing to condemn countless thousands to starvation in order to secure his political ends. When, in 1886, Tuke asked a 'political Home Ruler' why his party had never supported his initiative or worked for the improvement in the west themselves, he claimed he was given the answer: 'the fact is these districts and people furnish us with a very good "raison d'etre"'. This seemingly cynical exploitation of the misery of the poor to serve vested political interests was abhorrent to Tuke's strong humanitarian instincts.

The more successful the committee had been in securing government funding to supplement private subscriptions, the more it had played into the hands of the nationalists. They opposed such schemes, at times using the misery of the Irish poor to point an accusatory finger at the failure of the

British to provide a remedy, seizing on any adverse report of the condition of the Irish emigrants, or whipping up anti-British fervour by claiming that it was government official policy to depopulate Ireland. Tuke was infuriated, claiming that this was no more than political propaganda and would not help the people most in need.[36] However, the nationalist voice began to make itself heard. Westminster initially acknowledged the success of Tuke's scheme and granted additional funding of £100,000 for emigration purposes. This sum, however, was subsequently reduced to £50,000 through the persuasion by the Irish Parliamentary Party that funds should equally be made available for migration within, not emigration from, Ireland.

Then there was the hammer blow delivered by the Catholic bishops. Having vigorously opposed the Tuke Scheme from the start, they published a resolution, in July 1883, against assisted emigration: 'state-aided emigration as a means of ending this evil (congestion) is unwise and impolitic, and tends only to promote disaffection amongst the Irish race at home and abroad.'[37]

This resolution led to the archbishop and twenty-five priests from Tuam stating their opposition to assisted emigration. It should, they said, be opposed by every local and constitutional method available. Other local priests followed suit.[38] This gathering opposition was the beginning of the end of the scheme. As an outsider and Englishman, Tuke had relied heavily on the support of local clergy to gain the confidence and trust of the people.

The third knock was the deepening ideological differences between Tuke and the local Board of Guardians. The high ideals of the Tuke Committee in the selection of emigrants soon fell foul of the guardians. The latter were more concerned with emigrating as many people, particularly paupers, as possible, for the least amount of money. Tuke knew this would ultimately lead to the failure of the scheme. In his opinion, the emigrants had to be carefully selected and adequately provided for, before and during the voyage, as well as on arrival at their destination. He had learnt that when emigrants arrived penniless and were left to fend for themselves in a new country, they were likely to fail. However high the cost, he was committed to their welfare.

By 1884 the flow of applications for emigration started to dry up. A major contribution to this stemming of demand was the upturn in the harvest in the summer of 1883. There was less need and less destitution than in the preceding years.[39] This upturn coincided with a downturn in agricultural activity in Canada, where increasing mechanisation depressed the need and wages for agricultural labour.[40] Exacerbating the situation was the particularly severe Canadian winter of 1883/84, which made conditions harder for the emigrants to contend with. On 13 February 1884 the Department of Immigration in Ontario expressed concern to the Tuke Committee regarding the poor condition of many of the emigrants sent out in 1883. It was claimed that they, together with groups sent out through other auspices, were dependent on charity. This situation, which inevitably invited comparison to the influx of poor Irish during the years of the Great Famine, was invoking hostility from the local people.[41] There was a suspicion amongst the Canadians that their country was again being used as a dumping ground for unwanted Irish paupers:

> an emigrant … who leaves for Canada because he has his passage paid, a new suit of clothes given him, and money put in his pocket by Mr Tuke's Committee – such men can scarcely be said to be following out natural economic impulses leading them to better their condition and thus indirectly to benefit the world at large. Emigration is no longer culling and bringing to us the cream of the working classes, the men of energy thrift and enterprise which reaps the profits of transportation. It is as likely to be the indolent, vagrant and vicious who will go, as the thrifty, industrious and energetic. To go on receiving them, without check or control, is like attempting to guide a heavily loaded wagon downhill, with wheels greased and the brakes off, because it has been done before successfully with the brakes on.[42]

Such reports were made much of in the nationalist press. No differentiation was made between the Tuke emigrants and others, such as those sent out by the Poor Law Unions. Tuke determined that the allegations be investigated and he dispatched Howard Hodgkin and Ruttledge-Fair to Toronto. The result of their investigation revealed only three Tuke emigrant families who were struggling.[43] Out of the totality, cases of families that had returned to Ireland were few. The reasons were usually either the failure of expected support from family and friends or the death of the breadwinner which gave the family no option but to return.[44]

The Scheme Suspended

However, the damage to the Canadian people's willingness to receive the emigrants, and to potential emigrants' dreams of a promised land of work and plenty, had been done. In March 1884 the Canadian government withdrew support from the project. On 13 June 1884, Tuke published a resolution to suspend the work of the committee, concluding: 'any funds under their control which may be available for the assistance of emigration should be held over until a more favourable opportunity.'[45]

That favourable opportunity never materialised. Tuke did not reactivate his emigration scheme, in spite of the return of bad harvests and resulting distress in the late 1880s and early 1890s. He gave his support, instead, to other schemes, such as his work as a member of the Congested Districts Board. He had always claimed that emigration was only one remedy for relieving the distress of the people. However, the end of the scheme for emigration must have come as a great disappointment. The poor still queued up to leave the west. Each year from 1884 to 1891 he assisted, out of his own pocket, some 100 people to emigrate from Clifden and Belmullet. The esteem in which he was held by the people of Connemara is demonstrated by a petition presented by them in April 1886. They, 'mindful of your advocacy of us in the Press and with the Government', wish to 'take advantage of your presence amongst us today to express to you our profound and hearty gratitude for your beneficent labours on behalf of the impoverished and starving people of the West of Ireland'.

The petition, with over 200 signatures, requested Tuke's help to support 'the only permanent and real remedy which lies in the development of the resources of Connemara, and in particular the under-taking of the railway'.[46] Two years after the official end of the emigration scheme, the people recognised the potential for the development of local resources, and it was to Tuke that they turned. Their confidence in Tuke's ability to get things done was not misplaced. Within seven years the railway was fully operational, connecting Clifden with the rest of Ireland.[47]

'Beneficent Labours on Behalf of the Impoverished and Starving': How Successful was the Tuke Scheme?

To what extent can the Tuke Scheme be considered a success? There is sufficient evidence to indicate that it did benefit the emigrants. Reports from a range of key people, from immigration authorities, churchmen and agents, as well as the letters from the emigrants themselves, indicated that his emigrants were succeeding in their new lives. They were working, well-fed, able to climb up the social ladder and saving money, as well as sending home remittances. These opportunities would not have been available to them had they stayed in Ireland.

Did the Tuke Scheme benefit the west of Ireland as he had hoped? A key benefit was that it provided the people of the area with access to emigrant remittances. With its low level of emigration during the years of the Great Famine, the west had largely been denied this source of funding. Many emigrants sent money home to bring out family members, thus setting up a chain migration. In other cases, it was used to pay off debts and pay rents. It was estimated that Tuke emigrants in 1883 and 1884 sent back £2,000 in remittances to friends and family in the Clifden Union. By 1888 this sum had increased to £8,000.[48]

The Irish Parliamentary Party, under the leadership of Parnell, remained bitterly opposed to emigration. To them, Tuke's scheme amounted to nothing more than forced emigration, part of a government plan to further control the country through the depopulation of Ireland's 'best and brightest' – its potential leaders – leaving only 'the poor, the weak, the old, the lame, the sick, the blind, the dumb, and the imbecile and the insane'.

A key strand of Tuke's Scheme was the benefit of the consolidation of holdings through the emigration of entire families. In his reports, emphasis was placed on providing data on the outcomes. In the 1883 report on the Belmullet and Newport unions, Ruttledge-Fair acknowledged the importance of the disposal of holdings as 'a question of vital and paramount importance to those who remain, and one upon which the permanent success of the movement depends':

> It will be observed that of the 293 holdings vacated, 149 have passed to neighbouring Tenants; 106 have reverted to the Landlord, either by eviction or by possession being voluntarily surrendered by the outgoing Tenant; 18 holdings are 'waste', the emigrants not having given up possession, and the Landlord not having yet taken the necessary legal steps to obtain the same; while only 20 have been purchased by new Tenants.[49]

He concluded that in 273 out of 293 cases, the emigration of families had led to a consolidation of holdings. These figures, he claimed, 'conclusively prove the absolute falsity of the statements which have been made to the effect that the committee was digging fresh graves for the people'.[50] However, this was putting a gloss on the figures in order to paint the best possible picture. In reality, a high percentage of vacated land either reverted to the landlord or went to waste. The committee had little or no real influence other than persuasion.[51]

Continuing distress and the change of emphasis of support following 1884, demonstrated that the consolidation of holdings had not had the desired effect of making the remaining holdings more viable. At best, it served to avert worse congestion rather than facilitate consolidation.[52] In many areas most of the farms still remained under 20 acres. This land remained poor and unproductive, highlighting the importance of other sources of income. This was the direction that was adopted by the Congested Districts Board in the 1890s. Their work supported and encouraged local light industries, such as fisheries, and, importantly, improved railway links to connect the west with the rest of Ireland. No longer was the west cut off, neglected and forgotten.

Ultimately, the scheme, although ambitious, proved impracticable. Assisted emigration alone did not, and could not, solve Irish poverty. Numbers were too few and the timescale too short to make a real difference. It was an ambitious scheme which had been driven by humanitarian concerns and Tuke's belief that assisted emigration formed one part, although an important one, of providing a solution to the endemic poverty of the west of Ireland.

Yet in the end, emigration is all about people. To 'his' emigrants, Tuke was a hero. Applications for emigration outstripped places. The people went willingly, with no traditional 'wail' but with rousing cheers. For those starving people who were taken out of desperate poverty, the rewards were great. For this alone Tuke's scheme can be celebrated. It is a Tuke emigrant, who is left with the last word:

> In regards of Tom's appetite, he can consume 3 large bowls of tea, half-a-dozen of eggs, one pound of beefsteak regularly on each meal, together with many more choiceable vegetables on table – So you see, he improved a bully man in appetite since he left the old sod … I, myself, am getting rather too stout for hard work.

Notes

1 *The Galway Vindicator*, 20 May 1882, p. 3.
2 James Hack Tuke, *Distress in Ireland* (London, 1847).
3 James Hack Tuke, *A Visit to Connaught in the Autumn of 1847* (London, 1847).
4 James Hack Tuke, *Irish Distress and its Remedies: The Land Question. A Visit to Donegal and Connaught in the Spring of 1880* (London, 1880).
5 *The Times*, 27 March 1880, p. 3.
6 Invitation from the Duke of Bedford in Manuscript Collection: Religious Society of Friends (London, 1882). MSS 363.1.
7 Edward Fry, *James Hack Tuke: a Memoir* (London: Macmillan & Co., 1899), pp. 157–8.
8 H.F. Gregg, 'Two Nineteenth Century Quakers and the Irish Question, James Hack Tuke and Jonathan Pim 1846–1896', MA Thesis (Canterbury: University of Kent, 1984), p. 103.
9 Ciara Breathnach, *The Congested Districts Board of Ireland, 1891–1923: Poverty and Development in the West of Ireland* (Dublin, 2005), p. 21.
10 Fry, *James Hack Tuke*, p. 221.
11 *The Observer*, 12 September 2007, p. 24.
12 Gerald Moran, 'James Hack Tuke and assisted emigration from Galway and Mayo in the 1880s', in Mary Clancy (ed.), *The Emigrant Experience* (Galway, 1991), p. 74.

13 Ibid., p. 37.

14 These included Howard Hodgkin, Sydney Buxton, Miller Christy and William Rathbone.

15 Extracts from the Immigration Report of 1883 in Sessional Papers of 47 Victoria 1884 (14) at http://ist.uwaterloo.ca (accessed 12.09.2007).

16 Ibid.

17 Both the use of 'shteamer' and 'spidalling' suggests a humorous 'in-joke' between the major, Tuke and probably his wife, who accompanied him in his work.

18 *The Times*, 12 January 1883; 29 January 1883; 24 December 1883.

19 *The Times*, 5 February 1883, p. 3.

20 Sara Smyth, 'Tuke's Connemara Album', in C. Breathnach (ed.), *Framing The West: Images of Rural Ireland 1891–1920* (Dublin, 2007), pp. 29–47.

21 The 'wail' of departing emigrants was a feature of emigration during the Famine.

22 James Hack Tuke, 'With the Emigrants', *The Nineteenth Century*, Vol. XII (London, 1882), p. 152.

23 D. Fitzpatrick, *Irish Emigration 1801–1921* (The Economic and Social History Society of Ireland, 1984), p. 42.

24 Ibid.

25 'Reports and Papers Relating to the Proceedings of Mr Tuke's Fund for Assisting Emigration from Ireland, during the years 1882, 1883 and 1884'.

26 Gerald Moran, *Sending out Ireland's Poor: Assisted Emigration to North America in the Nineteenth Century* (Dublin, 2004), pp. 199–200.

27 Emigration from Ireland, 1882, 'Reports and Papers Relating to the Proceedings of Mr Tuke's Fund for Assisting Emigration from Ireland, during the years 1882, 1883 and 1884', p. 10.

28 The Royal Commission on the Depressed Condition of the Agricultural Interests, Minutes of Evidence, H.C. (c2778i) Vol. X, pp. 119–20.

29 Second Report of the Committee of Mr Tuke's Fund, 'Reports and Papers Relating to the Proceedings of Mr Tuke's Fund for Assisting Emigration from Ireland, during the years 1882, 1883 and 1884', p. 8.

30 Ibid.

31 Emigration from Ireland: Second Report of the Committee of Mr Tuke's Fund, 'Reports and Papers Relating to the Proceedings of Mr Tuke's Fund for Assisting Emigration from Ireland, during the years 1882, 1883 and 1884', p. 14.

32 Letter from Bishop Ireland, 'Reports and Papers Relating to the Proceedings of Mr Tuke's Fund for Assisting Emigration from Ireland, during the years 1882, 1883 and 1884', p. 15.

33 Letter from William Rathbone to Howard Hodgkin, 16 November 1882, MSS 369.

34 Kerby Miller, Reviewed Work: G. Moran, 'Sending Out Ireland's Poor', *Journal of Social History*, Spring 2005 (accessed 13.08.07).

35 *The Times*, 11 December 1883, p. 11.

36 James Hack Tuke, News from some Irish Emigrants, 'Reports and Papers Relating to the Proceedings of Mr Tuke's Fund for Assisting Emigration from Ireland, during the years 1882, 1883 and 1884', pp. 436–7.

37 Fry, James Hack Tuke, p. 197.

38 *The Galway Vindicator*, 10 November 1883, p. 4.

39 Emigration from Ireland; being the Third Report of the Committee of Mr Tuke's Fund (London, 1884), 'Reports and Papers Relating to the Proceedings of Mr Tuke's Fund for Assisting Emigration from Ireland, during the years 1882, 1883 and 1884', p. 21.

40 *The Nation*, 1 December 1883, p. 4.

41 Lord Brabazon, 'State-aided Emigration: its necessity', *The Nineteenth Century*, xciii (London, 1884).

42 Richmond Mayo Smith, 'Control of Immigration', *Political Science Quarterly*, Vol. 3, No 1 (Toronto, March 1888), pp. 46–77.

43 James Hack Tuke, Memorandum 13 June 1884, 'Reports and Papers Relating to the Proceedings of Mr Tuke's Fund for Assisting Emigration from Ireland during the years 1882,1883 and 1884' (London, 1884).

44 Emigration from Ireland: Second Report of the Committee of Mr Tuke's Fund, 'Reports and Papers Relating to the Proceedings of Mr Tuke's Fund for Assisting Emigration from Ireland, during the years 1882, 1883 and 1884', p. 14.

45 'Reports and Papers Relating to the Proceedings of Mr Tuke's Fund for Assisting Emigration from Ireland during the years 1882, 1883 and 1884' (London, 1884), p. 91.

46 Address from the People of Clifden and Connemara to James Hack Tuke (April, 1886), MSS 273.

47 This work was accomplished through the Congested Districts Board, of which Tuke was a founding member.

48 Moran, *Sending out Ireland's Poor*, p. 148.

49 Captain Ruttledge-Fair, Report on Emigration from Ireland: Second Report of the Committee of Mr Tuke's Fund, 'Reports and Papers Relating to the Proceedings of Mr Tuke's Fund for Assisting Emigration from Ireland, during the years 1882, 1883 and 1884', p. 31. Captain Ruttledge-Fair later became a major.

50 Ibid.

51 Moran, *Sending out Ireland's Poor*, p. 187.

52 Fitzpatrick, *Irish Emigration 1801–1921*, p. 21.

7

Irish Hard-Rock Miners in Ireland, Britain & the United States

Graham Davis & Matthew Goulding

Migration histories are usually written from within a cultural framework that reflects how individual countries view their own national story. Emigration from nineteenth-century Ireland has generally been understood as the result of poverty, a lack of capital investment and an unfair system of landholding all within an oppressive British administration of Ireland following the Act of Union.[1]

Irish immigration into Britain has more often than not been viewed within a negative framework.[2] The major settlements of poor Irish in Liverpool, Manchester and Glasgow were invariably associated with a host of social problems – poverty, overcrowding, disease, disorder and political violence.[3] The urban crisis of the 1830s and 1840s enveloped British cities undergoing a rapid expansion through industrialisation. At the same time, municipal government lacked the administrative means to deal with problems of inadequate housing, crime and epidemic diseases. It was unfortunate that mass Irish migration into Britain occurred during the period 1830–60. Poor Irish migrants became scapegoats for the myriad social problems arising from rapid urban expansion.

Once established by contemporary commentators, a negative stance towards the Irish could ignore the evidence that adult Irish migrants were generally healthier than the local populations of Liverpool and Manchester, or that considerable benefits accrued for the British economy in the provision of a highly mobile and adaptable workforce among Irish migrants, who included seasonal harvesters and railway navvies.[4] However, recent research on the Irish in Britain, summarised by Roy Foster, suggests that the old myths and stereotypes that have held sway for so long have largely been discredited.[5]

Irish immigration into the United States, after initial native hostility to poor famine migrants, has generally been perceived in a relatively positive light, as the Irish succeeded in a process of upward social mobility. The Irish integrated into American society and contributed to the rebuilding of the nation after the Civil War. Irish-American historians naturally celebrate the Irish contribution to the building of railways, their roles in the growth of the Catholic Church and as female teachers in the school system, their successes in the fields of sport and entertainment, and their role in local and national politics. Irish success in the longer term proved their worth as immigrants, but also demonstrated, to evident national satisfaction, 'the greatness of America'.[6]

Hard-Rock Miners

The central proposition in this chapter is that hard-rock miners migrated in response to economic factors at home and abroad: the classical 'push' and 'pull' factors. Notwithstanding the cultural filters of national histories, this truism holds good for migration within Ireland, between Ireland and Britain, and among the most numerous group that settled in the United States.

The starting point for understanding the reasons for migration to Britain and America must be conditions in Ireland, but also how those conditions have been represented by historians. Despite the evidence of the physical remains of old engine houses and abandoned mine shafts, the history of mining was erased from Irish school geography textbooks.[7] It did not fit the dominant narrative of agrarian poverty. In nineteenth-century Ireland, coal, iron, zinc, manganese, sulphur and gold were mined, but the most important centres were the copper-mining districts of Avoca in County Wicklow, Knockmahon in County Waterford and the Beara Peninsula in west Cork. Mining in Avoca and Knockmahon had begun in the eighteenth century and on the Beara Peninsula in 1812. By the mid-nineteenth century, Avoca directly employed 2,000 people, while Knockmahon and the Beara employed a further 1,200 respectively.[8] The copper mines brought additional employment and capital to the mining districts and an important supplement to poor agrarian economies. Alongside the miners who worked on the contract system below ground, half the workforce operated on the surface. These workers included blacksmiths, carpenters, stable-hands and carters, steam engineers and their labourers. The mines also employed significant numbers of women and children who prepared the ore for shipment and smelting across the Irish Sea in Swansea. Employment for women and children contributed an important element to the household economy of mining families. The miners also kept their smallholdings for growing food and, when the loss of the potato crop devastated south-western districts, Henry Puxley, the owner of the Allihies copper mines, arranged to have food imported to sustain the continuity of employment of his workers.[9] A retrospective report of 1889 claimed that £2,000 per month used to be paid to miners and labourers by Mr Puxley when he worked the Berehaven mines, and he cleared for many years, prior to the 1860s, £30,000 to £37,000 per annum profit. His income derived from mining was of paramount importance on his estate of 7,300 acres, described as of little agricultural value and situated in a poor mountainous district.[10]

Population loss during the famine was relatively small compared with most of south-west Ireland, which suffered greatly in those years.[11] Without employment in the copper mines afforded to the Beara Peninsula, an even greater loss of population, through death and emigration, would have occurred. Samuel Hussey, the Irish land agent, suggested in 1883 that 'nearly 2 millions of Irish could be employed on the fertile lands of America or in the colonies without allowing an acre in Ireland to go out of cultivation'.[12]

Population pressure was at its most severe in west Cork. In six western unions, population density regularly exceeded 600 per square mile of cultivated land, and in Castletown Union, it reached almost 1,400 per square mile – a figure higher than anywhere else in Ireland outside the urban unions.

As late as 1870, more than 80 per cent of the holdings in the Poor Law Unions of Castletown, Skull, Bantry and Clonakilty did not exceed £15 in value. Comparable figures in east Cork were under 55 per cent.[13] These indices of poverty provide an important context for the subsequent migration of copper miners. When the mines fell into decline, there was very little alternative employment in the area of west Cork, leaving the only prospect of taking mining skills and knowledge to other mining sites abroad.

Contemporary descriptions of the living and working conditions of the miners at Allihies present a picture of wretchedness, almost beyond imagination. However, such descriptions usually have an accompanying agenda so they need to be adopted with some care. The classic example is taken from a letter written by the Rev. G.T. Stoney to the *Cork Examiner*:

I have frequently visited the log shanty of the slave on the cotton plantations in South Carolina … I have knelt on the mud cabins on the mountains

of Connemara and the bogs of Roscommon, but never 'till I came to the
Berehaven mines did I witness such wretchedness of eye-revolting poverty.[14]

The date of the letter, 1868, is significant in that the miners were in dis-
pute with the Castletown Board of Guardians over the rejection of miners'
applications for admission to the workhouse. The Rev. Arthur Moynahan had
attempted to speak on behalf of the miners and Stoney was adding his support. Stoney was subsequently relieved of his position as curate of the mines
for his defence of the miners. This was not only a letter written in a highly
charged situation, but at a time when the miners were leaving for a new life
in America. Certainly, those left behind were living in desperate conditions.
While migration from the Beara began in the 1840s and can by association
with the famine years (1845–52) be connected with the poverty and poor
living conditions of the copper miners at Allihies, other global forces were at
work in prompting this movement from west Cork to mining districts in the
United States, first to the Keewanaw Peninsula in Michigan and later to Butte,
Montana. This was a movement that accelerated in the 1850s, 1860s and 1870s
and can be explained, not so much by poverty and famine in Ireland, but by
the severe challenges posed by the appearance of large quantities of Chilean
copper on the world market. This had the effect of depressing the price of
copper and reduced the scope for the employment of hard-rock miners in
Ireland and Britain. Nevertheless, Puxley's mines continued to be profitable
until he sold them in 1869 to the Mining Company of Ireland. Thereafter, the
mines became increasingly unprofitable and ceased working when they were
closed down in 1884.[15] In the mid-1850s, the price of copper was £140 per
ton, but by 1878–79 it had fallen to £90 per ton. It is important to recognise
that copper prices did not fall off a cliff but began a slow decline that affected
the livelihood and the employment prospects of the Allihies miners. The pattern of migration, a gradual increase in numbers over a generation, reflects
the changes in global copper prices rather than the conditions in Ireland.
Cornish tin miners were similarly affected by changes in the global price of
ore, and the opening up of new mines in South America, Australia and in the
United States prompted a parallel migration of 'Cousin Jacks', as they were
known, in search of alternative mining employment throughout the world.[16]
Comparisons between Irish and Cornish miners cast doubt on the conspiracy
theory of British imperialism as the determinant of labour migration incorporated into the nationalist narrative of events.

The Irish in Britain

There is plenty of scope for replacing old verities with new ones, substituting contemporary comment, with its built-in prejudice and political agendas, with hard data on the actual condition of the Irish in Britain and recognising that Victorian Britain contained very diverse regions and communities.

Roger Swift and Sheridan Gilley have done much to present the 'state of the art' on the Irish in nineteenth-century Britain in three collections of essays and a volume of contemporary documents. They have also proposed an agenda for further research. This includes a need to know more about Irish settlement, especially outside the areas of greatest concentration, demography, in and out migration, social mobility, employment patterns, particularly amongst rural workers, and mixed marriages. Until further regional studies are undertaken, Professor Swift has argued, 'there will always be the danger that the experience of the Irish in south Lancashire – especially Liverpool – will continue to unduly colour, if not dominate, our understanding of the Irish in Britain during the period'.[17]

Some of the issues identified above are addressed, in the first instance, with two regional studies of the hard-rock miners of Cornwall, in the south-west of England, and of Cumbria, in the north-west. They are based on a study of the 1861 census at the high point of the recorded Irish-born in Britain. In England and Wales, 601,634 Irish-born (3 per cent of the population) were recorded in 1861 and a further 204,083 Irish-born (6.7 per cent of the population) were recorded in Scotland.[18]

Few studies have attempted to capture all the Irish rather than the more conservative category of Irish-born. A new definition goes beyond the Irish-born to include other family members. It has long been held, but never tested, that the true figure for the Irish in Britain can be arrived at by doubling the Irish-born totals. This has always looked to be a very crude figure and is unlikely to be a true reflection of the varied economic and social structures of different communities where the Irish settled. For example, we know that the gender balance varied significantly between male-dominated mining communities, such as Camborne in Cornwall or garrison towns such as Plymouth in Devon, and female-dominated towns, such as Bath where Irish domestic servants were prominent.[19] Different family structures would surely follow but will require more precise analysis before we can offer a more refined amendment to a simple doubling of the Irish-born totals.

In addition to casting a wider net to include the children of Irish parents born out of Ireland, the movement of families is traced through the location of child births, so identifying the pattern of movement from Ireland to

Britain. The practice of Irish migrants to keep moving on in search of better opportunities elsewhere presents particular problems, along with the inadequacy of the census data in providing places of origin in Ireland. However, some clear patterns are still discernible in the movement of Irish miners to different parts of Britain.

A diversity of experience defines the Irish in Britain. Set against the Irish poor found in the slums of Liverpool, Manchester and Glasgow, Professor MacRaild points to the prosperity of the Irish in the north-east towns of Newcastle and Gateshead and the Cumbrian community of Cleator Moor.[20] Before an Irish community in one census date can be compared with those at a later date, it needs to be recognised that high levels of physical mobility make it difficult to provide a straight comparison. The Irish recorded in the census in 1851 were not the same people as those recorded in 1871.

Donald Akenson argues that the Irish in Britain should be studied in the context of the Irish diaspora – accepting that Britain acted as a vital hub between Ireland and the rest of the world – and the interconnected nature of Irish migration worldwide.[21] Irish migrants that settled in Britain probably accounted for between one-fifth and one-quarter of the total of Irish emigrants – a figure of 4 million was recorded by the registrar-general in the period 1852–1910.[22] Others were short-stay migrants in Britain en route to the Americas or Australasia from British ports. Some of these are captured in the census returns, located in emigration depots (as in Plymouth, for instance); others are not. Then there were around 60,000 harvesters who came to earn money to pay the rent on their holdings back in Ireland. The latter rarely showed up in the census returns, mostly taken in March–April, before the summer harvest season had begun. Such anomalies bring into question the reliability of census totals, but also pose a challenge in using census data more comprehensively.

Differential Movement from Ireland to British Centres of Mining

Our purpose is to set alongside the Irish experience in Cornwall with Irish miners in Cumbria. This involves identifying patterns of migration and settlement, age and household structures, and the competition for skilled work within the mining industry.

Cornwall, as Louise Miskell has shown, scarcely features on the map of the Irish in Britain and neither have Irish migrants been regarded as worthy of detailed study by Cornish historians, despite the central importance of mining

in the county.[23] Her study of Camborne, 1861–82, is concerned with the settlement patterns of Irish miners and their families, and adds an alternative case
study to the well-known examples of dense inner-city living in Liverpool and
Manchester. Miskell provides a local context to the mix of mining and agricultural life among Irish migrants and to the anti-Irish riot that took place in 1882.

Miskell uses the evidence of the 1861 census for Camborne to show a pattern of migration from the south-western counties of Ireland, such as Cork,
Waterford and Limerick. This confirms a regional pattern of Irish movement
found in other south-western cities, such as Bristol and Bath.[24] The migrant
Irish were a predominantly young group, as mining was a job for young men,
fit and able to do the work. The presence of some older children born in
Ireland compared with a majority of younger ones in Camborne suggests
that few Irish families had been in Camborne much longer than ten years.
However, by 1881, a settled Irish community clearly existed with established
family groups. There was also a change in the pattern of migration. The Irish
in Camborne in 1861 had often come via southern English counties, such as
Kent, Sussex, Gloucestershire and London. This pattern was less evident in
1881, when the Cornish copper- and tin-mining industry was in decline.

A broader view of Irish miners in Cornwall can be constructed from a county-
wide analysis of the census data in 1861, extracted heroically by the late John
Perkins. The census records 3,135 Irish living in Cornwall. This includes the
Irish-born and men, women and children of mixed descent. Only 317 of this
total can be clearly identified as part of the mining industry, including women
recorded as tin dressers, who continued the Irish pattern of women's work.
The total numbers, including family members of miners, came to 759 – 144
separate families, in all including 29 lodgers. Irish communities were most
prominent in the district of Kerrier, with 71 per cent of Irish miners and their
families, a total of 536, living there. Camborne (123 Irish), Illogan (101), Brea
(96) and Redruth (76) were the main centres within Kerrier. A further 127 or
17 per cent were found in the district of Carrick, with St Agnes (41) having
the largest numbers of Irish outside Carrick. The census does not record con-
sistently the precise nature of miners' occupations, but it is clear that the Irish
were employed predominantly in copper and tin mining.

The great majority, 240 of the 317 miners, were born in Ireland. The
remaining 77 were a mix of children born in England and old enough to
work in the mines (21), of half-Irish parentage (27), or born in Ireland but
of English descent (11). The remaining 18 were children of Irish parents but
born outside England or Ireland. These patterns point to the movement of
Irish miners to Cornwall before 1861, but also suggest a smaller movement of

Cornish mining families who had spent time in Ireland, where their children were born. The presence of Cornish miners who had worked alongside Irish miners in Ireland also suggests where Irish miners would have acquired the knowledge of Cornish mining sites. While the census provides limited evidence on birthplace in Ireland – most miners were recorded as born in Ireland – the specific places mentioned have a clear logic to them. Cork was the most commonly recorded birthplace. This suggests, even from the small numbers involved, that miners migrated from the Beara Peninsula to Cornwall where they could use their mining skills.

From the birthplaces of children, born to twenty-eight Irish families, we can trace the migration routes to Cornwall. London was listed six times and Wales five times, with the remaining seventeen spread out over places in southern England, with the exception of France, India and Bolivia (another mining centre). This pattern confirms the southern route from Cork, via South Wales, to Bristol or London. A specific example of such family migration is the Keeffe family. Daniel Keeffe was born in Ireland in 1801 and his wife, Catherine, was also born in Ireland in 1815. Their eldest son, Richard, aged 17 in 1861, was born in Ireland in 1844; the next son, Thomas (15), was born in Bristol in 1846, so pinpointing the family's arrival in England between 1844 and 1846. Another son, Daniel (12), was also born in Bristol in 1849. The father, Daniel, and his three sons were all recorded as tin-mine labourers in the 1861 census. The youngest son, John (4), was born in Camborne in 1857. So we can point to the second-stage migration from Bristol to Camborne between 1849 and 1857. An obvious economic advantage for the Keeffe family in moving to Camborne was the employment opportunities available for the sons as well as for the father, so enhancing the household income considerably, at least for a time.

Taken together, the evidence of the numbers of the first children born to Irish mining families in Cornwall points to a doubling of the totals during the 1850s, with an all-time high in the year 1860. Not surprisingly, the Irish population of Camborne was predominantly young, with 71 per cent aged under 30.

Cumbria in 1861 had a far larger Irish community than Cornwall. There were 17,471 Irish living in the county, with 1,569 or 9 per cent recorded as miners. Irish miners included 700 coalminers (44 per cent), 655 copper miners (41 per cent), with 41 miners (3 per cent) unspecified. Again, as in Cornwall, the Irish population was predominantly young, with 72 per cent aged under 31. The migration pattern was, however, shaped by a quite different geography. The short distance and ease of transport between Ireland and Cumbria, and the close proximity to Scotland, show up in the chosen routes. Of the 17,471 Irish and their families, 454 were born in Scotland (107 were Scottish wives and 269 were either sons or daughters). Of the 6,860 Irish living in Cumbria born in England, 91 per cent were born in Cumbria and only 624 were born elsewhere in England. This information reinforces a direct route from Ireland to Cumbria or via Scotland. But from where in Ireland did they originate?

The lack of specific Irish birthplace data in the census is frustrating, but what survives is interesting. Of the 10,113 Irish-born, 9,333 were given no specific birthplace. The place that had the highest recorded entries (292) was County Down, in the north of Ireland, in close proximity to north-west ports such as St Mary's and Workington, as well as to coastal transport to the west of Scotland. Other places that feature in the census record – Antrim, Belfast, Dublin and Armagh – link the east of Ireland with the north-west of England.

The exception to this was the south-east county of Wicklow, second only to County Down, with ninety-six entries. This endorses the idea of mining skill migration, with a link between the mining centres of Avoca in Wicklow and the mining centres of Cumbria, such as Cleator Moor.

Cleator Moor, in Cleator Parish, was a rural parish with a linen mill in 1801.[25] Its population of 362 grew to 818 by 1821, with growth coming via employment opportunities in the flax mill. This was short-lived, as the Birley family, owners of the mill, went bankrupt in 1830 and the population was reduced to 487 in 1831. Population growth resumed with the reopening of mining in 1842, along with the Cleator Moor Ironworks. By 1861, the population was 3,995, dependent on iron ore mining, coal mining and a reopened flax mill, in addition to employment in agriculture.

What is interesting in terms of Irish migration and settlement in Cleator Moor is the initial influx from Ireland of female labour employed in the flax mill. The women came first followed by the men working in the mines. Thomas Ainsworth, the flax mill proprietor, established two smelting furnaces on the far side of the moor. His links with Ireland, purchasing flax from the country, may also have prompted female migration from the northern counties of Down and Antrim, which were experiencing problems for the domestic industry in the mechanisation of the linen industry centred on the Belfast region. Brenda Collins has identified an important skill migration of textile workers from Irish counties to Scotland.[26] A parallel movement looks to have occurred in the case of Cumbria. There is some evidence that Irish migrants to Cumbria may have come via Scotland as well as into north-western ports, such as Whitehaven and St Mary's. The migration of female flax workers, followed by male mine workers, reinforces the point about family structures and the benefits to household incomes from the opportunities for women to add to male earnings.

At the time of the 1861 census, the population of Cleator and Cleator Moor was 3,995. By one measure that included the Irish-born, those married to an Irish person and the children of at least one Irish parent, 2,073 or 51.8 per cent could be described as Irish. It is important to recognise the question of intermarriage between the Irish-born and their non-Irish partners, which is as much an indication of integration of the Irish in British communities as a wider definition of Irishness. Certainly the children of Irish parents need to be included in the process of obtaining a fuller picture of the Irish population in Britain.

Facilitating the ironworks at Cleator Moor was the railway link in 1855 with Frizington to Whitehaven, Egremont and Barrow, and also the Bessemer process for steel making that gave a boost to the industry in west Cumbria. With the lowest phosphorous content in the country, iron ore in west Cumberland held a monopoly in the market. Iron ore production rose from 200,788 tons to 400,306 tons between 1855 and 1859. There were now more Irishmen: 794 Irish-born males compared with 664 Irish-born females. Mining families had large numbers of children: 746 children under the age of 14, with 206 born in Ireland and 407 born in Cleator, 379 of them born since the previous census in 1851. Census data on the children's birthplaces points to the key migration of Irish families to Cleator during the 1850s.

Mining dominated occupational distribution. Among those with specified occupations, 374 or 40.9 per cent were employed in the iron ore industry (plus ten masons and two bricklayers), who might have also been attached; 67 or 7.3 per cent in the coal mines; 166 or 18 per cent worked in the flax mills; and a further 163 or 17.8 per cent were described as general labourers. Another twenty-eight were employed in agriculture as carters or farm labourers. Most women and children, 151, worked in the flax industry. Others found employment as servants (67) or made a living taking in their fellow countrymen as lodging-house keepers (11). There were 358 households within the Irish community, with 337 born in Ireland, and families formed the dominant household structure. Alongside family structures, there were also significant numbers of lodgers, 332 in all, out of which only twelve were living with their spouse and fifty were married.

Rapid population growth was not matched by improved sanitary provision and other amenities in Cleator Moor. In the absence of a market, its inhabitants travelled to Whitehaven by train on Saturdays to do their shopping. The Irish in Cleator Moor had a reputation for lawlessness and drunkenness in 'a terribly rough and semi-barbarous community'.[27] Such descriptions, however, have proved to be more informative of the authors than their subjects. The Irish could not be blamed for the lack of amenities in Cleator Moor, but were invariably scapegoated in a negative association with poor conditions.

United States

'The Irish were a rural people in Ireland', as William Shannon succinctly put it, 'and became a city people in the United States'. This view forms part of the dominant narrative of Irish America in the post-famine era. David Doyle confirms that the incoming Irish became the most urbanised people in the world, while Americans remained a mostly rural population until 1914.[28] And following Oscar Handlin's pioneering urban history, over four-fifths of regional literature on the Irish has been centred on towns and cities. However, sizeable numbers of Irish were found outside the main centres in California (50,000) and Louisiana (17,000), living in urban, industrial or mining communities.[29]

The Irish progressed more rapidly in west coast communities like San Francisco in comparison with the plight of poor settlers in Boston or New York.[30] Early Irish migrants, such as merchants in New Orleans or ranchers in south Texas, became part of a social elite.[31] It should also be recognised that huge personal fortunes were made by Irish mining entrepreneurs in Nevada.[32] These stories remain outside the main concentrations of Irish population in America and outside the mainstream of the meta-narrative of Irish America. A focus on the migration and settlement of hard-rock miners adds to the diversity of Irish experience and further qualifies the usefulness of a dominant, American narrative.

At the same time that employment opportunities were decreasing on the Beara Peninsula, new mining operations were starting up in the early 1840s in the Copper Country on the Keweenaw Peninsula, Michigan. The Quincy Mining Company, near Hancock, and the Calumet & Hecla Mining Company, around Calumet, were large-scale operations that ultimately produced major quantities of copper for the American and world markets, and employed thousands of workers drawn from many different nationalities. In the period 1840–80, the Michigan copper district was responsible for around three-quarters of US production.[33]

Professor Bill Mulligan suggests that the investment behind these mining operations originated largely from Boston, a well-established centre of Irish settlement. Moreover, the Boston newspapers provided extensive coverage of the Michigan mines, so alerting Irish migrants to the prospects for employment.[34]

To add to this speculation, we trace the movement of Irish families that settled in Calumet, in Houghton County, one part of the Keweenaw Peninsula.[35] A micro-analysis of Irish-born families in the censuses of 1870 and 1880 provides evidence of the direction of migration and the rate of movement of Irish miners to America. The two censuses confirm a considerable presence of Irish-born miners in Calumet, alongside miners from England (primarily Cornwall), Germans, Scandinavians and some French, Canadians and Italians.

In 1870, 276 Irish-born adult names were recorded, 141 described as miners, 84 as labourers. The distinction is important because it is indicative of skill levels among Irish migrants and dispels the old myth that only the Cornish were skilled miners and the Irish were merely labourers. In addition, a further twenty-one male occupations included carpenters (4), engineers (2), black-smiths (5), and employees in stamp mills (3), who were all probably employed in mining. The total number of Irish-born females with specified occupations was 154; 132 of them were described as keeping house and 12 as domes-tic servants. Unlike in Ireland, females were not employed in the American mines. Families were dependent on male earnings or were supplemented by women providing board and lodgings for single miners.

Arrival dates in the United States have been calculated from the birth years of children born to Irish parents. Out of 100 recorded entries, thirty arrived in the 1850s, twenty-six from 1855 onwards, seventy during the 1860s, fifty of these between 1864 and 1869, suggestive of an American Civil War effect on reducing the level of immigration. Other states show up en route to Michigan that illustrate the pattern of movement among Irish mining families. Predominantly, Irish miners came into the north-east ports of entry, Boston and New York, and out of seventeen recorded instances, five listed births in Massachusetts, two in New Hampshire, Ohio, New York and Illinois, and one each in Iowa, Rhode Island, New Jersey and Virginia – evidence of a clear, geographical path en route to Michigan. There is little evidence of Irish miners having spent much time in England judging by examples of intermarriage and the location of child births. Overwhelmingly, the migration of Irish miners was directly from Ireland to the United States and primarily to Michigan.

As expected, the census data confirms that mining migration was pre-dominantly a young man's game. Of 100 entries where age of entry can be determined by the births of children in the US, seventy-four were aged up to 30 and twenty-six over 30. If we include the numbers aged 31 to 35, the numbers increase to eighty-nine in total. Virtually nine out of ten migrants who entered America were in the age group up to 35. Of the 101 entries for boarders in lodging houses, eighty were in the age group up to 35. Predominantly, migration occurred among men in their twenties. What is also significant about the 1870 data is that more young men lived as boarders (47) than in family structures (18). This suggests that single young men went out to become established with work in the mines before starting a family or bring-ing their wives and children out with them. Also, of the 276 males, 114 or 41 per cent had become US citizens, so indicating an intention to stay in America.

The problem of a lack of evidence of the Irish county of origin in the census record can, to an extent, be countered by the use of surname frequency.

The highest name frequencies shown in the 1870 and 1880 censuses point to a strong connection with west Cork: Sullivan, 38 and 24; Harrington, 16 and 15; Shea, 12 and 9; and Murphy, 8 and 6. These surnames match the most popular Cork names, as Timothy Neill has shown.[36] In comparing Irish surnames in 1870, seventy-seven different names were recorded, and sixty-one in 1880, with forty-one names in common at both dates. This suggests some differences in the structure of migration as well as some common elements.

The biggest difference observed between 1870 and 1880 is the change in living patterns. Whereas in 1870 considerable numbers of Irish miners were living in lodging houses, paying for their board and lodging, by 1880 this pattern had disappeared. Of the total of 141 Irish-born adult males, all were living within a family structure. In fifteen cases, additional family members, such as mothers and brothers-in-law, were also present. In a further five cases, boarders were taken into the family unit, providing additional household income. What can be deduced is that miners that stayed in Calumet had families who had joined them later. Other single men looked for better prospects in other mining centres in California, Nevada and Montana, or took their chances in less hazardous forms of employment.

Miners invariably had large families which meant that their wages had to sustain large numbers of women and children. High wages were undoubtedly a factor in inducing large numbers of Europeans to migrate to the mining districts of America. An unusual comment was inserted into the 1880 census for Calumet which provides evidence of miners' wages at the time. It reads: 'All labour marked on these schedules when not otherwise designated are working at the Copper Mines on $30–35 per month + 12 months of the year.' Miners were among the highest paid workers in America. It was hard, physical and hazardous labour, but for young men it was an attractive option compared with comparative wages in Ireland. In 1880, miners, plus their wives and children, totalled 921 people in 141 households. In addition, there were a further 37 relatives and lodgers, making a total of 958, producing an average household size of 6.8 persons. The most common size of family was in the six to eight range, classically husband, wife and children, adding up to a total of 280 people or 29 per cent of all families.

The American census also provides information on the wealth of families. This may not be all that reliable – most likely the figures underestimated the true state of things – but, nevertheless, it does offer evidence of a few individuals who stood out from the mass who had little to declare. Most entries showed estate property ranging from $50 to $500. Five entries showed estates worth over $1,000:

Bartholomew Shea, aged 29, deputy sheriff, property valued at $1,000. Michael Ryan, aged 40, labourer, with a wife and three children, five boarders and a servant. His property was valued at $1,200 and personal wealth at $200.

John Ryan, aged 42, Mining Captain, with a wife and 5 children and a servant. His property was valued at $3,000 and his personal wealth at $10,000.

Hugh McGuirk, aged 31, a gardener, an English wife and 36 boarders. His real estate was valued at $3,300 and his personal wealth at $2,000.

James Kirwin, aged 30, a general merchant, with a wife and daughter. His real estate which must have included the store was valued at $45,000 and his personal wealth at $3,000.

What is evident here is that the way to acquire wealth was to take in boarders or to sell goods to the mining community. It is well known that fortunes were made in the Californian Gold Rush from providing services in hotels and boarding houses or from selling shovels and clothing – rather more than came from panning for gold. The most enterprising of immigrants moved out of the dangerous life of the miner and took up alternative ways of making a living. For others, having lost their physical strength and endurance, less arduous work became a necessity.

Similar results on age structure were found in the 1880 census. From data derived from the births of children born in the United States, 72 per cent of the total of 120 arrivals were in the age group up to 30, and 28 per cent were over 30. On the states or countries found en route to Michigan, Massachusetts led the way with six entries, followed by New Jersey with four, and Pennsylvania, Maryland and Kansas with one each. England, with Cornwall mentioned once, also had four entries. Overwhelmingly, Irish miners made their way directly to the United States. Out of 116 miners traceable to their year of arrival in the United States, twenty arrived in the period 1856–64, forty-nine in the years 1865–72 (post-Civil War) and forty-seven during 1873–80.

We also know that with the decline in the numbers of Irish-born miners in Michigan between 1870 and 1880, overtaken by native Cornish and Canadians, Germans and Scandinavians, there is evidence of a further migration to Montana, where the Irish built up a strong presence. O'Neill has also qualified the old skill argument that used to distinguish Cornish (skilled) miners from the allegedly unskilled Irish miners. While Cornishmen were overwhelmingly classed as miners (433) rather than as labourers (40), a majority of the Irish were differentiated in the same way (456 miners and 398 labourers). In comparison with Germans (115 miners and 260 labourers), Americans (19 miners and 147 labourers) and Canadians (9 miners and 422 labourers), the Irish had a markedly superior skill ratio.

Comparisons with the Cornish miners suggest that while a rivalry existed, it was not so much over religious differences (Methodist and Catholic), but rather in terms of acquiring the most skilled and lucrative mining contracts. In Michigan, both groups were prompted by the same economic conditions as at home and by new opportunities abroad to improve their earning power. After 1870, Irish miners began looking for the benefits of a near-monopoly in Montana, where competition with the Cornish for the most skilled work was less of a factor as Irishman Richard Daly was the self-styled 'copper king' of the biggest mine in America.[37]

Conclusions

A study of the migration of hard-rock miners from Ireland to Britain and the United States is interpreted within the framework of cultural filters that apply to national histories in all three countries that possess their own meta-narratives. A negative view of an 'oppressed' Ireland informs the view of migrants forced into 'exile'. A pessimistic approach to the 'problems' associated with Irish immigrants has dominated much of the historical discourse in Britain. A more long-term, positive attitude to the Irish and their contribution to the building of America colours much of the Irish-American historiography.

The focus on the movement of miners opens up some of the regions in Britain and the USA that have received less attention from scholars in the past. Placed alongside the parallel movement of Cornish and European miners, Irish miners may be seen as part of the global forces of new discoveries of ore, dramatic price changes, new investment and cheaper transport. Fundamentally, miners were economic migrants engaged in a process of skilled migration, with individuals and families looking for better pay overseas. Irish mining skill and experience were transferred to British and American centres of mining along recognised shipping routes: via the south-west English ports of Bristol and Plymouth, and into north-west English ports, sometimes via Scotland, and into the north-east American ports.

Notes

1 Liz Curtis, *Nothing but the Same Old Story* (Belfast, 1996); Tim Pat Coogan, *Wherever Green is Worn: The Story of the Irish Diaspora* (London, 2000).

2 R. Swift & S. Gilley (eds), *The Irish in the Victorian City* (London, 1985); *The Irish in Britain, 1815–1939* (London, 1989); *The Irish in Victorian Britain: The Local Dimension* (Dublin, 1999); W.J. Lowe, *The Irish in Mid-Victorian Lancaster: The Shaping of a*

Working-Class Community (New York, 1990); Donald M. MacRaild, *Irish Migrants in Modern Britain, 1750–1922* (Basingstoke & London, 1999).

3 F. Neal, *Sectarian Violence: The Liverpool Experience, 1819–1914* (Manchester, 1988); J.M. Werly, 'The Irish in Manchester 1832–1849', *Irish Historical Studies*, Vol. 18 (1973), pp. 345–58.

4 Graham Davis, *The Irish in Britain, 1815–1914* (Dublin, 1991).

5 Roy Foster, *Paddy & Mr. Punch: Connections in Irish and English History* (London, 1993), pp. 285–6.

6 W.V. Shannon, *The American Irish* (New York, revised edn 1966); Dennis Clark, *The Irish in Philadelphia* (Philadelphia, 1973); T.H. O'Connor, *The Boston Irish: A Political History* (Boston & London, 1995).

7 Des Cowman, 'Life and Labour in Three Irish Mining Communities circa 1840', *Saothar* (1983), pp. 10–19.

8 Ibid.

9 James S. Donnelly Jr, *The Land and the People of Nineteenth-Century Cork: The Rural Economy and the Land Question* (London & New York, 1975), p. 165 note 150.

10 *Cork Constitution*, 6 February 1889, quoted in Donnelly, p. 165.

11 The population decline for the county of Cork continued from 1841 through to 1891: 149,000 labourers and servants and 41,000 farmers were reduced to 34,000 labourers and servants and 29,000 farmers, amounting, as Donnelly claims, to 'a social revolution'; Donnelly, p. 229.

12 *The Times*, 30 April 1883, quoted in Donnelly, pp. 867–8.

13 Donnelly, p. 230.

14 *Cork Examiner*, 4 March 1868, in Colman Mahony, 'Copper Mining at Allihies, Co. Cork', *Journal of the Cork Historical and Archaeological Society* (January 1987), pp. 71–84.

15 Colman Mahony, 'Copper Mining at Allihies, Co. Cork'.

16 Sharron P. Schwartz, 'Brooking "The Great Divide": The Evolution and Impact of Cornish Translocalism in Britain and the U.S.A.', *Journal of American Ethnic History*, Vol. 25, No 203, pp. 169–89.

17 For details of Swift and Gilley's work, see note 2.

18 Census of England and Wales, 1861. Census of Scotland, 1861.

19 Colin Pooley, 'Segregation or integration? The residential experience of the Irish in mid-Victorian Britain', in R. Swift & S. Gilley, *The Irish in Britain, 1815–1939*, pp. 60–83. Pooley identified Colchester, Winchester and Barrow as having the highest male/female ratios of Irish-born (314.2, 235.6 and 233.8 respectively in 1871), and Bath, Bury St Edmonds and Preston as having the lowest in the top twenty towns in Britain (48.4, 58.0 and 60.0 respectively), Table 2.3, p. 69.

20 D.M. MacRaild, *Culture, Conflict and Migration: The Irish in Victorian Cumbria* (Liverpool, 1998).

21 Donald H. Akenson, *The Irish Diaspora: A Primer* (Belfast, 1993).

22 Cormac O'Grada, 'A Note on Nineteenth-Century Irish Emigration Statistics', *Population Studies*, 29 (1975), pp. 143–9.

23 Louise Miskell, 'Irish Immigrants in Cornwall: The Camborne Experience, 1861–1882', in Swift & Gilley, *The Irish in Victorian Britain: The Local Dimension*, pp. 31–51.

24 David Large, 'The Irish in Bristol in 1851: A Census Enumeration', in Swift & Gilley, *The Irish in the Victorian City*, pp. 37–58; Graham Davis, 'Social Decline and Slum Conditions: Irish Migrants in Bath's History', *Bath History*, Vol. 8 (2000), pp. 134–47.

25 Amanda Shephard, 'The Irish in Cleator Moor', transcript, West Cumbria College, Cleator Moor Library.

26 Brenda Collins, 'Irish Emigration to Dundee and Paisley during the First Half of the Nineteenth Century', in J.M. Goldstrom & L.A. Clarkson (eds), *Irish Population and Society: Essays in Honour of the late K.H. Connell* (Oxford, 1981).

27 Quoted in Amanda Shephard, 'The Irish in Cleator Moor'.

28 David N. Doyle, 'The Remaking of Irish-America, 1845–1880', in J.J. Lee & Marion R. Casey (eds), *Making the Irish American: History and Heritage of the Irish in the United States* (Glucksman Ireland House & New York University, 2006), pp. 213–52.

29 Doyle, 'The Remaking of Irish America, 1845–1880', p. 225.

30 R.A. Burchell, *The San Francisco Irish, 1848–1880* (Manchester, 1979).

31 Earl Niehaus, *The Irish in New Orleans, 1800–1860* (Baton Rouge, 1965); Graham Davis, *Land! Irish Pioneers in Mexican and Revolutionary Texas* (College Station, 2002).

32 Dom De Quille, *The Big Bonanza* (Borzoi Book, 1947).

33 William H. Mulligan Jr, 'From the Beara to the Keweenaw: The Migration of Irish Miners from Allihies, County Cork to the Keweenaw Peninsula, Michigan, U.S.A., 1845–1880', *Journal of the Mining Heritage Trust of Ireland*, 1 (2001), pp. 19–24.

34 Ibid., p. 23.

35 The American Censuses, Calumet Precinct, Houghton County, Michigan, 1870 & 1880.

36 Timothy O'Neil, 'Miners in migration: the case of the nineteenth-century Irish and Irish-American copper miners – Statistical Data included', *Eire-Ireland: Journal of Irish Studies* (spring–summer 2001), pp. 124–40.

37 David M. Emmons, *The Butte Irish: Class and Ethnicity in an American Mining Town, 1875–1925* (Urbana & Chicago: University of Illinois Press, 1989).

8

Reconstructed Memory: Irish Emigrant Letters from the Americas

Graham Davis

With emigrant communities everywhere the memory of homeland has to be kept in aspic. The perspective over one's shoulder must remain identical to that recorded by the parting glance – even if that happened two (or more) genera-tions back, and even if the remembered impression is spectacularly contradicted by the mother country itself as experienced on return visits.[1]

As Roy Foster points out, when the last generation of Irish historians exam-ined the way in which their history had been written up, some of the most agonised responses came from the émigrés themselves.

Surviving Irish emigrant letters represent a small proportion of the many thousands originally written. In turn, surviving letters are not a true reflec-tion of the millions of Irish who left their native land. Inevitably, the illiterate did not have a voice, although the semi-literate did manage to set down their own thoughts and experiences. Protestant letters outnumber those written by Catholics despite the great majority of Catholics in Ireland and amongst Irish migrants from the 1840s onwards.

Among historians, the ownership of received historical memory is fiercely guarded. Kerby Miller, a leading American specialist on Irish emigrant letters, has identified a culture of exile among the Irish abroad. The idea of enforced exile became incorporated into the mindset of many Irish emigrants, serving as a rational explanation for their departure and continued absence, even long after they had prospered and had no realistic intention of returning to Ireland.[2] The way migration was understood belonged to an oppression history in which migrants are depicted as unwilling victims of English rule. The open declaration of the motive of individual advancement was unacceptable in a traditional, rural environment where community and family loyalties were dominant. The culture of exile was a cloak to disguise individual aspirations. In reality, Miller has argued that Irish emigration was surrounded by conflicting pressures, and emigrants themselves possessed highly ambivalent attitudes. Many farmers and tradesmen believed emigration was essential for the process of modernisation, a process synonymous with increasing bourgeois dominance and made possible only by a clearing out of the poor cottiers and landless labourers from Ireland. Emigration reduced the fear of potential agrarian violence in opposition to the consolidation of tenant holdings among the large farmers. For parents on smallholdings, it eased the way for the painful disinheritance of children without the prospect of unbearable family conflict. Miller has suggested that the theme of emigration as exile, manifest in speeches, newspapers and, most especially, the emigrant songs of the period, provided a way of reconciling tensions and anxieties.

Michael Kenneally, a Canadian literary scholar, has identified a need to employ the techniques of textual criticism to emigrant letters, not merely to extract historical detail. Letters can be examined as linguistic and rhetorical forms of self-expression. In the search for identity and nationhood, it can be revealing to focus on the tone and tenor of language, the stock phrases, the omissions and silences. His trawl through unpublished Canadian sources reveals shifting notions of home, a nostalgic remembrance of interior space and the importance of familiar things recalled. A more limited life in Canada meant that heaven became the real home, a place where the family would be reunited. Over time there was a discernible evolution of self revealed in letters to Ireland.[3]

Edmundo Murray is the leading historian of the Irish in Argentina and is also the editor of a collection of emigrant letters.[4] What is particularly interesting about Murray's interpretation is the act of 'becoming Irish'. Emigrants were not Irish, he argues, because they were born in Ireland. They had to undergo a process of transformation that gradually modified their values over time. When they made the transatlantic journey to Argentina, an informal colony of the British Empire dependent on British imported goods, they became *Ingleses*. It suited them to adopt an English identity as British subjects in a country ruled by an Anglophile elite that believed in the superiority of the races of northern Europe. From the early twentieth century, with nationalism becoming dominant among the Argentine governing elite, it became fashionable to discard English ways and garments, and adopt the manners and garb of the *gaucho*. The Irish followed in becoming Argentines. A century later, with their native Ireland experiencing an economic miracle that now has petered out in the financial maelstrom of 2008, it became acceptable again to become Irish – to celebrate St Patrick's Day, to decorate their houses with shamrocks and once more to be moved by stories of the Great Hunger (a tragedy that by no means affected all their families in the past, as some came from the relatively prosperous counties of Westmeath, Longford and Wexford). Murray shows convincingly that identity and the memory of the old country were subject to a surprising fluidity and captures the ability of Irish emigrants to adapt to new circumstances.

This last insight has quite a modern ring and ties up with the work of Mary Corcoran, a sociologist. She has interviewed returning Irish migrants after spending time working abroad during the 1990s, returning to a more prosperous Ireland enjoying the benefits of the Celtic Tiger and forming part of an increased return migration process – a reversal of population loss over many decades. She writes of Irish migrants reconstructing their identity as a result of the migrant experience and being often critical of Irish ways that now seem old fashioned in a slower pace of life.[5]

These four, not mutually exclusive, ideas – the memory of Ireland kept in aspic, the culture of exile, a discernible evolution of self and an invented or reconstructed Irishness – form the context of an examination of a selection of nineteenth-century Irish emigrant letters, drawn from Canada, through the United States to Mexican Texas and Argentina in the south.

First, however, it is important to recognise that the emigrant experience extended to several million people. A small and unrepresentative sample left the trace of a written record in the form of letters and journals. They wrote as individuals and their stories represent a wide spectrum of experience. The journey of migration and settlement involved great hopes, much privation, heartache, many setbacks and, it should be acknowledged, the prospect of a better life in the New World, if not for the individuals themselves then most likely for their children. Emigration was commonly a family strategy, mostly self-funded and often involving several stages of movement for different family members. So, we should be wary of an all-encompassing meta-narrative that tells the story of the Irish in Canada or the Irish in America. Irish emigrants were not a homogeneous group and their experiences were diverse rather than uniform. It really did matter *where* you came from in Ireland, *when* you left the country, *what* you took with you in the form of skills and capital, and *where* you settled. Opportunities could be immense for pioneer settlers in territory that was opening up in parts of Canada, Australia, Argentina or Mexican Texas, and very few for those who arrived in settled communities in the east-coast cities of the United States, with little but physical labour to offer the job market.

Letters

The first letter is taken from the first Peter Robinson state-assisted emigration scheme from Cork and Kerry to Upper Canada in 1823. It was written by Catherine O'Brian, from Ramsay Township, to her brother on 20 February 1824.[6] It contains the familiar presence of formulaic phrases in the opening paragraph: 'I embrace the opportunity of writing to you these few lines to let you know that I and my family is well, thank God for his kind mercies & hope that this will find you in the same.'

The unusual reference to 'a most agreeable passage' and to being 'amazingly well treated' may owe something to a loyalty to the organiser of the scheme, Mr Robinson, who was 'kind and attentive' in administering 'to our comfort and convenience', and a genuine gratitude that 'we are now most agreeably situated on a good lot of land with good neighbours all around in a flourishing settlement'. The letter also contained the obligatory detail on wage levels, as an encouragement for other family members to join them:

> Thos. has got and has the prospect to get plenty of employment at one dollar per day of wages and found in board and lodging, but he is more inclined to work on his land, and notwithstanding working out considerable [sic] he has got about four acres chopped down and hopes to have an acre or two more again spring and we have every prospect of doing well and of having plenty … The wages for labouring men is from ten to twelve dollars per month and found or by the day from two shillings & sixpence to three shillings.

The letter continues in a generally buoyant tone: 'This is a most delightful country I believe none in the world more healthy no sickness of any kind affects us, nor any of the settlers here, no want of bread, for all have plenty and to spare, and no man living willing to work but may live happy.'

The purpose of the letter was to encourage her brother Robert to come out to Canada on the next Peter Robinson scheme in 1825, 'embrace the opportunity for you may never have the like again'. Practical advice was then given on what to bring – 'plenty of clothes both for bed and body for that is our greatest want in this country' and also 'all the pots and pans earthenware & other cooking utensils that you have'.

However, the most telling section of the letter refers to brother John who was not encouraged 'to come to this country if he would not resolve to work better than he did at home', and 'if he would keep from the drink he might do well, but the rum is cheap four shillings and sixpence per Gallon and a great many of our settlers likes it too well which may prove their ruin, for a drunkard will not do well here'.

This last passage reveals a significant attitude to the new home in Canada. What accompanied the act of migration and settlement into a new land was the belief in a new start, not merely the opportunity to make a more plentiful and prosperous life, but the leaving behind of what some migrants saw as the curse of old Ireland: the inveterate fondness for alcoholic drink.

Catherine O'Brian does not reveal any lingering nostalgia for the land of her birth, but there is plenty of evidence that this was a common feature of emigrant letters, suggestive of the pain of separation from family, friends and familiar surroundings in Ireland, but also a means of keeping the connection with the old country. In the following account, a passionate desire to remember and return to Ireland is most keenly felt by the next generation, what the Rev. M.B. Buckley described in Montreal as 'a transmitted passion':[7]

I met several people from Cork, and they were overjoyed to meet me, who could tell them the history of the beautiful citie for the last generation. To some I spoke the Irish language and their delight was inconceivable. I may here remark that wherever I go I find the love of Ireland amongst the Irish to be the most intense feeling of their souls – an all-absorbing passion, running like a silver thread through all their thoughts and emotions. They think forever of the old land, and sigh to behold it once more before they die. One man who drove us one day for an hour refused to take any payment. He was from Ireland and we were two Irish priests, and that was enough for him!

'What part of Ireland do you come from?' I asked. 'From Wicklow, sir; I am 32 years in the country.' 'And do you ever think of the old country?' 'Think,' he exclaimed, 'Oh! yes sir, I do think of the old country, not so much by day as by night. In my dreams at night I see as distinctly as ever the lanes and alleys where I played when a boy. I fancy I am at home once more, but I awake and find I am in Montreal, and am like never to see my native land again.'

This dreaming of Ireland I found quite common, many people would give all they have in the world to get back again and live in Ireland steeped in poverty, rather than flourish wealthy in this strange land. And what is stranger still, is that amongst the young people, those love Ireland most who are born here of Irish parents. Their love is far more intense than the love of those who were born in Ireland. Philosophers must account for this; it appears to me to be a transmitted passion; they hear their parents constantly speak in terms of affection of the land of their birth.

Speaking to a visitor from Ireland was similar to a letter written home and for transmitted passion we can identify a reconstructed memory, a longing for identity that was fabricated and a generation old, to the extent it was mediated through what parents could remember of the Ireland they left behind.

In Arnold Schrier's collection of emigrant letters, he quotes the advice of the Rev. John O'Hanlon, the author of the most popular Irish emigrant guidebook of the period. He asked them to remember when writing home that 'Utopia of the imagination is not the United States of our experience', and that by substituting 'fancy for judgment, romantic hopes are first formed to be afterwards destroyed'.[8] As an example of the first flush of enthusiasm, a young girl's first letter home from New York in 1850 is cited:

> My dear Father I must only say that this is a good place and a good country for if one place does not suit a man he can go to another and can very easy please himself ... any man or woman without a family are fools that would not venture and come to this plentyful Country where no man or woman ever hungered or ever will and where you will not be seen naked.[9]

By implication, enthusiasm for the New World meant a rejection of the old country. Other letters, however, qualified the unlimited prospects available in America. A young worker in Philadelphia in 1854 wrote to his uncle, a farmer in Ulster:

> I have got along very well since I came here and has saved some money. I never regretted coming out here, and any young person that could not get along well there would do well to come here, if they intended to conduct themselves decently ... but old people have no great chance here.[10]

These sentiments were echoed by others: America was a young person's country with little reverence for old people. Economic opportunity came at a price. Old people were still respected in Ireland. Also, along with the premium on youth, sobriety was another condition of success. Anyone who could not cure himself of the drink habit had better stay at home. Age distinction was accompanied by an element of class disdain. Delany, a young lawyer who arrived in Washington, DC in 1849, wrote to his uncle four years later distancing himself from many of his fellow countrymen:

I am sorry to have to say it that by their fighting and drunkenness they are disgracing their country in the eyes of Americans. Generally speaking, Americans dont drink [sic], they are for the most part very temperate and disregard – detest the drunkard. Now instead of saving their wages, which are good, living orderly, keeping themselves and children clad, well, and clean, they are continually fighting among themselves: the Kerry men, and Clare men, and Limerick men: and for no other reason than this, because they were born in these different counties. But they have money to spend thus. So they have.[11]

Delany was not uncritical of life in America (he was hostile to the institution of slavery), but he clearly felt embarrassed by the continuation of old Irish habits of drunkenness, fighting and inter-county rivalry that he considered unworthy of immigrants in the United States. The very act of migrating to the New World required, from his point of view, a rejection of the worst of the habits associated with the Old World, a social distancing from the country of birth.

In contrast, the next letter is taken from Kerby Miller's huge collection and fully exemplifies the nostalgic element in the sense of loss in the 'culture of exile'. Mary Ann Rowe (*c.* 1860 – *c.* 1899) in the 1880s was a domestic servant living in the suburban community of Dedham, Massachusetts.[12] Her letter is in two sections: one strongly nostalgic for home, looking back and remembering good times; the other reassuring those back home that life was good, and looking forward to a better future.

Instead of the ritual, formulaic opening, Mary Ann begins awkwardly and apologetically in writing to her friend: 'It is not through any lack of friendship that I stayed so long without writing to you. I do feel so bad when I go to write to home. I don't be the better of it for a long time.' This suggests the possible pain of leaving Ireland but also, having left, there is a difficulty in trying to reconnect with home. Part of this may be the feeling of homesickness evident in the next section of the letter:

I would never have left poor Dunnamaggan if only I thought I would be so homesick. I cannot banish the thought of home out of my mind. There is not a night but I do be dreaming about you or someone from home. I dreamed last night that little John was dying. I fancied I was looking at him and had the pleasure of kissing him before he died. I hope and trust nothing is the matter with any of them.

The letter continues with the pleasure of remembering former days – Sunday afternoons playing with little children in Ireland. However, the tone of the letter changes abruptly with a description of Mary Ann's happy situation in America:

Yet I am living with a very nice family here in Dedham, Massachusetts [sic].
They are very nice people. I would not be allowed to go outside to put out the
clothes even when the dew was on the grass without rubber boots on me, my
mistress is so very careful of me. And I am within two or three minutes walk
from the church. There is a splendid church here in Dedham and three priests. I
can go to mass every Sunday and to confession whenever I want to. Dedham is
a very nice place and is a country looking place – when you look around, there
is nothing but trees.

What is revealed here is an acceptance of her new situation, representative
of so many young Irish women who began to dominate domestic service
in the United States and replaced native black domestics in the process. The
conditions female domestics enjoyed were invariably superior to conditions
back home in Ireland and also allowed Irish servants to save enough money
to pay for remittances, often in the form of prepaid tickets for passage to
America, and also to save for the proverbial 'bottom drawer', an investment
in marriage prospects that were superior to those in rural areas of post-
famine Ireland.[13]

Irish female migrants, while representing half the migrant stream out of
Ireland during the nineteenth century, did have different experiences from
Irish men, even from the same family. This is because separate spheres operated in the world of work. Working conditions remained very different for
domestic servants, the archetypal woman at work, primarily living in middle-
class households, and men who worked predominantly, and more visibly, in
outdoor labouring employment. Often such labouring work involved continued migration in search of further employment or better prospects. This was
especially prevalent in the field of hard-rock mining in the United States. It is
well documented that from the 1880s Irish copper miners from Bearhaven in
west Cork took a well-trodden path in a process of skill migration to mining
centres in Michigan, Utah, California and to Butte, Montana, the biggest
copper mine in the world run by Irishman, Marcus Daly.[14]

Three letters, taken from the Hurley Collection in Cork Archives, reflect
changing conditions in the far west of America in the 1880s and 1890s, not
least from the perspective of an itinerant miner.[15] Michael Hurley, writing to
his sister Kate in Ireland from Shasta County in California, on 5 December
1886, excuses his failure to write home as he was not permanent in any one
place. He promises to compensate with the price of a new dress. He then
compares the problems of Ireland with the prospects in America, becoming
quite lyrical in describing the Californian climate:

I am sorry that times are so bad in Ireland now, next year might be good if a couple of weeks of California Climate was in Ireland last harvest it would be very much need there never is any rain here in summer time and sometimes very little in winter cant see a cloud the sun shines here not as in northern climes obscurely bright but one unclouded blaze of living light.

With sun as a metaphor for good times in California, the tone of the letter is largely negative towards life in Ireland, viewed from 6,000 miles away. Michael dismisses the advice his sister has given him to return home on economic and political grounds: 'You were advising me to come home a few years ago if I did I might be like Patrick and Tim Hurley now living in misery trying to raise the rent to pay the tyrant Lords I hope the time will come when they can't collect no more rents.' Even his smug dismissal of Irish relatives in San Francisco carries with it a rejection of the old curse of the Irish – itself a rejection of the habits of home: 'The Hurleys of Castelview have come down in the world. John in San Francisco is not doing well either, he likes his beer too well.'

On 13 January 1891, Michael Hurley wrote to his mother in Ireland from Spokane Falls, Washington. Writing from long distance gave him the courage to admonish his mother for buying a farm: 'I was astonished to see that you gave (£)750 for that place. I think you must have been out of your mind no wonder times would be hard in Ireland when people are that foolish to pay so much for such a little place and such rent after.' Then there is the contrast with life in north-west America that carries a certain smugness despite his own rollercoaster experience: 'I have got that much money after all I have lost but I don't want to give it all for that place and then going into debt for stocking it. I can do better here.'

News from Ireland, even for an itinerant miner, was freely available, but it only confirmed his sense of fatalism and negativity about Ireland's future: 'Things look purty badly messed up back there now Parnell & Mrs. O'Shea have caused some trouble I am afraid it will delay home rule for a while Ireland never was on the point of gaining anything but something happened to prevent it.' By contrast, America was booming, and was obviously the place to be and accept becoming American: 'The wilds of America are becoming Civilized rapidly a few years ago there was nobody but Indians where this town stands and now there is about 30,000 people in it 6 and 7 stories [sic] high.'

Michael concluded his letter with a message to his younger brother: 'Tim you are better pin up the collar of your shirt and get married and run that place yourself I don't want it hoping this will find you all in health and happiness I will conclude for the present.' Michael, while continuing to take an interest in Ireland and his family's welfare, sees his future in America. It is a

reminder that emigration for many was not merely about individual advancement but was part of a family strategy.

By 12 March 1894, when brother Dennis Hurley wrote to his mother from
Carson City, Nevada, the boom times were over in the silver mines:

> Very bad times in United States, everything low with a great scarcity of money
> and work. Nevada and other silver producing states, who owing to the low
> price of silver which in place of selling at 129 cents per oz. is now selling at
> 59 or less than half of the par value. Archbishop Walsh of Dublin has written a
> book on this subject which is highly praised by friends of silver the world over.
> I am still at work but retaining it very insecure now.

Like his brother Michael, who had not written to him lately, Dennis was not
averse to giving advice to his younger brother in Ireland:

> Tim, my dear brother, you should look more to other requisites in a wedded
> partner than L.S.D. It is not like going to the bakers after a loaf of bread, all
> much the same. Some girls are better for a man to marry, even without a shil-
> ling than others with a good fortune. Look to qualities of head and heart, thrift,
> intelligence, cleanliness and cheerfulness, no lazy untidy old mope. Do not
> postpone what you intend to do as you are not getting young.

The letter also contains other family news that links up with Michael's earlier
letter: 'John Hurley, Castleview, died in San Francisco Dec. 19 leaving 8 children to mourn his loss. Wife and self are well thank God, and hope this will
find you all well.'

The next set of letters form part of an emigration scheme to Mexican Texas
in the years 1829–34. The first group of Irish settlers were recruited in New
York, Philadelphia and New Orleans by two Irish *empresarios*, or agents of the
Mexican government, John McMullen and James McGloin, to move to San
Patricio on the Nueces River, in the province of Coahuila y Texas. The main
attraction was the promise of land grants of 4,428 acres per family, surely one
of the best deals available to new settlers in the Americas in the nineteenth
century.[16] As part of the practice of boosterism in encouraging migration,
letters home were included in the emigrant guides of the day. Jemima and
Mary Toll, who came from New York to settle in San Patricio, were quoted to
endorse settlement in the new colony:

> I found this country equal to what was said in the hand bills and better again …
> really I was astonished when I came amongst the colonists to see them all full of

comfort, plenty of Corn, bread Mush Butter Milk and beef and what perhaps those who sent false reports never enjoyed before. As for pigs and fowls they are as numerous as flees … Do not be daunted the prospect here is good … you'll have no work, your daughters can milk 50 cows for you, and make butter which is 25 cents a lb here, in Matamoros 50 cents. A cow has 2 calfes in 10 months a sheep and a goat 3 yearlings in 15 months. The healthiest country in the world. The richest land will show like Gentlemens domains in Ireland. Fine wood and water as in any part of the world. As for fowl and fish of every kind no man can believe, but those that see.[17]

Clearly there is some hyperbole in this account, not in the description of plenty or in the reproductive capacity of animals able to graze all year round in the pastures of the Texas Coastal Bend, but with regard to health which ignored the hazards of cholera, malaria and yellow fever, or the more obvious dangers to homesteads from hostile Indians and Mexican bandits in a frontier zone. Yet, the key sentence reveals the aspiration to own sufficient land to become like gentlemen in Ireland. It could not be more clearly expressed that emigration, or in this case a further migration from the United States to Mexico, was seen in terms of social and economic advancement. In a number of cases the dream was fulfilled, as 4,428 acres was to become the basis for building up large estates.

The second group of Irish settlers were recruited directly from Ireland by *empresarios* James Power and James Hewetson for the colony Refugio, located on the Mission River, a few miles inland from the Texas coast. Power returned to his native county Wexford to encourage would-be settlers to go to Texas with him on the promise of abundant land and future prosperity. As proof of the great deal on offer, he took members of his own family: his married sister, Elizabeth, and nephews, Martin Power and Thomas O'Connor. Surviving letters between Martin Power, a young cripple who was duly assigned his land grant in the Power-Hewetson colony in 1835, and his father, Daniel Power, back in county Wexford, reveal an emotional tug-of-war between father and son.[18] In Martin's first few years in Texas, he witnessed a cholera outbreak in New Orleans en route to Texas, shipwreck off the Texas coast, the destruction of property and massacres of settlers in the Texas Revolution of 1835–36, and further depredations and killings by Comanche Indians. Daniel Power, on hearing of all the disasters that befell the colonists, urged his son to return to Ireland.

Despite all that happened that might well have persuaded him, Martin resisted his father's pressure, and in a letter of 1839, revealed his true motives for going to Texas and staying there:

The only thing that ever caused me to leave was the dulness of the times and fearing not with standing all my brothers off duty and hard labors to add to little stores – that they would be at least tore to pieces by making two farms of one. I have thought deeply for the past two years I spent there you know were getting mity [sic] little better and we all doing everything in our power. I have for my time at least 80 pound a year since I left Ballinhash to present date … I know you would not at this time insist on me to go home … and not only that but see the door open to make an independent fortune in a short time.

Martin's memory of home and family in Ireland is bound up with the pressure of subdividing the land among the sons that was being resisted in south-east Ireland to preserve the viability of tenant holdings. This produced its own pressure for younger sons to emigrate and look for a better life in the New World. The chances of tenant farmers owning their land in Ireland at that time were remote. The opportunity to own a sizeable amount of land in Texas was an attractive alternative, even when all the hazards had been encountered. Martin stayed and died in Texas without fulfilling his dream. However, his cousin, Thomas O'Connor, mentored by his uncle James Power, was to become 'the cattle king of County Refugio', building up a vast ranching empire of 500,000 acres and becoming one of the richest men in Texas before his death in 1887. His eldest son, Dennis O'Connor, himself a millionaire rancher with his brother Tom, wrote a draft letter to the *Galveston News*, dated 22 December 1888.[19] In a long letter written in crayon he revealed the extraordinary journey he had made in terms of his allegiance and identity, as he looked back on his roots in Ireland and Texas. It is an exceptionally revealing example of the evolution of self:

I was born in this Refugio County in the Republic of Texas in 1839 of Irish parents of the colony of Power and Hewitson. Enlisted and served as a Confederate Soldier throughout the rebellion. When in military camp I read Gen. Grant's terms of surrender to Gen. Lee + army I expressed myself thus – I believe it not, for the history of man gives no record of such magnanimity but if it be true then I intend to become a loyal citizen of the great nation whose servants met such acts. We disbandoned [disbanded] I went home and dispassionately watched the proceedings of my southern brethren. All my political schooling was democratic, had voted for S.A. Douglas. My father [Thomas O'Connor] was a slave owner. I registered as a voter, took the amnesty oath and had as I expressed it, a country again.

'Yes, Sir, I decend [sic] from the Emerald Gem of the ocean and I am proud of that decent [sic] next in point of esteem to my citizenship of the United

Dennis O'Connor

St Denis Chapel, O'Connor ranch, Victoria, Texas (Author's collection)

States, the Galveston News to the contrary notwithstanding. I can spread out the tail of my coat widely and most defiantly under these suns and your Queen's police dare not tread thereon lest they tramp upon Uncle Sam's striped and starry handkerchief not so safe an undertaking as collecting rents in the land of the shamrock. It is scarcely worthwhile to say republicans are not dynamite advocates. But I must presume to suggest that you dealt in that commodity superfluously ... I will concur with you by answering you that if I were compelled to choose between the occupation of using dynamite on English landlords in Ireland or elsewhere by word or insinnuation [sic] deride or slander a downtrodden people I would certainly prefer the former especially if it would terrify one of the oppressors of mankind but for one single moment.

In one life, Dennis O'Connor had moved from being a citizen of the Texas Republic to a citizen of the United States after annexation. He then fought for the Confederacy during the Civil War and once again became a proud citizen of the United States, thanks to the magnanimity of the surrender terms. In politics he became a Republican even though his father, Thomas O'Connor, had been a slave owner. However, what is most striking is Dennis O'Connor's passionate identification with Ireland, another example of reconstructed memory, but most specifically with the poor oppressed Irish tenant farmers. Clearly, this sense of oppression history had been handed down from his father, whose family were tenant mill farmers in Kilmuckridge, County Wexford. At the time of writing the letter, Dennis O'Connor was a powerful, millionaire rancher and landowner with many tenants of his own on his estate that extended into several Texas counties. In economic terms, he had far more in common with landlords in Ireland than with poor, 'oppressed' tenants who, following Gladstone's Land Acts in 1871 and 1881, were in a much better system than in 1834, when Thomas O'Connor left Ireland at the age of 17. The O'Connor farm in Kilmuckridge was eventually purchased under the provisions of Conservative legislation which enabled tenants to acquire their own farms over time. The current owner of the 100-acre farm is Dennis O'Connor, a direct descendant of Thomas O'Connor's elder brother, Dennis.

If cattle ranching in Texas offered immense opportunities for wealth creation, that was no less true of some of the Irish migrants in Argentina. Edmundo Murray's collection of letters offers insights from Irish families that prospered in their new homeland, and, in the process, acknowledge changing perspectives to the land of their birth. A moral distancing was added to the physical distance that separated Argentina from Ireland. The greater opportunities available to Irish men in the New World posed a stronger contrast with old, discredited ways in the Old World. This showed itself in a tone of near

A Celtic cross at the O'Connor ranch, Victoria, Texas (Author's collection)

contempt for 'an oppressed and ever distressed country' and a frustration with family members who stuck stubbornly to their poverty in Ireland.

John James Murphy was a successful sheep farmer in Salto, Argentina, and engaged in an extensive correspondence with his brother and family back in County Wexford. Though he returned to Ireland twice, he made Argentina his home and prospered in a way he would have found difficult in Ireland. He wrote to his brother Martin Murphy in 1864:

> I am well aware that your desire that I should live amongst you are such as will lead you to think that I under any circumstances might remain at home and my desires in this respect are no less great but what to determine as is. Whether in this country or that we should choose to pass together the fine happy years that may be left to us. In this country we live like fighting cocks, plenty of the best of mutton any way you choose to cook it, in every house, particularly those with a family, has plenty of fowl, eggs, milk, butter, catchup, daily of their own making, and brings from town each year a supply of all the other necessities, even English sauce, pickles & CC, which is before every day with plenty of all sorts of vegetables and potatoes, the latter two crops in the year.[20]

Murphy was describing the bounty of frontier life which struck a primitive note back in Ireland, but for him the scale of his economic success in Argentina outweighed all other considerations. He also expressed his irritation that bad times in Ireland did not induce his brother to look for a better future in Argentina:

> There are many causes which induce people to remain at home longer than they should. The fear, or rather shame they so foolishly entertain of being thought by those neighbours of being under the necessity to leave. But what may I ask in what form do they profit by this foolish simplicity? In none whatever, but finally becomes caught in their own net. There is another class of people that entertain a prejudice to every thing foreign, and cannot believe anything real but what is within their own sphere of knowing. They cannot believe that happiness can be formed in any place but where themselves really are, though at the same time if they could but see their position as others do, they would fancy themselves the most miserable beings under Heaven.[21]

Prosperity achieved in Argentina brought with it an increasing irritation with family members who insisted on remaining in financial difficulty in Ireland, and the old country itself became 'that distressed and ever oppressed country'.

Conclusions

The letters discussed here, extending in time from the 1820s through to the 1890s, and drawing on the experience and perceptions of Irish emigrants in Canada, the United States, Texas as part of Mexico – as an independent republic and as part of the United States – and Argentina, illustrate the themes with which this chapter began. The memory of Ireland could be frozen in aspic and fiercely defended in the New World. It could also be rationalised as part of a culture of exile, with the dream of one day returning to Ireland, or at least be reunited in heaven with family members at home. There is the phenomenon of a transmitted passion for Ireland, stronger among the generation that had never been there but had acquired a reconstructed memory from Irish parents.

Negative memories of Ireland could also justify fulfilling a dream of enjoying better times in the Americas, even to the extent of communicating an irritation with the ways of the old country and its prolonged destiny of enduring hard times. What is also apparent is a reconstructed memory of Ireland that becomes incorporated into a journey of self-discovery: the old self in Ireland, oppressed and restricted, and the new self in a dynamic America and South America, taking advantage of better opportunities to prosper.

Notes

1 R.F. Foster, *Paddy & Mr. Punch: Connections in Irish and English History* (Allen Lane, The Penguin Press, 1993), p. xiii.

2 Kerby A. Miller, *Emigrants and Exiles: Ireland and the Irish Exodus to North America* (Oxford: Oxford University Press, 1985), pp. 125–6.

3 M. Kenneally, 'Textualizing Irish Immigrant Identities in Canada: The Emerging Landscape', conference paper, Canadian Association of Irish Studies Conference, Maynooth, Ireland, 22–26 June 2005.

4 Edmundo Murray, *Becoming Irlandés: Private Narratives of the Irish Emigration to Argentina (1844–1912)* (Buenos Aires: Literature of Latin America, 2006).

5 Mary P. Corcoran, 'The Process of Migration and the Reinvention of Self: The Experiences of Returning Irish Emigrants', in Kevin Kenny (ed.), *New Directions in Irish-American History* (Madison: University of Wisconsin Press, 2003), pp. 302–18.

6 Peter Robinson Papers, Cork City Library.

7 Rev. M.B. Buckley, *Diary of a Tour in America*, edited by his sister Kate Buckley (Dublin: Sealy, Bryers & Walker, 1886), pp. 50–1. I am indebted to Professor Michael Kenneally for this source.

8 John O'Hanlon, *The Irish Emigrant's Guide for the United States* (Boston, 1851), p. 12.

9 Arnold Schrier, *Ireland and the American Emigration, 1850–1900* (first pub. 1958, rep., Chester Springs, PA: Dufour Editions Inc., 1997).

10 Andrew Pauley to his uncle, 21 August 1854, Philadelphia.

11 Thomas Bernard Delany to his uncle, 29 August 1853, Washington, DC.

12 Letter of Mary Ann Rowe, 29 October 1888, in Kerby Miller and Paul Wagner, *Out of Ireland: The Story of Irish Emigration to America* (London: The Aurum Press, 1994), p. 76.

13 Hasia Diner, *Erin's Daughters in America: Irish Immigrant Women in the Nineteenth Century* (Baltimore: John Hopkins University Press, 1983); Janet Nolan, *Ourselves Alone: Women's Emigration from Ireland, 1855–1920* (University Press of Kentucky, 1989).

14 David M. Emmons, *The Butte Irish: Class and Ethnicity in an American Mining Town, 1875–1925* (Urbana & Chicago: University of Illinois Press, 1989).

15 The Hurley Letters, Cork City Archives, Ireland.

16 See Graham Davis, *Land! Irish Pioneers in Mexican and Revolutionary Texas* (College Station, 2002).

17 Jemima and Mary Toll letter, New York, reprinted in David Woodman Jr, *Guide to Texas Emmigrants*, 1835 (Reprint, Waco: Texian Press, 1974).

18 Martin Power to his father Daniel Power, County Wexford, Ireland, 1839, Power Letters, Hobart Huson Library, Refugio, Texas.

19 Dennis O'Connor, draft letter to the editor of the *Galveston News*, 22 December 1888, O'Connor Family Papers, Victoria, Texas.

20 John James Murphy to Martin Murphy, 1864, in Murray, *Becoming Irlandés*, pp. 42–3.

21 John James Murphy to Martin Murphy, 20 August 1865, in Ibid., p. 65.

A shorter version of this paper was published in Britta Olinder, Werner Huber (eds), 'Place and Memory in the New Ireland', *Irish Studies in Europe*, Vol. 2 (Trier: Wissenschaftlicher Verlag Trier, 2009).

Index